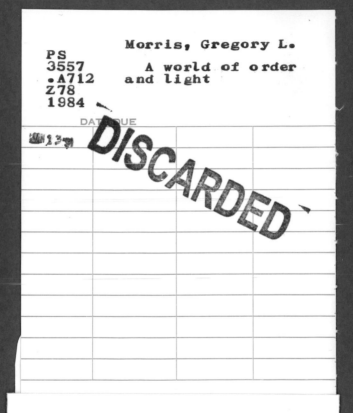

A World of Order and Light

Gregory L. Morris

A World of Order and Light

The Fiction of John Gardner

The University of Georgia Press  Athens

Copyright © 1984 by the University of Georgia Press
Athens, Georgia 30602

Set in Galliard

Printed in the United States of America

The paper in this book meets the guidelines for permanence
and durability of the Committee on Production Guidelines
for Book Longevity of the Council on Library Resources.

Library of Congress Cataloging in Publication Data

Morris, Gregory L.
   A world of order and light.

   Bibliography: p.
   Includes index.
   1. Gardner, John, 1933–1982—Criticism and
interpretation. 2. Philosophy in literature.
I. Title.
PS3557.A712Z78 1984   813'.54   83-9195
ISBN 0-8203-0696-7

To Gayle

Contents

Acknowledgments

It's a long list of people to whom I owe debts of gratitude, who hold my markers, who could, if they wished, dun me (but won't). However, my particular thanks must go to the following: to my wife, Gayle, for her inordinate patience and encouragement and insight, for her skill as a first reader, and for deluding me with the belief that I would some day finish this work; to Sallie Sherman, James Bashore, David Goldsmith, Virginia Leland, and Patrick Kurp, for making this sort of thing—this business of books—appealing and promising to me in my years as a beginner; to Lee Lemon, John Howell, Robert Bergstrom, and Thomas Bestul, who, with their invaluable professional advice, saved me from all sorts of literary chaos; to my family and friends, who contributed to the completion of this work with their shows of support and confidence; to the family and friends of John Gardner, as well, who were consistently generous with their time and knowledge; and especially and finally to John Gardner, who in a tragically brief lifetime made something special and magical of this world, who gave to it much love and concern and kindness, who taught us all a little bit about life and art and our own imperfect, but marvelously human natures.

A World of Order and Light

Prologue

No one knew better the world's fragility than John Gardner. He realized that existence is a delicate balance between calm and chaos, between the secure and the accidental. There were no guarantees in life, only precarious truces. Gardner's private peace with the universe was shattered the afternoon of September 14, 1982, as he rounded a curve in a Pennsylvania mountain road near his home in Susquehanna, his motorcycle—and his life—sliding out from under him. Surely there was a stillness, there in the Endless Mountains, and a darkness as when the ground gives way in the depths of a forest.

While death left Gardner's life in fragments—a marriage just four days from celebration, a major novel laboring towards completion—time did allow his work to come, in an ironic sort of way, full circle. Both his first published novel and what is presumably his last—*The Resurrection* and *Mickelsson's Ghosts*—had as their protagonists professors of philosophy, men who physically symbolized Gardner's trademark as a philosophical novelist. Both novels were also critical failures, unfortunate beginnings and ends to Gardner's artistic life, the worth of all that came in between barely compensating for the deprived sense of promise from what might have been.

It is ironic, too, that John Gardner established his early reputation on his two novels *The Wreckage of Agathon* and *Grendel*. Both were politically and philosophically timely books, and they were easily misinterpreted as additions to the bleak and cynical literature that marked the 1960s. The idea of John Gardner as an existential comedian seems outrageous to anyone who has read the greater body of his work (and who possesses ten years of valuable hindsight), but that is how he was viewed by the critical press at the time.

Today, however, the world of John Gardner is a much clearer one. The Gardner universe is one organized by a belief in what he calls "emotional metaphysics," in a sort of "felt" philosophical system that is as dependent upon the heart as upon the head. In *On Moral Fiction*, Gardner's critical manifesto, he says that art "is essentially serious and beneficial, a game played against chaos and death, against entropy."[1] Metaphysical collapse, the "twilight of the gods," the winding down of the universe, is always around the corner, almost inevitable. Art and life are games, or perhaps more aptly, jousts between existence and death, order and chaos, virtue and sin; opposites charge, battle, resign, in a continual challenge to each other. What makes it more than a game and ultimately so serious, of course, is the ineluctability of death, chaos, and extinction.

Human beings, naturally, have their choice in this scheme. They may submit to the metaphysical despair of it all, "go nihilistic," and contemplate suicide. Or they may summon their courage and their madness and struggle against the darkness, confront the dragon, and "go heroic." Gardner's heroes never enter the battle empty-handed. They go armed with the lunacies of love, faith, intuition, and art—the weapons of humanistic thought and the tenets of emotional metaphysics. These are lunacies because only a lunatic would enter the lists against the forces of chaos— the monsters, the trolls, the Grendels—and expect the world actually to be the better for it. Only a lunatic would put so much stock in such an assortment of abstractions—but then, "all heroes are crazy." The hero acts out of love for man and his community, and acts with what I call applied faith, or a faith that is both religious and practical, that puts to work the sentiment and discards the dogma. Moreover, the hero (and we all could very well be heroes) acts upon an intuitive intellect that in some mysterious and indefinable way feels and ferrets out the proper, heroic course of action; these heroes act rightly because something inside them, something that they know is reliable and consistent, tells them they are acting rightly and morally.

That intuition, that hunch, moreover, has been nurtured by what Gardner calls the tradition of moral art, a tradition that "seeks to improve life, not debase it. It seeks to hold off, at least for a while, the twilight of the gods and us."[2] This, says Gardner, is what all of the artists of the great tradition—Homer, Dante, Shakespeare, Tolstoy—have felt and believed and worked from. And it is from this same humanistic, moral aesthetic that Gardner writes and creates. The artist is one who labors to preserve this metaphysic and this cosmology "of god and man." He is both singer and priest, and he creates his art from a specific Aristotelian model that stresses character, *energeia,* and honest experimentation. Authentic art "imitates nature's total process [and] in sworn opposition to chaos, discovers by its process what it can say. That is art's morality."[3] True art admits no cheating, no deceit, no falsification of action or motive. And what the artist and the reader should discover (and here is where it all becomes contentious) is that the world, though an annoying mixture of good and evil, of progress and stasis, of belief and negation, is finally holy and humane and purposeful. Both nonartist and artist work through this emotional metaphysic, employing compassion, love, intuition, and a vaguely religious impulse, and arrive at an affirmation of the world and of existence.

While any attempt to gather several artists under one convenient label is naturally difficult and disquieting, I believe that there are certain people who do clearly share Gardner's humanistic aesthetic, who represent a combination of the already variegated threads of what might be called neohumanism. In music, composers such as John Corigliano (whose "unfashionably Romantic music" and concern for the audience put him at the center of this revival), Warren Benson, and Joseph Baber (Gardner's friend and operatic collaborator) have been at work creating a musical style that builds upon the old traditions, ultimately the emotional traditions in music history. In the visual and plastic arts, one might include sculptors such as Henry Moore and Thomas Mallory, as well as Gardner's friend, the late Nicholas Vergette, a potter and sculptor. One might also mention painters such as John Napper (a friend of Gardner and illustrator of one of his novels), Wayne Thiebaud, Karen Moss, and Jack Beal (who has been clearly marked by the critics as the leader, somehow simultaneously, of this drive toward social realism and the New Sentimentality in painting).[4] All are artists who celebrate a sort of reality of the eye and heart, who maintain the perceptions of both to be accurate and dependable. Finally, writers such as John Fowles, Larry Woiwode, Mark Helprin,[5] and Nicholas Delbanco all work out of a concern for the continuation of the universe (with its history), and seek the preservation of those forms and ideals that have come to shape the great tradition.

What separates Gardner from these artists, however, and what makes his best work of true significance is his ability to transcend the realism of his material, to create what one might describe as "magical landscapes"—environments for his fiction that combine the identifiable with the fantastic. The physical details of these landscapes are intensely accurate, almost literary facsimiles of the geography. The town and farms of Batavia, New York; the countryside around Carbondale, Illinois; the streets and monuments of Bennington, Vermont: you walk these places and you recognize them in Gardner's fiction—there's no mistaking their reality.

Gardner makes them magical, however, by infusing them with that strange and mystical and illuminating quality of light that shines throughout his fiction. It is a light that transmogrifies perception into intuition. The mundane, the real, is for the moment blessed and transfigured. The world is changed, and it is the light that brings that change—a change which Gardner profoundly believed possible. All of Gardner's finest work reflects this light, mirrors those magical landscapes.

In the end, Gardner and neohumanist artists like him do two things. They return to art a content, a human subject that is real and living. And they turn Romanticism on its head by admitting the apparently chaotic nature of the universe at the same time that they affirm the power of art not to *make* order where none may have existed but to *discover* order. Gardner insists that order, however invisible it may be most times, exists in reality. Gardner says that what the artist does is necessary not for the realization of the order but for the salvation of a mankind that struggles in a confusing universe. The artist does not make order "more real" in a cosmic sense, but he presents its reality to the human beings who need it so desperately and miss finding it so often.[6]

What is most satisfying about Gardner's own art (at least to many people) is that he is so faithful to his own aesthetic and to his metaphysics of the heart. His fictions function by legitimate process and development; Gardner allows his characters to act and to think and to sometimes fail as they humanly should. There is no naïveté, no convenient turning of the back on what is real in the world. The real is what drives his characters to act, and to act genuinely. That reality might be located in various sectors of time and space, might be historical, mythical, autobiographical, or contemporary, but it is ultimately real and believable and discoverable. John Gardner has been faulted for many things—a bourgeois realism and moralism, a reactionary aesthetic, an obnoxious sentimentality—but like his lunatic heroes, he must be admired for the valiant effort he puts forth in his art: the effort to keep the world sane and loving and convinced of its own moral value. It is the philosophical consistency and quality of this luminous vision which is Gardner's artistic hallmark and, as I intend to show in the succeeding pages, his artistic achievement.

Chapter 1

"The Old Men"

Dead brother, give me your hand,
materialized once more in the strange gray room:
bend down and breathe into my dry mouth,
as if with love, the earthsmell of your cold
invulnerable indifference to the world.
                    —"The Visitor"

John Gardner completed "The Old Men" in 1958 as his doctoral dissertation at the University of Iowa. Apparently the direction by Ralph Freedman was rather loose; it was a looseness, however, that Gardner appreciated and exploited because he

> was writing something that was different from what other people in the workshop were writing, and at that time it was a lot *worse* than what the people at the workshop were writing. But I didn't like what they wrote, and when I got good I didn't want to be like them when they got good. And so I sort of wrote privately and took medieval courses, and at the last minute some very kind professors let me do a "creative Ph.D.," that is to say, a novel, and I had been taking workshops. I had a very nice deal with the workshop there; there were very good teachers at that time, in fact, some of the best writers in America—Saul Bellow was there, and Herb Gold, and Robert O. Bowen and Marguerite Young and Spencer Tyler and Vance Bourjailly—and I would write and turn in my stories into their mailboxes and not go to any classes, and at the end of the quarter get back my papers with the "A's" on them and no comments. And that was very nice, I didn't want any comments because some writers really want to learn how to write correctly.

> What that really means is that they write exactly like everybody else.
> There's another kind of writer who may be worse, sometimes is,
> who's absolutely stubborn about what he's going to do.[1]

Gardner's insistence on going his own with this dissertation-novel is perhaps the reason it shows those qualities most typical of him as a novelist: the confidence, the broadness, the somewhat brusque individualism. He was convinced of the worth of his style, though it ran counter to the accepted grain, the slick postmodernist cynicism of the black humorists. Gardner was after something more in the American tradition—in the grand tradition—a realistic and faithfully told story, one with credible characters and ideas solid enough to endure.

At the time of its writing, Gardner was reasonably satisfied with the quality of "The Old Men," but the twenty intervening years dimmed, in his eyes, the book's value. He has described it as "a bad book . . . full of flaws and weak writing."[2] In many ways this is true. It is an ambitious book, perhaps overpopulated and sprawling, barely structured, with many of its resolutions unearned. The writing is at times naïve, embarrassingly overcomplex and overplayed, and shamefully melodramatic. Still it is an important work in that it reveals the shapes of things to come. It is, certainly, "early Gardner," the product of a twenty-five-year-old writer, but it is buttressed by nearly ten years of fiction apprenticeship, of story-writing and story-telling.

Part of the importance of "The Old Men" lies in its relation to the remainder of the Gardner canon. It is the touchstone for comparison, for from it can be traced certain patterns of development, various growths and recessions. It is an obvious source for subject and idea in the later works; places, names, and themes spring up in more recent novels and stories that first appeared in this dissertation-novel. Gardner, quite early on, seemed to know where he wished to go in his fiction, and "The Old Men" serves as a literary roadsign, pointing out thematic direction to his works to come.

Most apparent is the mere geography: the Catskill Mountains. "The Old Men" is part, one might say, of a Catskill pair whose other half is the novel *Nickel Mountain*.[3] The Mohawk Valley of New York provides the setting for both novels, and in both books we find looming over the characters the forested humps of Crow and Nickel Mountain. The names are invented, but the awesome physicality of the mountains is authentic. For Gardner, as for Cooper, the Catskills and their environs offer a proving ground for the testing of men and women and their ideas.

Among these ideas is the inevitability of old age and death, of mortality. Beneath the near agelessness of the hills, all too age-conscious humanity struggles to outwit (or outwait) the finality of dying. It is a theme later dealt with in *The Resurrection, Grendel, Nickel Mountain,* and *October Light,* and is perhaps Gardner's prime philosophic concern.

Also present is the notion of ghosts and visions, of dreams and nightmares. The human imagination is a creative force and is shaped, so Gardner maintains, by personal belief and development. The ability to envision the immaterial and the questionable is important for Gardner. His visionaries are special and peculiar people, ones marked for private but important destinies. We see this idea played upon again in *The Resurrection, Nickel Mountain, The King's Indian, October Light, The Art of Living,* and *Mickelsson's Ghosts,* wherein certain characters possess certain imaginative qualities that are explored and annotated.

There also are characters in almost every Gardner fiction, and beginning in "The Old Men," who are forced to confront the shocks of accident and grief. The universe is causal, but surprising; events are related to one another in causal sequence, but that sequence does not always reveal itself to human rationality or knowledge. The seer is the rare talent who can reach back far enough into history, unravel the connections, and make predictions and pronouncements upon the future. Most of us, however, are caught unawares by the mishaps of the cosmos and so often assume unnecessary responsibility for actions that hold no relation to us. In "The Old Men," as well as in *The Resurrection, The Wreckage of Agathon, Grendel, Nickel Mountain,* and *October Light,* people know logical and illogical suffering, the kinds of pain that come in a volatile world.

To combat this felt anguish, Gardner offers love—an old solution, but not, in Gardner's case, a sentimental one. Wounds are salved by strength of community, constancy of faith, temperance of ideals. Love and hate spring from the same source, and are often the weird progeny of each other. Such love-hate relationships are at work in "The Old Men," where they generate much of the book's physical and psychological action; and they reappear in every one of Gardner's later works of adult fiction.

Finally, there are other, lesser ideas that randomly turn up in Gardner's fiction and that first appear in "The Old Men." There is the notion of youthful perversity and iniquity (*The Resurrection, Nickel Mountain, October Light*); the sterility of institutionalized religion (*Nickel Mountain, The King's Indian, Freddy's Book*) and the revitalizing force of art, particularly music (*The Resurrection, Grendel, The King's Indian, October Light, The Art of Living*); and the idea of "modeling," or character formation based on role models (*The Resurrection, October Light*). In short, there is an impressive quantity of technical and intellectual substance that has made its way from "The Old Men," in whatever recarved form, into Gardner's later writings. "The Old Men" is a marred work, but hardly one to be benignly swept off into a corner, mused at as a curious but ultimately jejune piece of craft.

"The Old Men" is set within the Catskill Mountains, in Slater, New York—a small town with a small university. It lies cordoned by mountains: to the north, Crow Mountain; to the south, Hood Mountain; and to the west, "the local giant," Nickel Mountain. Nickel Mountain is just one of the haunters of Slater; its past is mysterious, its origins so unclear that "No one could say how the mountain had gotten its name. Perhaps it was a distortion of some pre-Monhawanta Indian name, or perhaps it was that once, near the mountain's base, a mine shaft had been sunk in search of nickel. None had been found. Instead, the miners had made the vaguely disquieting discovery that Nickel Mountain was hollowed out inside, like a meeting place of the gods."[4] Nickel Mountain rises, ghostlike, over the town, an enigma to the men who live at its base. "It was not simply that men had hanged themselves on Nickel Mountain or that the dead had been seen walking there, palpable, gray-white, thoughtful, for the mystery had come earlier, was perhaps implicit in the mountain's lines or in its two lakes, set close together like huge misshapen eyes" (p. 4). The mountain is a malign presence that commands awed attention.

Slater is also pervaded by the spirit of age, of infinite and tiresome years. As the title suggests, the town is peopled with "old men," men who have drawn out their lives in Slater, men who will die in Slater. They are farmers and professors, fanatics and skeptics, but they are all aged, and all share the same retrospective vision that comes with time and experience. The "old men" are the keepers of the legends, the storytellers, the preservers of myth. They are bent-spined old men in search of a tale and a truth as they drift off toward death. They are lined and grizzled, some wise and some crazed. Some are like living ghosts, men who have already passed through "the gentle decline toward the grave."

Amidst the legends and ghosts and near-ghosts walks the spirit of Lawrence Emery Leigh, Slater's "great man." The town, like all else, had been dying in the mid-nineteenth century when Leigh appeared. A "dentist and Methodist preacher," Leigh quickly established a seminary (later to become Leigh University—also dying) and generally looked after the spiritual life of the town, until, as one of Slater's men tells it, "Leigh was murdered in a Nickel Mountain tavern, where he'd gone to preach. It seems as he lay there, or kneeled there, dying . . . he promised to keep an eye on Slater, alive or dead. Promised to come back from the grave to keep the town righteous" (p. 47). And to many of the men and women in Slater, Leigh is indeed still keeping the village honest.

Naturally, there are believers and nonbelievers. Those who accept the legend accept it in varying ways. Sam Ghoki is an aging Jehovah's Witness, a doctrinaire and a visionary, but his visions are forced. His morality is strict and overbearing, and he seeks to repress and obscure, instead of cultivate pure instinct. He is a man caught in the sweep of time, a man so bundled up in his blind belief and mortal guilt that he cannot deal with the realities of the present life. He is a tyrant to his daughter Ginger, a sixteen-year-old whose precocity only torments old Ghoki the more. He sees the world in spiritual symbols, as emblems of a warped theology: "He, old Ghoki, like Nickel Mountain, and like the ghost of Lawrence Leigh—like both, for the two were one, and one with himself and one with Almighty Jehovah—he was another kind of metaphor, and he went his way" (p. 8).

Ghoki's is just one type of belief, a narrow and egotistical sort of belief that denies the legend's impressive power. A broader and more imaginative sort of belief is that held by Professor Utt, an aging man who earnestly seeks to maintain the wonderful essence of the myth. He affirms the presence of the ghost, exalts its purpose, and refutes its mere whimsicalness. Leigh appears to those who are faithful to him, who have the sensitivity (whether conscious of it or not) to detect his coming. Says Utt:

> "These young people, and the baked old men you see rocking on their porches, *believe* in Leigh's ghost. The thing's a force, a bullwhip for evil in a world where none of us knows, for sure, what's evil and what's not. That's the terror." The definition—the exact location of the basis of terror—was good, an insight he hadn't expected. And the light of the insight drove him on. He knew, well enough, what was happening to him; it had happened many times. Nevertheless, he leaned forward farther, punching out his words with the stem of his pipe. "I've seen strapping eighteen-year-olds run like sheep till they fell down sobbing, beating the shale, because they'd seen Leigh's face." (pp. 49–50)

Cynics enrage Utt, as do the quantifiers and logicians of myth. He rails against "the scientification of ghosts: poetry not as search but as lament" (p. 51). In their ability to envision, Utt and Ghoki are kin, but Ghoki's vision is pernicious, while the professor's is healthful and restorative.

Among the skeptics is old Lorward, like Utt a professor at the university. Lorward is a scientist, a wizened and wise old man, "deep-brained" and owllike with "Merlin's eyes." His perceptiveness is unnerving; it travels beyond deduction to near mind-reading. He is Gardner's oracle and seer, though his visions are not always blessed. He neither accepts nor rejects the folklore of Lawrence Leigh, but he approaches it doubtingly, a hand kept behind his back. What is most strange, though, is Lorward's clear resemblance to old Leigh himself. Like Leigh, Lorward is bearded, hook-nosed, and gray: "Lorward's black coat, in the mirror image, sank from his humped back to a point a few inches below each shoulder, and the tip of his frayed, dark vest, just visible under the beard, was loose, revealing behind it a frayed white shirt with yellowing buttons, sagging from the old, hollow chest; unreal. The voice, though, was as deep and full-bodied as the voice of the cello" (p. 41). He is Leigh's avatar, a man who lives with gray cats in rooms with old furniture and cobwebbed picture frames. People are afraid to meet his eyes. He knows more than anyone around him.

Ginger Ghoki exists within this community of graybeards with all the subtlety of a reveler among mourners. She, too, is a believer in ghosts, a holder of visions, but they are not the kind commanded by her father. Hers is a secular mysticism that calls up not chariots and angels, but men and other earthly shapes. She is sexually informed; she enjoys the excitement of sexual contact, but in an unusual way. For Ginger, love and fright are bound together, the scare provoking the pleasure. The horrid in life beckons her passion, and the origin of this phenomenon is part of her search: "In some strange way they were tied together, terror and love, and if she could just make out why they were tied together, it came to her now, she would have found what she was looking for, waiting to become" (p. 61). Sexuality is a tool, a device for her exploration of a world that she is struggling to understand. Her nightmares are gnarled and border on the psychotic. There is a perversity about her that is cruel and cutting, but at times unwitting. Her treatment of her father, of the young Phil Empson, and of the older Quinn is puzzling and unconscionable. She hasn't yet discovered how to love properly. She is the young *belle dame sans merci* of the Catskills.

The relationship between Ginger and her father is an indication of the problems in her character. Sam is painfully strict, a deluded guardian of Ginger's lost chastity. He wants to keep her pure, sinless, ready for the kingdom to come. But Sam is battling temptations and urges of his own.

> Once, in a kind of waking nightmare, old Ghoki had found his daughter lying naked on the davenport, and for an instant he had considered incest. He was an honest man, and he did not pretend, now, that the thought had not come. Again and again, when the girl's head touched a certain angle, or when her lips bit tight, becoming her mother's lips, the memory of that morning returned. And so he had starved himself and had prayed, not sleeping, until a man had come to him and had said, "The darkness is safe. The night is Mine." And old Ghoki had been satisfied; there was no choice. The Father shall kill mankind. That was the law. (p. 19)

Sam's lust has faded, but the uncleanness of the thought shocks him into penance and purgation. He must deny the flesh that drags him down, starve it of its nature; only then will the visions and the visitations come. It is a warped sort of religious and moral attitude, one that is obviously repugnant to Gardner and his way of belief.

Father and daughter thrive upon a love-hate conflict. Sam despises Ginger's worldliness and whorish ways, knowing as he does the frailties of the body. Ginger detests her father's backwardness and Biblical whinings. Yet there is a caring between them that comes, perhaps, from the shared loss of wife and mother. Ginger must enter womanhood alone and unguided; her father's attempts at explanation are feeble and pitiable. It is, in fact, Sam's inability to handle Ginger's flourishing sexuality that finally kills him. Sam is forced to acknowledge the signs of his daughter's aging, the eternal changes which

> he knew were normal and emotional and physical changes, and though they disturbed him, made him feel unclean, he knew they were part of the tribulation of parenthood, mortality. Nevertheless, they meant that his girl was a full-blown woman now, or wanted to be. Living in a college town, beset by God knew what vile temptations, she was lucky to have kept her innocence at sixteen. He had told her—time and time again—of the sins of the flesh, of gluttony and lust. But what were his sayings? Words, the confusing admonitions of a John. He had not told her exactly what lust meant, had never mentioned, he thought angrily, the love that had made desire a sacred thing when he'd lain beside her mother. It was high time he said these things to Ginger. (pp. 139–40)

So he stolidly prepares himself for the interview between parent and child, but grows enraged at Ginger's distance and lack of interest. She starts for the door and for her boyfriend, her blouse unbuttoned invitingly. Sam rages at her, futilely; and as she leaves, his heart gives out and he plunges into the eventual darkness, carried off in the rush of wings and the wail of a fallen angel. When Ginger returns with Phil and discovers her father's body, they both flee into the rain, allowing Sam's soul to fend for itself. Sam Ghoki is a man whose motives, founded in love, are perverted by a strait-jacketing religious system. His inability to deal with the physical world destroys him; guilt and irresponsible conscience damn him.

But Ghoki is not alone among the damned and near-damned. Tucked away in his house of shadows is old Lorward, the observer and figurer. He recognizes the connection between Ginger and the young professor-poet Rosen, and seeks to sever it. Rosen's poetry is "despiritualized, hopeless," a reflection of his faded life. He has failed with his wife, has succeeded with the dean's, but feels some sympathy for Ginger, whom he wishes to warn of life's threats and hazards. He tells her tales, shocking ones of love and horror, and they send Ginger off into a vision of old Lawrence Leigh.

Lorward perceives a danger in their relationship, and so calls the poet to his lair for a dialogue (Gardner, here, is shaping the meeting between Grendel and the dragon in *Grendel;* he even reuses a line from this earlier scene in his later book). We find that the two men are frightfully similar. Rosen is a young man grown philosophically ancient. He possesses some of Lorward's perceptivity. And both have been hard on their women:

> At last, turning, lowering his heavy white brows over his spectacles, Lorward said, "I destroyed my wife some years ago. . . . The way we all destroy our women," Lorward continued sententiously, jerking the cover from the coffee-pot as he spoke, spattering explosive droplets of water on the range. "By pressing down into their vitals with our harder manly bones, sucking the blood of their sensibilities." He smiled, showing teeth as yellow as the eyes of the cats, but deader. "Now that she's gone I use a walking-stick."
> (p. 125)

What holds out salvation to Rosen, implies Gardner, is his concealed faith, his urgently denied hope for mankind. Though his poetry belies the fact, Rosen has elected (for the present) to live. It is what Lorward tells him:

> "You, my boy, do not believe in selflessness, happiness, justice. You do believe—as a poet—the Judaic-Christian 'myth,' as you'll call it. In the fall of Adam, capitulation of David, crucifixion of God's own son—dying in a lost cause, lost from the start—you find poetic representation, so to speak, of the world's great truth: one is born, one suffers, one dies. Theoretically, all men should die in the lost cause, and if they cannot die in it, must admit, at least, that not dying is wrong. There's your ethic. But breathing is good—and there are only two choices, join or live. . . . But you do not live by your philosophy," he said. "The same non-rational force which dictates your credo dictates your violations of it—your actions—gesture without meaning, like the clapping of a single hand. You believe that nothing, not even the mind, not even art, is any hope; but you act in spite of yourself with humanity." He raised his hand abruptly to forestall argument. "Not always. You slip. But at bottom you are moral. I pity you." (pp. 127–28, 129)

Rosen affirms what little he can. Lorward has ceased trying to affirm, and now exists solely to know, to understand, and to spin the webs of his rhetoric (like Bishop Brask in *Freddy's Book*). Rosen recognizes Lorward's predicament as the predicament of all agedness: "For the old men there are no alternatives, no escapes; only the long, slowly unravelling tight-rope strung across hell. There it was: the sense of humor was the first sense to die, and humorless, old men lost perspective: slipping on the sill of the grave, they clutched at straws and saw them as trees" (p. 132). What Rosen does not realize is that he too has begun the descent toward old, humorless age. Lorward "knows his pulse" because Lorward has traveled the same path. It is up to Rosen, then, to make the effort, to act morally.

It is the same lesson that Jay Corby must learn. Corby is a remnant of an old and decimated Slater family. As a child he saw his parents ruined by polio; more important, as a young man he suffered the suicide of his older brother Dale, a former professor at Leigh University. Blasted by his wife's apparent infidelity, Dale took his life—was destroyed, Jay insists, by the cruelty and connivance of the woman Dale had loved. Dale's death is Jay's ghost. Dale had believed in holding on, in loving; he believed "that being good was better than being evil, that even if you made a mistake, gave your love not to a woman but to a pig, you had to hang on—psychologically *had* to, because you might make the pig a woman by love, and once loving you had to try" (p. 158). Part "sentimental dung," part earthly necessity—but Dale was still willing to "break his back for something."

Not that Jay Corby is cold. He is humane, he is sensitive and insightful, almost to the point (like Lorward) of uncanniness. He can be loving and strangely caring; but he hasn't yet crawled out from under the weight of his brother's suicide. He needs, suggests Gardner, to pinpoint responsibility and guilt. And so he broods, and haunts the graveyard that holds his parents and his brother. He cherishes the solitude and silence as a way of coming to some sort of holy knowledge. His moodiness is deathful, but he is filled with intelligence.

This is why he is so quick to pick up on Ginger's sacrilege on the night of her father's death. As she feels the shock of her stricken father growing more and more real, the familiar terror begins to sweep through her once more. As before, the terror keys her passion; and with her dead (or dying) father on the floor below, Ginger and Phil make rapid, blasphemous love in her bedroom above.

This guilty memory becomes Ginger's "sin," and the manipulation of this memory drives the novel onward. It is a shared transgression, known not only to Phil and Ginger but to Jay and Rosen as well. Ginger is surrounded by knowing "old men, old fathers." Sam Ghoki's ghost points a thin bony finger at her and whispers, "I know, I know." And so she turns to Rosen for salvation, and to Corby she turns for commitment. From Rosen she learns of an identical connection between love and terror, of blood rising against blood; their peace is one without sense and contact. In Jay she sees something unusual and frightening, something she has known in no man, young or old, before. His shadowed profile spurs her into nightmare and into vision, and she half-believes that she can ride into humanness on his heels. Rosen becomes a brother, and Corby the Grail.

Ginger persists, however, in her perversion of human kindness. She taunts Phil with her "collies," rejects Utt's parental concern as senile humbuggery, and manages to twist fate unmercifully. The vengeance meant for her is wrought upon Wally Yopes, who had merely taken the trouble to care; consequently, in the struggle between Yopes and Phil's high-school vigilantes, Phil suffers a murderous beating that sends him to the hospital. From this come guilt and concealment, eternal human damnations. There is guilt on all sides; some of it is felt responsibly and some of it is not, and the way in which Gardner's characters work with and against this guilt is one of the novel's main concerns.

Human accident and tragedy necessitate responsibility; the assumption of guilt, says Gardner, is a part of human nature and, under normal circumstances, a healthy part. If people can think out the complexities of their feelings, establish the connections between events, then the guilt can be turned into something productive. When it preys, however, guilt debilitates. People lose faith; they despair and devour their innards. Such guilt distorts the causes of human action and breeds impotence (sexual and emotional), violence, and suicide. And there is not a single character in "The Old Men" who is not touched, in some way, with this type of guilt.

Part of this novel's intricacy and mystery lies in the nature of Ginger's character. She is moving toward a type of madness, beyond vision to unearthliness. At times she is unreachable and out of human contact; she is perched on a star's edge in space, seeing things that no one else can see, hearing melodies too high-pitched for the normal ear. People who misunderstand believe she is insane. But as one character explains, "It's guilt . . . that makes people see the ghost" (p. 369). Perhaps it is guilt that blends, like running colors, imagination and reality. All those who have met the spirit of Lawrence Leigh have had linen to hide, things unwished for.

But it is more. There are those with deeper insights. It is Lorward who (as always) looks farther, who lifts up the old boards to see what's crawling beneath it all. Says the hump-backed old seer: "That girl's got damnation in her. . . . Damnation and redemption like two poisons. A man can't tell which poison to fear more" (p. 465). Ginger is a latter-day Rappaccini's daughter, offering hope and despair, salvation and death.

To Rosen, Ginger is "a constitutional outlaw—an outlaw in her very genes" (p. 417). Her perversity is inherent and purposive and natural. She's "a fantastic mixture of little-old-woman and child" (p. 418), and the horror is that she cannot locate the solid ground in between. She is looking to be rescued, to be pulled away from the brink of insanity and given a chance to reconcile the ghosts and guilts that plague her. Rosen gives her books, gives her *The Golden Bowl* and *The Marble Faun* in hope that she will recognize the ambiguities in her spirit. At the same time, Rosen is attempting to save himself. The ruin of his own marriage and the ugliness of his affair with Mrs. Woodstock evoke despair; his life takes on deeper shades of gray, and the visions that come to him are of locked doors and pistols. Through Ginger he can act, make an effort, and preserve the life that he feels drifting from him. So he defends Ginger at the risk of his position. He understands what the reckless and cowardly brow-beating might do to her, how it might send her reeling, irretrievable. He later even admits to loving her. Jay tells Rosen it will kill him. "Maybe," Rosen replies. "I had an idea it would bring me to life. I suppose that was what I thought. But maybe you're right. Maybe you get killed anyway, though" (pp. 477–78).

But to save, without fully comprehending, is impossible (a lesson Gardner teaches again in *The Resurrection*). This is what hamstrings Jay Corby. Not only is he confused by Ginger's far-eyed questions and unfelt perceptions, but he has only recently uncovered the truth of his own brother's death. Dale Corby was a suicide not because of his wife's unfaithfulness, but because of his own multiple infidelity. This revelation at once illuminates and obscures; it explains more fully Dale's action and dissolves much of Jay's hate, but it clouds even further Jay's knowledge of himself. He must answer the questions Gardner asks of all his protagonists: What is there to affirm and respond to? Where does one rest one's faith? For a moment he sees his purpose in Ginger, in attempting to fathom and to aid her, and this is why he opens up to old Lorward, whom Jay sees as her ultimate benefactor. Jay has only a fraction of the knowledge and of the secret, for he partly knows "why Ginger Ghoki had lain with Phil Empson, the night of her father's death. Her hell-fire father had taught her his terrors, and her defiance had taught her answers to them, and defiance had taught her new terrors. . . . But it was beyond that now, hopelessly tangled" (p. 454). When Ginger's eyes glaze over in a vision of her father, Jay sees only black wall and candle flame. When the horror comes in the deep chambers of the church, Jay nearly takes her, nearly falls to her violence, though he cannot penetrate her mystery. He, like Rosen and Lorward, must wait for the answers to come.

Ginger has the fatal touch; everything she touches becomes endangered. She cracks the faith of those who trust her, like old Dr. Utt, who "always trusted his heart more than his head," who "believed, finally and emphatically, that life was good, beautiful, nature just and lawful" (pp. 469–70). Her wildness stirs the viciousness in men. Her sexless night with Jay hurls Wally Yopes into a killing fury, the sort of fury that battered Phil Empson. That same act results in Jay's expulsion, makes him an outcast, marks him. Ginger scars all the men she loves—Quinn, Rosen, Jay—scars them emotionally and physically. She sets people against others, and against themselves; people like Empson and Rosen destroy themselves out of a failure of hope and a ruination of faith.

The only man who remains to save her is Jay Corby, and he too is made to suffer. Jay argues for self-salvation and tries to persuade Ginger that the crazed can retrieve themselves. He snaps the thin band that checks her guilt over Phil's death and she strikes out, taking blood, leaving her mark:

> There were tears in Jay Corby's eyes, but he would not touch the stinging cheek with his fingers. And she could read—could suddenly read—his thoughts. *She does not own me; nobody owns me. I will die first.* And she saw—it was this that came to her—that by the scratch she had taken possession of him, had forced him to belong to her. For she was human. He could not treat her as a machine or a twig on a mountain that had unknowingly scratched his cheek. He had attacked her, had forced her to fight him, and she had scratched his face. He, they, had broken through coldness, calm friendship, to something that must either be love or hate. She felt, suddenly, responsible for him—responsible as she had not been even when he had held her in his arms at the hospital. And responsible for Rosen, too, and Quinn and Wally, and responsible for Phil Empson's death. She knew now why her father had been terrified by the vision of her mother writhing on brimstone. She, Ginger, whether enemy or lover, must not give pain, and her pain—her own pain—was his, or was theirs. . . . It was not frightening now that she had seen it, found words for it. But the hopelessness was still there, the no escape either as monster or princess. (pp. 514–15)

In these favorite Gardner images of monster and princess we see that it is part of Ginger's infernal nature to "give pain," to disrupt and destroy, just as it is in the nature of love to conceive hate. This, in particular, is what happens to poor Rosen; half-mad like Ginger, his salvation comes too late, comes in tragedy and blackness and the loneliness of suicide.

No, Ginger still has not learned the implications of her character and of the brand of love she spawns. It is (as in all of Gardner's fiction) a process. After Rosen's death, the ghost of Leigh comes to Ginger in her guilt, sits with her and judges her:

> *Jack Rosen shot himself tonight.*
> "I know."
> *That isn't enough, knowing. You failed to save him.*
> "But I *couldn't* save him. *Nothing* could."
> *That isn't enough.* (pp. 586–87)

Her punishment is physical and cruel, brutal penance for her perversity (and a distant echo of her father's own mortification). The barbaric and medieval chain-whipping that leaves her disfigured is a psychological purge, an attempt to expel all guilt—just as she uses the sexual act as an exorcism of her terror. The violence she inflicted upon others, she returns upon herself, pain for pain.

Ginger must scar herself as she scars the men in her past ("beauty must claw the beast"). Those "three white lines moving down her cheek" are symbols of her connection and bond with her victims. She has drawn into herself their spirits, their natures, as part of her process of growing. "I've become something—you just do, without realizing it. And what I've become is people, all the people I've known, even you. I have to hang onto that, you see?" (p. 669). For Ginger, this is the first step toward the world of the sane; it gives her something to possess and to own. In the agony of that night she "had awakened, had grown, at last, passionately sane" (p. 653).

The scourge serves for Ginger as the farm serves for Jay. Jay must decide what he is going to do with his life, what he means to "be." So he turns to the land, working to reclaim it and to reshape it in his image. As Mullen tells him, "It j-just makes a difference, owning and not owning" (p. 601). It is Gardner's idea of the agrarian myth. You must have something to give to the land (and to life), something to put into it before you can belong to it. You must, Gardner declares, have something to affirm, something that can extract from your soul all of its physical and emotional energy. You bend your back "because what you bought, what you owned was the right to half kill yourself building something and to find out you were building wrong and to switch, shift your footing, kill yourself some new way. Because you built or you shot yourself, like Rosen,—it was life or death, and the choice was optional" (p. 618). It is the essential existential dilemma.

Jay also learns that the past cannot be rebuilt, as can the farm—only remodeled or refocused. One can, perhaps, manipulate the memory, but not the truth. It is the tavern owner, Mrs. Spratt, who instructs him: "You take it or leave it, and if it don't fit, you don't wrench it. You never knew the man that brought that woman in here, and you never will. You knew somebody else. Make that fit, if you can. That's about all there's time for" (p. 616). Jay finally comes to realize that guilt only withers and bears no fruit, that your life comes with a built-in history, and that nothing you do, however excruciating, can change it. "So whether or not it fit, you bought it, owned it, because there was no one and nothing you could pay, ever, except the past, the land, and, if you were lucky, the woman you owned the right to spend yourself for, watch over, pay with new seeds to replace the ones that shouldn't have been planted. Making yourself old, breaking your bones" (p. 620).

In a similar fashion, Jay hopes that he can somehow take possession of Ginger and remake her, and their lives. His feeling for her is a loving one, though he doesn't yet totally understand her. He is confused by her explanation, unaware of how well Ginger understands *him*. She tells him:

> They can go crazy for thousands of reasons, and in thousands of ways, and most of the time other people don't even know it's happened. Sometimes you don't know yourself. There's nothing you can do, but you have to try. *I* do. Things keep working on you—trees, for instance, or the sound of waterfalls,—and you do things because of them. They become part of you too, like people. You become sort of involved in them, and sometimes it makes you good and sometimes not. You watch people, because it's people that are important, that bring you to life, and you do things, and what you do is all confused with mountains and trees and waterfalls and animals and people you've known before, and whether what you did was sane you only find out afterward, if you find out at all. You have to keep watching, both people and things, because to do something good you have to be pushed—but you see bad things, too, and good and bad things are all mixed together. So you have to be watched. You have to *make* yourself be watched, and by people that you matter to—and people who really know—because otherwise they watch the wrong way. That's why you used to come here nights, Jay. Because without even knowing it, you wanted to be watched. Except that with you it's mostly just the past that watches. That's the difference between us. (pp. 670–71)

Jay is caught up in time, Ginger in humanity. Because Jay has still to learn involvement and the freedom which it brings, Ginger cannot accept his marriage offer. Nor can Jay accept Ginger's blatant offering of her body, an opportunity for Jay to begin his possession—in physicality. Jay still cannot distinguish between Ginger's reality and appearance, her genuine desires and her "faking."

The tale is a truthful one, one told over in time, its medievalism attractive no doubt to Gardner. Ginger is the lost and wandering princess, and

> like the princess in the tale, she'd gone from the shepherd hut out into the forest. Had wandered from place to place—had gone to wolves and bears and to Rosen, the mad prince, her brother, and to Dr. Utt, myopic old priest who saw no visions but believed in them as surely as in food and good conversation, and each place she went she was taken in, blindly, on faith, as Utt took in the stories of Leigh. And she'd gone to Lorward, aged magician who did not believe anymore in visions or food or talk, but who had also taken her in, as though he had known her by her walk. And she'd gone to Jay, the knight, foreign prince who had come on some quest he could not quite remember, and Jay, like Lorward, had known her and taken her in, hating her because she kept him from his quest, but not sure, quite, that she was not a part of the quest. And she'd walked with him, guiding him without knowing where they were going. (pp. 656–57)

At tale's end, they go alone, each pursuing a separate bounty. They make their ways through the forest, one going east, one going west, but always with the expectation of meeting, always with the belief that their destinations are identical. As she heads off in the arms of old Merlin-Lorward, Ginger turns: " 'I'll come back for you, either way. . . . You must wait.' And maybe she would, he thought; would come to him in the night, with wild, gleaming eyes, old in her teens, with broken bones.—And yet maybe not. Somehow, watching her walk, he had a feeling that when she came—if she came—she would come quietly, glittering nervously from within, like one's first glimpse of water inside the mountain. He knew it was a wild hope. Wild and maybe insane" (pp. 674–75). A wild and insane hope. A typically human and Gardner-esque hope. They *will* come together—as visions, as ghosts, summoned by love and faith.

"The Old Men," after all, is a novel that deals with the reconciliation of past and present. Memory so often provides an obscured perception of a distant reality; facts and fictions mingle, merge, and generate a totally new version of one's personal history. As these perceptions are redefined, so is one's concept of present reality. Man's mental and physical character is shaped by what he knows (or thinks he knows) of the events before his time, and as these facts crystallize and harden into certainty, man's knowledge of his own nature becomes more real and familiar.

Quite often, this growth into knowledge is spurred by "shocks" or jolts of life's brutal realism. Death and accident, destruction and betrayal, flesh and bloody sinew—all are part of the world we occupy. We are challenged by these accidents to devise a system of belief in which we can place our faith, and by which we can restore some meaning to an inchoate universe. Professions of confidence and commitment must be made; man must order his world about something solid and substantial, and recognize the necessity of human connection. This is a theme played upon again and again in the fiction of John Gardner, one that he sees as central to the survival of contemporary humanity. It is an attempt to maintain a shred of idealism in "this fallen, traitor- and monster-ridden world."[5]

Chapter 11

The Resurrection

I believe in sense; but only a fool or child
believes mere sense a match for the crushing blood.
          —"Desire on Sunday Morning"

The Resurrection, Gardner once remarked, "was the book that I wrote for myself. In all the others I've been conscious of an audience. For instance, I now read my stuff to my kids, and if my daughter thinks something is too slow, I change it. But in *The Resurrection* I did everything the way I wanted to do it."[1]

One of the things Gardner "wanted to do" in this novel was to respond to the didacticism of Tolstoy's own *Resurrection,* a book Gardner had just recently read:

> I thought it was an awful, awful, just wicked book, and I meant to answer it point by point, but the answer is obscure. Anyway, it was meant to be about a person, but also people in general who love ideas to the exclusion of people, so that people become ideas. I like James Chandler, but he never really understands his wife or even looks at her, he doesn't understand his children, obviously; and he falls in love with a girl and doesn't have the faintest idea what the girl is like although he has a fatherly feeling about her. He abstracts, and as a result what he does is cause total disaster. . . . Basically I was answering Tolstoy, and I answered too slyly to make myself clear. Tolstoy hated rote behavior, including such behavior as is expressed by duty. Chandler shares his theoretical distrust of theory, but his body controls him exactly as a good theory would— but with more harmful effect. What I wanted to do is show that a theory against rote behavior and convention can be at least as

monstrous as rote behavior, that in fact it leads to the same thing.[2]

Gardner later clarified his objection to Tolstoy's novel in *On Moral Fiction,* writing that "the tirades against rote-religion and the like in Tolstoy's late *Resurrection* are ugly not because of their implicit fascism but because they show warped emotion. The immorality is incidental."[3]

To demonstrate the error of Tolstoy's thinking, Gardner peopled his novel with Nekhlyudovs, with characters who wish to save themselves by saving others, and who act out of this sort of "warped emotion." They seek a resurrection through self-glorification and through self-conscious abnegation of the present. Mad, old John Horne is a radicalized Tolstoy, preaching the doctrine of rebirth and sacrifice, and it leaves him solitary and despairing. Viola Staley works toward sainthood in her half-granted devotion to the Chandler family and in her ill-designed love for James Chandler, who ruins himself because of a poorly constructed moral belief, and whose memory is literally "resurrected" in the early pages of Gardner's novel, in the tableau of daughter and lover at Chandler's graveside. (Like *The Sunlight Dialogues, The Resurrection* begins with a prologue from which the narrator flashes back to tell the bulk of the story.)

Tolstoy's ethical egalitarianism, Gardner believes, is a fraud. At the end of *Resurrection,* Nekhlyudov realizes "that the only sure means of salvation from the terrible wrongs which mankind endures is for every man to acknowledge himself a sinner before God and therefore unfit either to punish or reform others."[4] Such an attitude leads to quietism, to a passive acceptance of fate and an irresponsible refusal to act and to decide. Equally poisonous is the notion that to act against convention, merely for the sake of the action and for its egotistical satisfaction, is to act morally. If there are affirmations to be made, says Gardner, let them be made from the heart and from intuition, from pure, not "warped" emotion. This is the key to Gardner's "emotional metaphysics." The loves that count for something in Gardner's novel—the love of Rose Chandler for her husband and her son, and the brilliantly intuitive love of Marie for James— are the loves that Gardner wants to preserve. Affirm the world, affirm the "buzzing, blooming confusion," but affirm it because it is good and lasting and blessed, not because it is an enticing idea.

Gardner does not deny, of course, that reason serves well as a basis for moral action. He does believe, however, that a sane philosophy can be perverted toward an immoral and illogical goal. That is what happens in *The Resurrection;* that is why Gardner's novel is so heavily philosophical, why his protagonist is himself a philosopher. Gardner has revealed, in fact, that *The Resurrection* is based upon the life of the English philosopher, R. G. Collingwood who, on being told at the age of nineteen that he possessed a terminal disease that brought with it deterioration of the brain, set to work on his philosophical structure, a structure that Gardner called the "best system since Kant."[5] Collingwood died from this illness at the age of fifty-two, and many of his critics claim that his work after 1932 (when his health began to suffer dramatically) reflects his mental and physical failing.

Three of his philosophical doctrines are worth noting here for their bearing on *The Resurrection:* "(1) that creations of the human mind, no matter how primitive, must be studied historically, not psychologically; (2) that historical knowledge is attainable; and (3) that history and philosophy are identical."[6] This emphasis upon the importance of history especially appeals to Gardner; it is the reason for his rejection of Sartre and the existential stress upon the present. Gardner has also been influenced by Collingwood's aesthetic theories, expressed in *The Principles of Art.* Collingwood's argument against "art as craft" and his regard for the imagination, intuition, and the Aristotelian mode are all traits reflected in Gardner's own aesthetic thought. Both men agree that (to quote Collingwood, as Gardner does), art is "the cutting edge of philosophy."[7]

Like Collingwood, Gardner's James Chandler is an idealist who, in the Kantian tradition, splits the noumenal and phenomenal worlds but retains a belief in metaphysical order. He is dogged, in the last three weeks of his life, by the puzzles of metaphysics and aesthetics, and when stumped he often invokes the ideas of Collingwood to help clear the way. For Chandler, ideas are preeminent; the center of existence is mind. Such things as family and worldly relationships are secondary to his achievements in the abstract. At the age of forty-one, "James Chandler felt secure, on top of things. He had reached the rank of Associate Professor; his articles and his book were beginning to be noticed; he was happily married and had three small daughters whom he loved very much, though he could not say he knew them."[8]

Chandler is a metaphysician, a dying breed in the positivistic twentieth century. His concerns are with "the old realist-idealist dilemma" and with the epistemological problem of dream and reality, and he sets about solving them in a Collingwoodian way, by relying on historical analysis. Chandler is "some second Thales tranquilly tumbling down well after well" (p. 8), stereotypically ignoring the mundane for the profound. In the spirit of Kant, he extracts an untainted delight from his work, a sort of "pure" joy. They call him "Professor Quixote" because

> his concern with metaphysics in the age of analysis made him a man born too late for his time, a harmless lunatic, all of whose energy

and skill went into a heroic battling, by the laws of an intricate and obsolete code, against whatever he could contrive in the way of dragons. His success, if he should prove successful, would not be success in some worthwhile endeavor but merely proof to himself and the esoteric world of his own quite superfluous discipline that he could manage a feat which, as everyone including James Chandler knew, was no longer worth attempting. (p.11)

Chandler is the first of Gardner's intellectual lunatics or intellectual heroes, though he undercuts his heroism with "warped emotion." Chandler's philosophical doubts are real enough and pertinent enough in the modern world. He is concerned with systems, with their usefulness and their breakdowns, with the shifting means of perception which they provide. He carries in his memory two quotations, one unidentified and one from Collingwood: "The twentieth-century philosopher (if we discount self-pitying existentialists) does not suffer from any profound metaphysical anxieties. Philosophers who happen to believe in God and those who happen not to, do the same sort of work" (p. 11); and, "For the Christian, as never any pagan, religion becomes an influence dominating the whole of life; and this unity once achieved can never be forfeited again" (p. 12). The first of the two is fundamental to Gardner's renunciation of the Sartrean *Angst,* and both quotations underline a trust in the moral framework of the universe. Belief or disbelief in God is incidental; what is essential is the suspicion of a design in creation. Human beings are systems-builders and they may build religiously or metaphysically, but the supportive ethos must be there to keep the system from immediate collapse. Further, humanity is the locus of its own system: "However man's view of the universe has changed, the macrocosm-microcosm concept of those wise old Greeks still held: One was, oneself, with all one's kind, the cosmic detonation. Or the cosmic rose, perhaps, as Collingwood had it" (p. 13). Humanity is the universe in miniature, its actions and ideas the igniting forces that keep existence in motion. The universe grinds on, producing, chewing up, reproducing matter and spirit, and mankind looks for some way to survive.

Survival (or even the hope of survival) is difficult, though, in a world where disease and decay can come so quickly and so unheralded. The news comes to Chandler as unexpectedly as a housebreaking:

He had, according to his doctor, aleukemic leukemia, on the verge even now of the blast crisis, an increase in the lawless proliferation of lymphatic-type cells that would swiftly and suddenly shift the white count from its present six thousand to something astronomical, perhaps near 500,000; there was, in effect, nothing to be done.

> And so it was settled. The limits of Chandler's identity (It was thus that he put it to himself, fleeing into the comforting arms of pedantic abstraction) were set. (p. 13)

The shock of the material, of the eternal corruption of the body is brought sharply home to Chandler. Suddenly, time and extinction press inexorably upon him. He discovers that he is finite and capable of passing out of this world as quickly as an old idea. It is the familiar medieval concept of "mutabilitie." As Gardner puts it, "One way or another, my characters are always set against the tragic backdrop, because values have meaning only insofar as they're mutable, we're mutable."[9] Death, Gardner has said, is the only thing that makes life serious. It alters our perceptions and molds relationships.

As a philosopher, Chandler finds the question of his mortality even more serious and more susceptible to examination than most people would, but in no way is he more capable of handling "the idea of dying":

> He himself had written long ago, when he was still young and in excellent health, "A philosopher is not better prepared than another man for the crises in life, for example, the coming of his own death; he is merely prepared to suffer more systematically, which is to say neither to suffer more nor to suffer less but rather to evade in a slightly different way," and lighting on this passage now—he was rereading all he'd ever written—he was surprised to see how right his guess had been. (p. 16)

A life full of ideas shrinks awfully when it confronts its end. Man cowers, whimpers, searches for a way to answer the darkness, but ultimately submits.

For Chandler, the first step toward understanding comes in a return to his personal history. The present, both temporal and geographic, becomes meaningless; it is the past which must be studied (as Collingwood would suggest), and that can best be done by going back to where it was lived. In Chandler's case, this is Batavia, New York, a small farm town in the northwest corner of the state.[10] His mother still occupies the family house there, alone, widowed by the suicide of her husband. There, too, are people and parts of his past that continue to throw shadows upon his present.

As Chandler discovers, the nearness of death changes one's angle of vision. Everything is cast in a new light: the town of Batavia is different; there is the influx of strangers and racial mixtures, newcomers from downstate and Italians and blacks and Poles. "Too much was changed, thrown into a buzzing, blooming confusion." Batavia is a town built on quicksand (though I do not believe Gardner wants the symbolism pushed); the town is shifting, and Chandler seems to hear the moans as it undergoes its "urban removal."

In his mother, however, Chandler sees the genuine impress of time. After "what might as well have been twenty years," Chandler faces her:

> She walked with a thick black cane; she was nearly blind; and she had a goiter. She stood smiling, holding out a shaking hand, and as he went to her, herding the girls ahead of him in his embarrassment, he remembered his grandmother in her black lace veil. She had been slighter, more genteel—you'd never have caught her with gray slip showing—but the shaking and the blind old eyes were the same, and he was shocked. (p. 20)

Days and years still wear most harshly on the flesh, and the coming-home of this reality grates at Chandler's soul. It breeds flashes of hatred for his family, quick bursts of irrational fury. Death begins to bare Chandler's nerves—death coupled with the nagging presence of time.

Time becomes "a visual dimension," a new way of defining experience. Chandler, haunted by this presence, attempts to escape time, to live, like a child, outside of time. Remembrance becomes for Chandler a new mode of thought. The past becomes blended and confused with the present, the distinctions grow dim. Chandler is aloof from time, poised on a balance-beam, observing with the distance allowed one who is certain of his death the actions of those around him. The future holds nothing now for Chandler and is of no concern (though he worries over the fate of his family). Instead, he seeks explanations for the conditions of things present, looks for causes and connections.

Chandler begins to brood. In Batavia's growth and change he perceives a symbol for the universe, and he questions the justness of it all, sensing that

> it was *not* all right that the narrow old brick street was gone. It was good, but it was not all right. There was not a trace of the comfortable old country town, nothing. Or if that was too strong, there was nothing that didn't stand out like a death's head, a Victorian gable singing *Memento mori* above a cheap, glossy storefront. He recalled, suddenly, Collingwood's phrase, *a process in which the things that are thus destroyed are brought into existence.* What was it, exactly, that was being built? Not even the brotherhood of man, because there were always new waves of strangers: "Nigger section," the driver had said, with a kind of laugh, as though he were showing a dirty picture. They too would be assimilated and would

assimilate, but then there would be still other strangers of some other kind—Nature is never spent—and the city would expand, all cities would expand, and the glossy storefronts too would fall, leaving only, here and there, a windy Sears to sing *Memento mori*. He remembered: *A lawless proliferation*. (pp. 36–37)

Like the murderously expanding white cells in his blood, like the explosive Einsteinian universe, things grow more numerous. All things change, all things are transient, all things die and are succeeded. Chandler is bewildered by the flux and the uncertainty of his world; he loses himself momentarily in the blackness of the existentialist pit, and is rescued (like Thales) by the chance and technically heavy-handed, but solid grip of a boy, another human being (p. 37).

Chandler also begins to dream. His recollections are conscious and subconscious; the visions come to him both awake and asleep, eyes alive and eyes dead, and they are troublesome. Visited by nightmares as a youth (they are one of his most vivid memories), Chandler, as a dying adult, has dreams equally as frightening and disturbing. Sleeping in the bed of his childhood, his first night back in Batavia, he dreams of his dead father. He sees him at work on his machines, "large and intricate machines, rickety conveyor belts with slats and holes like something used by Catskill farmers" (p. 23). Chandler's father was a "tinkerer," a craftsman of improbable mechanics; his one passion was for the perpetual motion machine that spun and hummed in his dusty workroom. He was a man loved by his son, who had "never seen anything anywhere so beautiful as his father's smile" (p. 23), and in his dream the smile and his father's face are as fresh and real as when he was alive. The past is becoming corporeal for James.

His second dream comes the very next night, and it takes a decidedly more threatening turn. In it he sees his three daughters standing high upon a railroad bridge, oblivious to the train hurtling its whistle from the tracks just beyond. He calls to them; they hear nothing, and so he runs after them:

> He drew near to them at last and called to them again. Anne, the one who had his face, turned and smiled. He realized abruptly that he had made a mistake: It was not Anne but an old, old woman with a toothless, wizened face like the face of a monkey. She had been expecting him. Her mouth was full of blood. He glanced down to see what time it was, then remembered, in sudden, stinging terror, that his wristwatch lay where he had left it, at home on the dresser. The old woman began to smile, her head tipped back to keep the blood in, and she reached out to stroke his cheek.

And now he felt, together with terror, a horrible, obscene delight.
(p. 39)

It is a dreadful vision, one that will haunt Chandler repeatedly. As a child,
his dreams were sharp and colorful, and "almost invariably he saw himself
in his dreams as heroic." But now, once again in his mother's house, "he
had nightmares worse than any he had met with since his childhood."
Time and experience have worked their gloomy magic on Chandler, as
they work it on us all. Remembrance becomes spectral and ghostly, popu-
lated by hags and witches and all of the grotesqueries that collect in our
past. For Chandler, it is the old woman who comes to him again and
again, caressing him, beckoning him, terrorizing him. She arrives twice
more, appearing successively on the following nights; on the fourth night
and in the fourth dream she comes as both a mental and a palpable
presence;

> He remembered standing in the children's room, listening with all
> his might, and remembering hearing something at last, a swishing
> sound, perhaps the sound of a skirt. He struggled with someone on
> a rooftop—dimly he recalled a dry, skull-like face, long hair, the
> scent of an old cedar trunk left for years in an attic—and then he
> felt himself falling and felt a burning pain shooting through his
> knee. When he awakened, early the next morning, he was cold and
> stiff. The window, which opened onto the porch roof, was partly
> raised, and when he got out of bed to close it, pain shot, once
> again, through his knee. In the bathroom he discovered with
> amazement that his face and chest were scratched and bruised. (pp.
> 44–45)

Appearance and reality, once clear to Chandler, have now become
blurred. The physicality of her presence is startlingly real and authentic.
He questions the nature of his dreams, whether they are in fact the
product of a night's fancy, or actual half-awakened dramas—and he cannot provide an adequate answer.

The challenge for Chandler becomes at once intellectual and personal.
He takes up his writing, returns to epistemology and to his study of
memory, though time stubbornly denies its completion. He tears up his
C. I. Lewis and all of his realist double talk, and commits himself to an
analysis of something that is fleeting, evasive, and ambiguous. But for
Chandler memory has substance and existence; the fabric of his present
life is woven from the past, from memory, and it is his key to understanding that same life. It is the same puzzle that presents itself to Jay Corby in
"The Old Men": the reconciling of the true past with the assumed past.

Part of Chandler's past in Batavia is housed with three aged, spinster sisters—the Staleys. They are the oldest living things in the town; their house is a museum, ancient and musty. Maud Staley was a painter in the "stock Romantic" tradition, her vision flowery and magical. Betsy Staley, Chandler's old piano teacher, still gives lessons to the children of Batavia and still curses beneath her breath at each missed note. And Emma Staley is the oldest and the craziest of the three. It is Emma who holds a special fascination for James—she is the misty lady of his dreams, though the vision is at first confusing to him:

> He'd had no idea how completely he had prepared himself to find
> Aunt Emma the mad old woman in his dreams. But he had been
> wrong. She was beautiful, almost more beautiful than she'd been
> when she was younger. She was a tiny, china-doll-like person
> dressed from head to foot in black: a black shawl of the kind his
> grandmother had worn, a long black dress, black shoes and
> stockings, and, oddly enough, black gloves. Her face was like a
> girl's: trusting, gentle, innocent. She looked at them all with the
> same friendly curiosity, as though she had never seen them before
> but was very much inclined already to like them. (p. 61)

Visually, Emma is wrong; there is too much beauty, too much softness. The woman of Chandler's visions is cragged and hoary. But Emma is Chandler's past: she is his mother and grandmother, his days as a child, the pale dusk of his father's workshop. She is the ambiguous memory: in daylight, she is the past glorified; in the darkness of his nightmares, she is the past scarified.

Her actions in real life mirror her actions in Chandler's visionary life: "Without warning, Aunt Emma reached up and touched Chandler's cheek very lightly with her dry, cold fingers. Chandler instantly recalled the similar gesture of the old woman in his dream, but he felt, now, no fright or revulsion, only a slight embarrassment and then a gentle surge of pity. It was as though it were indeed the spontaneous gesture of a child" (p. 62). In truth, she is a child, in mind-age, in the distant stare of her eye, in her relinquishment of time. She looks to Chandler and whispers, "I've been good. . . . Father, I've been *good*" (p. 66). She is Chandler's fourth and most complex daughter. "He saw her sitting erect and prim, waiting for a long-dead father—of God? was that it?—waiting for *him*, whoever it was, to lead her away; from her overpowering world of old mills and waterfalls and sundials of mossy stone" (p. 67). Her words echo in Chandler's brain and haunt him as vividly as her night-image.

There is also a fourth resident in this house of age: the niece of the Staleys, nineteen-year-old Viola Staley. She is their housekeeper, their guardian, their keeper of the keys. It is Viola who locks mad Emma in her room, whence comes the eerie scratching of nails against door-wood. It is Viola whom Chandler's mother, Rose, brands as "evil." James's first impression is twin-sided. He recalls her face with its peculiar power, and how he "was startled all over again by the green of her eyes. He couldn't tell whether a thing so unnatural was beautiful or terrible. She crossed to the double door opposite and was gone, leaving him still in his light coat, his hat in his hands. The young woman's eyes continued to molest his thoughts" (p. 51). Viola possesses a perverse beauty that draws and repels. She is an actress in a role, playing half-mad, half-sane, the seductress and the killer. She is the sister of Ginger Ghoki in "The Old Men," of Miranda in "The King's Indian," and is distantly related to Isabel in Melville's *Pierre*.

There is an element in her which is neurotically morbid. As a young girl, "she wanted more than anything . . . to be dead, or if not dead, a nun, then, cool and gentle and remote as a star" (p. 73). She craves the mystical in a twisted way, delighting in the intricate, almost sensual ritualism of the Catholic Church. "She'd been violently religious. She had read every book she could get about saints and martyrs, and she'd haunted the church and its lawn like a troubled ghost" (p. 74). She judges herself as "unfit for Nature"; she is emotionally and psychologically separate from the greater part of mankind. She wants desperately to save, to sacrifice her flesh for some larger cause, but her motivation is askew. Her desire is selfish and egotistical and blinkered. The salvation that she genuinely seeks is only for herself.

When James falls to the sidewalk, a victim of his disease, Viola drives him to the hospital. It is an instinctive act, yet for Viola there is something more deeply and more disturbingly satisfying about it, for "the truth was, she was glad she had been there, glad to feel his cold blood on her dress. Like one watching a liner sink or watching a new motel burn down, Viola felt intensely alive, favored by the gods, and her secret awareness that she was glad made her cheeks and forehead burn with shame" (pp. 80–81). Some black portion of her soul is nourished by violence, by death or near-death. It is as if she has ritualized the failure of flesh and substance, made it a part of her obscure and ghoulish litany.

By her act, also, she insinuates herself into the Chandler family. Now dual caretaker, she must look after a double trio of sisters: one threesome desperately old, the other invigoratingly young. She defines her feeling for the children as love, but the feeling is mixed with the vision of her dead father, coffined, pale, and candlelit. As terror evoked passion in Ginger Ghoki in "The Old Men," so death and anguish spark love in Viola. She is looking for some sort of defiled sainthood. She supplants

Marie Chandler as mother and protectress, siphoning off affection, transforming herself from saviour to threat. It is "a sickness of the blood," as deadly as James's leukemia.

Marie Chandler senses the unholiness about Viola. In her own way, she is every bit as insightful and intelligent as James. A teacher of English, both she "and her husband were not basically dissimilar. They were both, in the loose sense, idealists, though Chandler had words for it and his wife had only poems" (p. 100). Husband and wife are emotionally and philosophically hopeful, perhaps romantic, but straight-facedly honest:

> Both Chandler and his wife operated, as Chandler would have somewhat pedantically put it, not by the law of utility or by the regularian principle . . . but by the religious principle of conscience. R. G. Collingwood once wrote, in a passage James Chandler was fond of quoting, "Man's world is infested by *Sphinxes,* demonic beings of mixed and monstrous nature which ask him riddles and eat him if he cannot answer them, compelling him to play a game of wits where the stake is his life and his only weapon is his tongue." Both Chandler and his wife knew the truth about the sphinxes, and neither of them was on their side. But Marie was one of those people who are forever hoping that perhaps the game can be played not only by wits but by intuition, which is to say, one of those beautiful and good artistic people who fight courageously on the side of mankind and always get eaten in the end. What is more, she knew it. (p. 101)

Marie is the heroine of this piece, for she is the one who acts by intuition and whose metaphysics is emotional, not intellectual. Marie is the artist, Chandler the pedant—and Viola one of the Sphinxes, a man-eater, a devourer of spiritual goodness. Marie is furious that it was Viola, not herself who was by James's side, who had been there to witness the terrible privacy of his bleeding. She picks up the challenge that Viola (perhaps unwittingly) has laid down; her love for James is worth risking extinction for, certainly worth the intuitive effort she must expend to rescue the small bit of her husband's life that remains for herself and for her family.

James Chandler, meanwhile, lies apart from the intensity of emotion, strapped helpless to a hospital bed. Physically inert, Chandler allows his mind to roam eagerly, sometimes bizarrely, a result of the drugs being pumped through his body. In the hospital with Chandler is a man named John Horne, a philosopher-lawyer. Horne is a grotesque, clownlike, "goatlike" man who is marred and somewhat hideous: "He was enormously fat, with a large head. . . . His face was lumpy and horribly scarred on one side, as if he'd been burned, and his eyes were huge and far apart" (p. 106). He is one of Gardner's cartoon figures. Horne is a believer in spirit, in divinity, in faith, in resurrection. At the center of the universe, says Horne, is sanctified man:

> All that rushing and seeing and hefting is only the *way* we stay alive, not the reason for it. The reason is purely and simply self-love, the greatest power in the universe. And the true measure of human adaptability is man's power to find, despite overwhelming arguments, something in himself to love. It's not a thing to be scorned or to reprimand children for; a thing of beauty! Because at its root self-love is awe: Man looks at himself and says, "Great God, what a splendid thing!" Not vulgar egotism; nothing of the kind. Splendor! Honest and forthright recognition of the best there is in Nature. (p. 115)

A disfigured Walt Whitman, robustly singing himself and "the fact of love." Horne is a bit of a humane and heroic lunatic. He stoutly asserts that "life can be resurrected" through a spiritual embracing of one's personal holiness and dignity. His enthusiasm, however, is frightening and the props for his belief shaky.

Horne seeks out Chandler as a fellow philosopher and, even more so, as a confessor. Chandler wants to talk aesthetics, but Horne deftly shifts the discussion toward himself. "Atonement. . . . Art is the self-sacrifice of a man incapable of sacrificing himself in real life," Horne pronounces (p. 147). For Horne, art is the working out of one's spiritual squalor; through art, the canker is purged and the spirit sanctified and reborn. "Good poets atone for the evil in their lives, evil poets atone for the evil in their very souls, which they cannot help but continue to affirm. By writing the poem, the poet hopes to exorcise his devil. God help him" (p. 149). Art is religious, and the poet is priest. To affirm the aesthetic response, one must affirm "disinterested love," the love of the idealists. "A man incapable of love—incapable of aesthetic response—is a man congenitally damned. For such a man, providing he has the intellect to perceive his condition, life must be a continual but hopeless search for something he can find it in his heart to die for" (pp. 151–52).

It is a curious system, Tolstoyan in its moralism, but one that Chandler cannot accept. "You insist on finalities," he tells Horne. If not the final salvation then the final damnation, not mixture of judgments" (p. 152). Chandler destroys Horne with two lines from Blake: "O Rose, thou art sick; the invisible worm / That flies in the night, on the howling storm." But Horne's destruction is ambiguous. He is annihilated by his own absolutism. The world demands flexibility and leniency, and Horne's program of aesthetic moralism cannot last. Yet neither is Chandler totally blameless, for he ironically attacks the same "rose"—Collingwood's "cosmic rose"—that symbolizes the valued purity of the individual person. And so Chandler (and Gardner) leaves Horne abandoned, perhaps betrayed, sitting, spinning his theories to the blind.

For Chandler, however, there *has* been a sort of intellectual awakening. In dreams and in clear light, he has painfully built an aesthetic that he envisions as an answer to Kant. According to Chandler, Kant failed to see the disinterest in moral affirmation. Kant insisted that the aesthetic response be free of moral or practical interest, that for a thing to be beautiful it must be beautiful in and of itself. Chandler declares this separation of ethics and aesthetics a fatal mistake. Art as affirmation is inextricably bound up with morality. Chandler writes:

> I am suggesting that affirmations can be of two kinds, in Kierkegaard's sense *ethical* or *moral*. These kinds correspond precisely, though Burke did not notice it, to the two kinds of aesthetic experience elaborated by Edmund Burke, *viz.,* the experience of *the Beautiful* (the small, the curvilinear, the smooth, the pleasant) we may associate with the *ethical* (i.e., *social*) *affirmation;* that is to say, with affirmation of what is to be sought, what will "do," what must be tolerated (the harmlessly ugly or ludicrous), and what will not do in a given culture. All that belongs in Burke's realm of *the Sublime* (the large, the angular, the terrifying, etc.) we may identify with *moral affirmation;* that is to say, with human *defiance of chaos,* or the human assertion of *the godlike magnificence of human mind and heart.* (p. 201)

This is pure John Gardner; the entire first part of Chandler's essay is quoted or paraphrased in Gardner's *On Moral Fiction* (pp. 158–59, 161, 164). Chandler begins his essay as Gardner begins his, but along the way they part. Gardner, in fact, has commented on this portion of his novel:

> I believe that in a work of art, all the ideas are changed into people, places and things. It's true that in my fiction, characters argue philosophy, but as a matter of fact, I don't believe in the philosophy of the argument. They argue that philosophy because that's what's important to them and it expresses their feelings and positions. In *The Resurrection,* I've got a long section which is a paper that a character is writing about the aesthetic opinions of Immanuel Kant, and I actually think I know what went wrong with Kant's theory and I really wanted to say that, but I had a character who was dying of aleukemic leukemia, and one of the things that

happens with that is that your mind stops working well. And so
what I had to do was—I present the beginning of the argument
really well and then, in spite of the fact that I would like the world
to know the truth, and I would really like to write that essay, I have
to write an essay which imitates the deterioration of this man's
mind, and so it ends up a bad philosophical essay and gets worse
and worse and more and more inchoate and that's just the way it is,
that's the way fiction is.[11]

Gardner completed the essay he wished to write in *On Moral Fiction*,
and it helps reveal the flaws in Chandler's own argument. Chandler declares that the artist is one who "simplifies, extends, or reorders categori-
zation and choice for the rest of us, speeding up the painfully slow process of evolution toward what, hopefully, we *are*" (p. 202). This is only
partly correct, for Gardner would contend that the artist is no freak, no
oddity of consciousness; nor does the artist make the choices for us by
picking out what is more meaningful and presenting it to us through his
art. The essence of art is its susceptibility to sharing, its contagiousness, as
Tolstoy would put it. Good art is good because it strikes certain emotional and ethical chords that ring in all of us. Thus, Gardner writes that
"beauty is generalized human feeling (purity of heart) which is brought to
focus and released by the art object, a thing as indifferent to beauty, in
itself, as a radio tube is indifferent to the music of Schubert. Beauty in
art . . . is the same thing as beauty in life: it happens regularly, through
the conscious agency of some artist, if only because it is expected."[12] For
Chandler and for Gardner, there is "a delight without interest" that asserts man's potential for selflessness, "that projects action beyond the ego
and toward the universe."

Chandler's leap, however, from "delight beyond interest" to "aesthetic
wholeness" is fraught with logical misconnections and contradictions,
and is a sure sign of his mental failure. What was once a selfless aesthetic
becomes an exaltation of self, an approach to saintliness; it is an unlikely
mixture of Viola Staley and John Horne. Gardner himself makes the tie
between art and religion (again faithfully following Tolstoy), seeing simi-
larities between the two, but nowhere is there room for canonization of
the artist, nor of the intelligent perceptor.

This is not Chandler's only metaphysical problem: "His sense of being
in two places was constant now, a thing that should have been all to the
good" (p. 203). He is becoming more and more detached from spatial
and temporal reality. He feels madness creeping in, he grows all too
certain of the "dark woman's" existence. He can still affirm, still see the
blessedness of human faith and caring—this he can observe from a dis-

tance, aloft, unbound by the physical. But he keeps it apart from his personal suffering, from the headaches and the nausea and the sourness in his mouth. Beyond this still is the psychological pain that plagues him and sends him

> through periods of terror, a groundless quaking of the heart that came over him without warning or apparent cause and made him want to howl. A clot of white cells somewhere, perhaps. He would believe the old woman to be somewhere in the room with him, or standing downstairs in the middle of the night, listening. Or he would see her, even hear her speak, murmuring words that didn't quite make sense but hovered teasingly on the edge of sense. While the terror was on him he couldn't think and when it was gone, he was afraid to think back on it. He began to long ardently for death. (p. 204)

The wish for death is a wish for release. Moreover, it is a desire that dismally complements one other belief of Chandler's: "He saw with a shock what he had known abstractly for years, that the ultimate proof of love is premeditated self-destruction—the ultimate betrayal of love" (p. 164).

Self-destruction as an emblem of love is part of the Chandler legacy. The only cousin of James's father committed suicide; and "when his own time for choice came, he took with confidence the road his older cousin had taken" (p. 126). Suicide as a proof of love is a malign and irresponsible truth, the product of a physically or philosophically diseased mind, "the mistaking of the laws of one's own nature for absolutes" (p. 126). It is an act that hurts more than it cures.

It is a hurt that has twice been brought home to Rose Chandler, who has never understood the reasons for her husband's actions. In her old age, the past has become a means of existence; in a sense, she mirrors the sad debilitation of her son. She has wept for George, and now weeps for James, whose youth has proven no safeguard against mortality. She sees *things* crumbling about her, things she loves—her house, George's books (some slyly "authored" by Gardner's friends), George's machines—all shattering at a touch, toppling into rubbish. Rose wants desperately to understand her son, to communicate her love to him; but she works only through experience and action, through living—something to which James has still not yet found the secret.

James, in fact, is a man suffering from too much love. He feels himself tugged at from all sides—by Rose, by Marie, by Viola—and he has difficulty sorting and responding to these feelings. He is, quite literally, a man being killed by love. There is, as described above, the honest and long-nurtured love of his mother; there is the fierce and protective love of his wife; and there is the perverse, profane, and calamitous love of Viola. Ultimately, though, it is James's own distorted imagination that kills him—that and Viola's madness.

Driven by her lunatic passion, Viola abandons Emma and goes to the Chandler house to declare her love for James. His condition frightens her—his frame grown cadaverous, long lines of bone and thin skin. But the terror of it urges her on, sends her spinning into another world where the music is dissonant and where she is momentarily outside of herself and of time, where "for the first time in her life she knows what is wrong with her" (p. 225). Viola finally recognizes the corruption in her heart, and it jolts her. At last she sees her willfulness for what it is: a coal-black streak of inhumanness and egotism that turns people into objects and love into iniquity. Viola is catastrophe fleshed out.

James finally must choose between the sensible and the reckless, between the beautiful and the sublime—and he chooses wrongly. He makes affirmations, but affirmations that are grounded in sickness and misplaced sympathy and "warped emotion." He sees in Viola's act of will something generous and authentic, something that confirms his existence in "an intense present." His brain seems to clear as the idea rushes over him:

> All this time it had been there right in front of him—if it had been a snake it would have bit him—and he'd missed it! It was not the beauty of the world one must affirm but *the world,* the buzzing blooming confusion itself. He had slipped from celebrating what was to the celebration of empty celebration. . . . Again the nausea welled up in him. If he should have to vomit he would rip himself open, and the whole thing would be over. He closed his eyes, but that was worse, and he opened them quickly and fixed them on the cracks in the warped porch flooring. He thought: *One must make life art.* (p. 229)

James disastrously *mistakes* art for life, and so makes a grand gesture in an ungrand cause, hastening after Viola to make emotional amends. The deed must be commensurate with the motive and with the result, and in James's case neither need is filled. James dies at Viola's feet, his self-sacrifice unheeded by her eyes that stare beyond the window. Emma has escaped, the dream-woman gone; but the vision merges as Viola and Emma become one. His nightmare has destroyed him.

James's final claim—"No harm. It's done us no harm"—is tragically off-base. His virtual act of suicide, neither wise nor moral, brings everything—his family, his life, his ideas—crashing down around him. There is barely a trace of selflessness in his action, though he erroneously believes it to be void of egotism. He ignores the effect of his death upon those who truly love him, leaving them in darkness, distance, and absurdity, and turns the act of his death into a sadly meaningless and fruitless event. The hope of resurrection is lost for James Chandler. There will be a tombstone and flowers and infrequent visits from the women who loved him. They will at least keep alive his resurrected memory.

Chapter III

The Wreckage of Agathon

We're gathered, children, to learn of the ancient past.
                                                    —"History Lesson"

John Gardner's reputation languished after *The Resurrection,* his work finding little appeal to either public or publisher. With *The Wreckage of Agathon* (1970), however, Gardner's long apprenticeship began to pay off: "For a long period of time, my writing was not liked. It was very difficult for me to get published; it was a very long period of time before I did. Finally people began to publish my things. Actually, *The Wreckage of Agathon* broke it, and I got a sort of mild reputation—although it's a kind of terrible book."[1] Gardner was hailed as a political satirist, a black humorist, a writer (however oddly) in the Sartrean-Swiftian vein; and the novel drew nearly as much misinterpretation as *Grendel* later would. The book's wickedness lies in its deception and in its misleading turns of meanness. A handful of critics, though, did rightly perceive the novel's elemental strain of hope, and praised it for its humane achievement. The problem is that Gardner makes his protagonist too likeable, too approachable; his nastiness is overshadowed by his gruff and avuncular exterior. It is difficult to hate or even chastise someone who tells such wonderful lies.

Just where Gardner discovered his protagonist is uncertain, for like Plutarch (one of the major sources for this book)[2] Gardner is writing pseudohistory. In other words, while Gardner uses reliable historical fact, he augments that fact with convenient but telling fiction, padding "what did happen" with "what ought to have happened." It is the same technique he later uses in part of *Freddy's Book.*

As in his later epic poem *Jason and Medeia,* Gardner retreats to antiquity in *The Wreckage of Agathon,* to classical Athens and Sparta. The time is between 600 and 560 B.C., during the reigns of Lykourgos in Sparta and

Solon in Athens. To Sparta comes the Athenian seer, Agathon, friend and scribe to Solon and intended counselor of Lykourgos. Aided by his pupil, Peeker, Agathon becomes the scourge and demon of Lykourgos; he taunts him, insults him, plagues him beyond endurance, and finally is thrown into a Spartan prison for his pains.

Though there is no apparent historical record of such a person living at that time, the name of Agathon appears in several different places. In Plato's *Symposium,* for example, it is Agathon who hosts a party that includes Socrates and Aristophanes. At one point in the discussion a guest remarks, "Don't you know that Agathon has been abroad for many years?" which would complement the fictional Agathon's tenure in Sparta. Plato's Agathon is apparently the same man mentioned by Aristotle in his *Poetics* as the author of *Anthos*. Gardner's Agathon is also a poet ("once the most famous poet—or at least second most famous—in Athens"), though we do not know if he dabbled in drama. Obviously, Gardner's Agathon is not, strictly speaking, Plato's Agathon, who lived over a century after Gardner's fictional character. However, there is little doubt that this sort of creative anachronism and conflating of time might have appealed to Gardner.

One other possibility presents itself as well: Gardner may be offering an ironic contrast to Socrates, whose character differed so greatly from Agathon's. Socrates was beloved by his disciples, a courageous warrior (it was Socrates who saved the life of Alcibiades), and went to his death with glory. Agathon, on the other hand, was despised, ugly and distasteful, unforward in battle, and lowly in death. Socrates understood the significance of love and its nobility; Agathon never came to comprehend its meaning. Socrates was wise; Agathon was witty.

One final connection: in Plato's *Crito,* Crito attempts to sway Socrates into escaping and thus avoid death. Socrates logically argues the need for remaining in jail and for the delivery of his life to the hemlock. Agathon, also imprisoned, is also given the chance to escape. Being too plague-ridden to protest, his rescuers spirit him away in a farcical and parodic operation. It is this idea of imprisonment-escape, confinement-freedom that Gardner may be playing upon. Whatever the case, Gardner surely must have at least had in mind the life of Socrates when he created his pseudo-life of Agathon. What better way to illustrate the flawed intellect of his own philosopher *manqué* than with the echoing counterimage of Socrates's immutable heroism? The "good life" was more than an idea: it was a thing to be lived, and Agathon never managed to reach beyond and behind the concept.

While in jail, Agathon and Peeker ("semi-Seer") do manage to set down their thoughts, conversations, and remembrances in writing, and the novel is the product of their efforts. The book is a dual narrative, with

Gardner testing the reliability of both his narrators. The book moves through Agathon's early years in Athens, his education and experiences with Solon; through his political and intellectual battles with Lykourgos; to his relations with his Athenian wife and their Helot friends. It is a novel of contrasts and affinities; characters and camps are played off, one against the other, for a final distillation. What remains is a study in power, systems management, and corruptive egotism.[3]

Sparta is a city that has "been squeezed tight into one man's image—the image of a lunatic: Lykourgos" (p. 9). It is a city driven by duty and discipline, by a fanatical adherence to the rigors of law and order. Weakness and emotion are hunted out like sick cattle and destroyed. Art, music, and matters of taste are scorned and debased ("even pigs make aesthetic choices"), and reason is merely an excuse for cowardice: "Wisdom acts. Stupidity labors to explain itself" (p. 31).

Behind the system stands, indeed, the figure of Lykourgos, another of Gardner's "lunatics." It is Lykourgos who sets about the total reconstruction of the Spartan way of life. It is Lykourgos who turns gold into lead, who outlaws wealth and institutes widespread land reform; he makes iron into a weapon, makes it useless as a means of commerce and transforms it into the executioner's tool. He demolishes sexual difference; "he turns women into men," makes marriage a war game and the act of love an act of conquest. Men he turns into insensate machines for killing and attack, stripping them of personality and individual intellect. As Agathon describes them:

> They train naked, hour on hour in the summer heat or the winter wind, until their hides are like leather and their muscles are like pliant wood. They learn to fight, as they learn to march, with precision, every movement clean as the closing of a trap. The iren gives his signal and they draw their swords as if with one single muscle. He calls out again and they advance a step like the spikes of a single harrow. . . . When a man moves his hand by an inch too much, the iren signals him out of formation and bites his thumb. The man does not scream. Not a muscle of his face stirs. . . . As they march to the attack, the Spartans play their flutes, a piercing, deadly singsong thing in the Lydian mode, with no trace of joy, no faintest intimation of mercy. They destroy a city, kill everything alive in it down to the humblest dog, and send their ultimatum to the next. All this is Lykourgos's work. Only a fool would deny that it's effective. (pp. 81–82)

Lykourgos strives for uniformity and supremacy through constant refinement and selection. His is a Spencerian world wherein only the fittest are allowed to survive—to kill and to die.

The hallmark of the Spartan world is its law. It is Draconian in its severity; Lykourgos is fond of quoting Draco's comment on the necessity of capital punishment: "Even small crimes deserve death. . . . As for greater crimes, well, death is the worst I've got" (p. 115). The criminal nature is genetic, inherited, and it must be blotted out. Death "purifies the blood [and] that's the beginning and end of Law and Order" (p. 115). So necks are bent to and broken by the cold iron bars of the Spartan executioners; punishment is carried out in the public square, the eyes of children opened wide to the bloody object lesson.

This is the same law which has been abolished in Athens under the "new humanism" of Solon, poet and lawgiver. He is the opposite of Lykourgos in every way. Agathon recalls his first sighting of Solon's "imposing" figure:

> In walked the fattest, silliest-looking man I have ever met. (Only Kroesos himself is said to have been fatter, who weighed seven hundred pounds.) Solon was in his middle thirties, but nearly bald already. His nose was pink. No one needed to be told he was a wine merchant, without a drop of noble blood in his lineage—despite what people say now. His flesh jiggled like a mile-wide field of flowers in a breeze. He spread his legs and stretched his milk-white arms like a man meeting his concubines after long separation, and said, "Gentlemen, God bless you one and all!" (p. 70)

Where Lykourgos is lean, Solon is broad; where Lykourgos is controlled, Solon is boisterous. Solon makes his fame first as a leader of the Athenians in battle against the Megarians, whom he defeats by costuming his army as flower-laden women. Hardly in the Spartan mold!

Solon encourages commerce and artisanry, and welcomes foreign creative and monetary influence. His laws are compassionate and flexible. Crimes are punished with the least amount of blood and pain, and the penalties are assigned with a looser, less legalistic zeal. Solon's is a government by intuition. His poetic nature turns him toward a humane conception of political organization. Effective political power is extended down through the lower ranks, down to the farmer and laborer and craftsman. Solon opens up the world to the middle and lower classes, both politically and economically. He grants suffrage, cancels debts, and rewards industriousness. He is a lyricist and a lover of both men and women.

The two lawgivers are brought together under one roof, in the house of an Athenian nobleman (Agathon's father-in-law), for a historic test of political wills. Solon behaves with characteristic moderation (*sophrosyne*), neither attacking nor belittling. Agathon records one swatch of conversation:

> Says Lykourgos: "The trouble with a genius is that he dies. The state falls to ordinary men, and they destroy it." They were talking of Solon's wild improvising.
>
> Solon smiled. "I'd rather be destroyed by ordinary men than by System."
>
> "In my system," Lykourgos said, "there will be no ordinary men."
>
> Solon thought about it and nodded. "True, perhaps," he said. "And when you die, there will be no room for genius in all Lakonia except your grave." (pp. 84–85)

The problem, as we come to learn, is that *both* men are destroying themselves, both falling to their self-engendered systems. There is armed revolt in Sparta, and the Athenian upper class is grumbling over a weakening and collapsing society. It is a lesson that Gardner will teach several times more: all systems fail.

But there is an allure to Lykourgos's system, one that draws the then-young Agathon away from his Athenian teacher-lover and toward the Spartan nightmare. Agathon approaches it as a matter for examination and philosophical observation. His first impressions are revealing and not far off the mark, but they come to be modified with time:

> The truth is, I was much impressed by Lykourgos's Sparta when I arrived. Though I came full of scorn, even humanistic outrage— though also full of admiration for any man who could bring it off— I was impressed by the studied simplicity of the world Lykourgos had recreated. I saw his whole scheme, now that I was here, in the simplest and most lucid terms, and I was amazed at my former narrowness of vision. A matter of simple geography. Sparta was agricultural, required a huge labor force—not slaves but something almost slave, because that many slaves would be a threat to the master race—and required, above all, the reactionary temper which keeps a farmer regular of habit and stable. Athens lived by trade, a thing requiring liberalism, tolerance, flexibility. Neither was right or wrong, then: the Just Life was a mythological beast. I would study the world for its images of aspects of myself. (p. 87)

Agathon is writing economic history, and it is accurate in as far as it goes. It stops short, however, of the more significant differences that skulk beneath the surface. So Agathon stays on, long past his original intentions, and learns.

Our first acquaintance with Agathon comes after many years as official seer and foil to Lykourgos. With Lykourgos off on a visit to the oracle at

Delphi, Agathon and Peeker are arrested and packed off to prison. Agathon is a repulsive looking man, grown old and stale and contemptuous. Even Peeker, his third-year disciple, finds him unbearable: "He was the foulest man alive, by any reasonable standard: a maker of suggestions to ˙ ugly fat old cleaning ladies, a midnight prowler in the most disgusting parts of town—the alleys of the poor, the palace gardens—who searched out visions of undressed maidens and coupling lovers, especially old ones, and lived, whenever his onion patch had nothing in it but burdocks and brambles, by foraging in the garbage tubs behind houses" (p. 1). He leers, he farts, he stinks of onions and street sewage. "The old bastard's crazy as a loon," Peeker wails; he is a "god's fool," caught up in the divine madness of Shakespeare and Melville. He makes jokes of substance and lives on essence. When he laughs at Peeker's efforts to have themselves freed, Peeker rages: "I could have hit him with a chair, but I kept my temper. We had hope now. 'You're crazy,' I said. 'I mean *literally*.' And it came to me that it was true. He was a great Seer, yes, and he was a good old man, but he was out of his mind, insane. I'd been cowed by him before. I hadn't realized that a genius can be as stupid as anybody else at one or two points; but I knew now" (p. 51).

Indeed, it is Peeker who shows the only concern with outward reality. He is Agathon's guardian and preserver-from-harm. Despite his anger, Peeker cannot abandon the old man, cannot allow him to rot in jail alone. He is compassionate toward Agathon, understanding of his lunatic visions, barely tolerant of his flouting of the material world. Agathon judges Peeker: "Helot through and through, my poor disciple, and not even one of the revolutionist crowd: one of those who, instead, endure, blindly imagine that by suffering and piety they will prevail. They too will be bloodied" (p. 10). Peeker is the realist and the lover; he is the balance to Agathon's top-heavy "idea-ism."

Agathon, like James Chandler in *The Resurrection*, is a man in love with ideas. He is a trained observer and commentator, but he has difficulty with feeling. His prejudice and failing is self-admitted: "But this is clear: I loved my wife—loved her second only to adventures and ideas" (p. 58). For Agathon, there is a connection (with echoes of an Alfred North Whitehead title) between adventures and ideas. The creation of a concept is the only authentic adventure in this world; all action is but the retelling of an idea. Good actions are reflections of good ideas, bad actions the products of bad ideas.

Such a philosophy immobilizes Agathon, renders him incapable of reaction and response to the brutality around him. This crazy-eyed indifference sets Peeker fuming and drives him to his own near-madness: "People die right in front of your eyes and you just fart around, tell stupid shit-ass stories about girls and old dead politicians, and people are actually *dying!* There's some things a human being doesn't have to stand" (p. 78). Agathon's neutrality is unhinging and unhuman, strong on speculation but thin on sympathy. He does nothing to stanch the progress of a bad idea, as if afraid of destroying something holy. It ultimately turns him into a betrayer, something that his lover, Iona, perceives:

> "You'd give up anything, anybody, for an interesting idea, even a monstrous one like his." Her voice was half serious, half mocking. Coming straight at you (except with questions) was Iona's last resort.
> "An idea or an adventure," I said.
> She lay still, looking at the stars. I could feel her baffled annoyance, and it pleased me. At last, with a brief, ironic smile, she said, "All right, smart one, explain."
> "It's nothing," I said, still mysteriously uneasy but also tingling with something more than sexual pleasure. "It's a cliché I have. Ghost of my youthful metaphysics. What is the ultimate reality? Adventures and ideas. An adventure is when someone pokes you in the mouth. An idea is when you think pokedness." (pp. 99–100)

Lykourgos's Sparta is just the place for such detachment. Agathon is fascinated with the *idea* of such a system, with the way it continues to run on the strength of just one man. He is the court jester, the "wise fool," always a flayed skin's breadth away from death, but somehow protected. Agathon points the finger at Lykourgos's contradictions, political and personal. He shows up the flaws in Lykourgos's adoption of Alkander, the boy who made Lykourgos a cyclops, in its exception to the Spartan rule; he goes farther, mocking Lykourgos's supposed intimacy with a woman, claiming, "She faked it!" This is Agathon's role, to mock and make sport. Incapable of any sort of emotional depth, he resorts to derision. He is one of Gardner's unblessed lunatics. Oddly enough, Agathon later is genuinely shocked by the realization that Lykourgos actually hated him, that he was jailed because Lykourgos finally decided to avenge the insults and indignities: "Lykourgos must have hated me all these years, hated me so devotedly that tyrannizing me in life was not enough" (p. 221). Peeker, who is growing into the true seer, recalls a confrontation indicative of Agathon's relentlessness:

> "We're old men, you and I," Lykourgos said. "Let's come to truce."
> "O deathless gods, hear what he asks of me!" Agathon said. "O motionless mild Apollo, behold this indignity done my old age!"

He was wrong. Any fool could see it. Even if Lykourgos was all he said, an enemy to the laws of earth and heaven, still Lykourgos was a man, had rights. He could burn cities with one word, but he couldn't get justice from Agathon, yet was too just a man to destroy him. (p. 95)

Agathon's vision is every much as single-eyed as Lykourgos's and Solon's. All three are, in their separate ways, tyrants.

For just as Lykourgos and Solon rule over their respective city-states, so Agathon dictates his personal relationships. With his wife, Tuka, he is callous, sometimes cold, and always ultimately ungiving. She is an artist, a harpist of remarkable and entrancing skill; as Agathon remarks, "She was un- if not anti-philosophical." She has a captivating beauty that was made even more chilling by her fits of abstract cruelty and oddness, by her playing at "Tuka-not-quite-sane." It is part cleverness, part viciousness, and part madness, and it baffles Agathon and drives him to distraction. Yet he loves her, as deeply as he might.

Their marriage is further complicated, however, by their involvement with their well-heeled Helot friends, Dorkis and Iona. Dorkis is a powerful man; his physical presence compels attention and respect, and his intellect is rugged. He is a relativist, a man who views the world as changing and metamorphic. Reality is like air, "You have to ride it, like a bird" (p. 47). Absolutism is fatal, a blind man's approach in which the multiple truths of the universe are ignored until too late: "Pursue one single truth, never glancing to left or right, and *pow!*" (p. 46).

Dorkis's relativism extends to a belief in "selective promiscuity"; says Agathon of him: "Religion . . . was one of his fascinations. Sex and wine, sad proofs of life's caducity, were the others" (p. 45). Dorkis sees nothing corrupt in the sexual swapping of like and commensurate types. This, then, admits a familiarity between his wife, Iona, and Agathon, an acquaintance that develops precipitously into love. Iona is strong willed and a thinker, a mover. She believes in the bold, sometimes unreasoned act. It is Iona who foments rebellion among the Helots and tries to enlist Agathon in their cause. Agathon teaches her to write (an ultimately fatal act), and Iona attempts to instruct Agathon in loving, but he is blocked by his egotism. He is torn between the two women, torn by a confusion between love and lust, but it is a pain which he relishes. He is, he says, in love with two women who were

goddesses in the only sense of the word I understand. They were embodiments of heavenly ideals—conflicting ideals—that my soul could not shake free of. Tuka, even on those awful occasions when her mind came unhinged, had the precision of intellect, the

> awesome narrowness of purpose, of a mathematician or a general.
> She knew, beyond any shadow of a doubt, what she wanted from
> life and why she wanted it, and she would stalk her desire with the
> single-mindedness of a carpenter driving a nail. Iona wanted not
> some one thing but everything; she had a mind as wide, as devious
> and turbulent, as a poet's, and she went for what she desired like a
> swarm of blind bees in a windstorm. (pp. 55–56)

Agathon's allegiances are warped by his weakness. He fails to see the
eventual responsibility that comes with emotional involvement. His later
affair with Thalia demonstrates for Agathon, though apparently not
clearly enough, the damage and danger that come from poorly considered
commitments. A marriage is destroyed by infatuation and physical attraction, but Agathon emerges from it all barely changed. This, says Gardner,
is his sin: he is indiscriminate and irresponsible. He cherishes Tuka for
her fire and jealousy, but pursues Iona for her wit and savvy and plotting
power.

Gardner implies several causes of Agathon's problems. Peeker, with his
characteristic insight, points in one direction:

> He's philosophical about death. Good. But I hear how he groans
> and whimpers in his sleep, and I see how goddamn scared he is
> when he peeks out through the cell door, watching the fires. He
> jokes about how when they drag him away he'll bawl like a baby
> the ephors have decided to throw from a cliff for its sickliness, but I
> see through the jokes: he really will bawl, and stupidly, hopelessly,
> he'll try to bribe them, and when they lift the execution rods over
> his head he'll die of terror. So would I, maybe, though I don't think
> so. The difference between us is that he hates himself for it, hates
> himself for everything, and hates everybody else that shares his
> faults. As simple as that. Agathon, the great lover, hates people.
> (pp. 163–64)

Agathon's philosophical indifference fails him when he stares at the gray
shade of his own death. He has nothing to support him; his legs grow
rubbery and his humanness evinces itself in nervous tics and tears. He
mistakenly hates the people about him because he believes they share his
cowardice.

Agathon finally cannot act, and action is a mainstay in Gardner's system
of emotional metaphysics. He can think, he can joke, he can fondle, but he
cannot make the necessary human effort toward action. Instead, he suffers
and betrays. He lives with the memory of his brother's death (crushed
beneath the hooves of Agathon's horse), and the guilt twists him. He

recalls his betrayal of his childhood friend Konon, whom he sends to his death after revealing his plan to assassinate Solon; it is an act derived only partly from love for his mentor—the rest is pure egotism. Again it is Peeker who senses the flaw: " 'You haven't suffered,' Agathon tells me. 'That's the problem.' Not like him, thank God, not by betraying everything I ever loved without lifting a goddamn finger. He made his beautiful Iona ugly, and drove his wife Tuka home to Athens, and all by mere Nature, without a malicious thought. He'll wreck me too, if his luck holds out. I should strangle him, and save the whole human race!" (p. 167). Agathon believes that suffering is the key, that mankind must be bent beneath some sort of pain, guilt, humiliation before it can make a claim upon life. This is partially true, says Gardner, for the universe in its chaos inflicts suffering and pain and guilt (the death of Agathon's brother is reminiscent of the death of Gardner's own brother, Gilbert, and the guilt Gardner long felt over it). Humans must endure and vanquish the sorrow. With Agathon, however, the suffering only pushes him further away from mankind. It robs him of his qualities of grace.

Agathon looks at Dorkis, a blessed one, and marvels, puzzled at how his

> absolute and simple faith filled the room like autumn light, like a sea breeze. Even when his ideas were crazy, the man had sophrosyne, as they used to call it in the old days. There are men in this world—wizards, witches, people like Lykourgos—who spread anger, or doubt, or self-pity, or the cold stink of cynicism, wherever they walk: the sky darkens over their heads, the grass withers under their feet, and downwind of them, ships perish at sea. And then there are men, here and there, like Dorkis. God only knows what to make of them. Their ideas are ludicrous, when you look at them. Peasant ideas. Childlike. But what tranquility! (pp. 152–53)

Agathon, in his sterility, cannot get past the simplicity of Dorkis's ideas. He cannot see the grandeur of his belief in a world that ultimately works correctly. Dorkis is an illuminator, a bringer of "autumn light" ("October light"?). He is a Gardner *hero:* he affirms, he acts, he builds, he confronts death with courage. It is Dorkis who saves Agathon from the wrath of the mourning Helots when Agathon cruelly ignores their suffering to gather the charred remains of his "scrolls of dead knowledge." Dorkis tells him, "You care more for knowledge than for people," and though Agathon denies it, Dorkis is right.

When the time comes for Dorkis to die, after he has revealed his complicity in the Helot plot, he dies "like a God." Even Agathon is struck by his aura when Dorkis stands before Lykourgos:

I was impressed; in fact, awed. Shackled, beaten, Dorkis seemed more powerful than all of them. It seemed to me for an instant that he had learned something of unspeakable importance, but the next instant I doubted that—it struck my silly philosopher's prejudice, that power comes from knowledge. It struck me (God knows what I meant by it) that Something had learned Dorkis. It was as if one of his gods had gotten inside him, had taken over. (p. 196)

Dorkis sacrifices himself for a belief that is honest and dignified and provable. He relinquishes his life to save Iona's, the actual figure behind the rebellion. His execution becomes a martyrdom, something nearly holy and mystical. Again Agathon narrates:

As for Dorkis, he seemed to be beyond waiting for anything judgeable by our kind of time. He knelt with what seemed infinite patience and something I'm almost embarrassed to give its name: tenderness. He was separate—totally, absolutely—separate from everything around him. It was as if he had at last, without thinking about it, accepted something, and the choice had transmuted him. I tried to think, snatching at straws to keep my feelings dead, what it was that made his kneeling different from that of a condemned Spartan, but I couldn't get hold of it. Then the iren went to him and asked him something, and Dorkis nodded, gently, as if to a child. And suddenly I knew. He had accepted evil. Not any specific evil, such as hatred, or suffering, or death, but evil as a necessary principle of the world—time as a perpetual perishing, space as creation and wreckage. (pp. 197–98)

The world's pain and grief, says Gardner, wrecks and disfigures most men. The hero, like Dorkis, however, is emotionally and physically transfigured, transmuted. Dorkis's belief in a good beyond evil lends him strength and vaults him beyond mere mortality. He becomes a legend, a myth; he is "the Snake," a source for poetry and confidence and hope. He is transmogrified into Art.

Suffering also teaches and instructs. In Peeker's case he learns more from Agathon's tales of sorrow and hurt than from his metaphysics. Peeker endures, suffers himself, acquires patience and tolerance, and most important, a vision. He is educated in the idea of love, in its power and its abuse. His master's life is a vivid lesson which Peeker more often correctly interprets than does Agathon. Peeker ties together all of the loose ends, preserves and passes on the history, and makes sense of it all. His fondness for the common and the practical, and his willingness both to listen and to act, supply him with a certain worldliness—or at least with an understanding of the worldly. Peeker embraces and believes, and his ability to love makes of him a true seer.

Suffering can do other things as well. For Tuka, suffering is a testing, a "refiner's fire" (to borrow Mark Helprin's phrase) that scars and marks her for life. Her battling with Agathon eventually becomes too brutal and frightening; they discover that each is capable of killing the other, no matter how much love they feel. When Peeker visits Tuka after Agathon's death, her tenderness and compassion light up an airless, dreary room. Tuka has left Agathon for his own sake, to save him from even more guilt and corrupted suffering. With Dorkis and poor Peeker, Tuka is one of the few people in the novel who is capable of loving and understanding and forgiving. She, in her own way, has made her sacrifice.

For others, suffering turns flesh into stone. Iona allows her love for Agathon, with all of its energy and force, to be misdirected into a bad idea. She becomes single-mindedly driven by the notion of revolution; politics and power and reprisal overtake her potential as a human being, and transform her into a conniver. Iona is no better than Solon or Lykourgos in her tyranny and in her devotion to an absolute ideal. She can only now approximate loving; she denies the truth in Agathon's history, calls it "a senseless, complicated lie." She simply refuses to accept her part in it all, to accept her responsibility for events and effects. Like Agathon, she dons a mask behind which she can bury all of her actual feeling. People keep their masks like they keep neckties or necklaces; they wear a different one for every occasion, dexterously switching them—two, three, four at a time—when circumstances require it. Masking is simply another form of cowardice. It is an unwillingness to demonstrate a true belief.

At its worst, suffering turns people into wolves. This is, perhaps, the dominant metaphor in the novel. Gardner quotes Schopenhauer in his epigraph: "Therefore with the same necessity with which the stone falls to the earth, the hungry wolf buries its fangs in the flesh of its prey, without the possibility of the knowledge that it is itself the destroyed as well as the destroyer." *The Wreckage of Agathon* is full of wolves, of people who in their obsession with force and conquest and in their certainty of vindication go about the destruction of their very own systems. Lykourgos creates a society that thrives on death and rapaciousness, that exalts the firm jaw and the cold eye. Once set in motion, it mauls everything in its path and Lykourgos is powerless to stop it, so he abandons his system and starves himself to death at Delphi, a sacrifice to god and state. Solon, who begins right-mindedly, watches his reforms backfire and turn. He takes Athens into war, nurtures political chaos, and survives to see the dismal harvest of his idea. Democracy sinks to dictatorship as part of the endless cycle of rise and fall. Iona focuses her vision upon upheaval and ends up destroying Dorkis, the man most important to her, and sending Agathon to a grubby, rat-bitten death. She knows she literally killed her husband, though there is something prideful in her knowledge. She also knows she is killing herself, that a life of hiding in caves and feeding off stolen corn is merely another form of dying.

For Agathon, finally, suffering nearly brings him to the realization of his "wolf-ness," of his tyrannical, devouring nature. Like all the others, Agathon follows one idea unfailingly to the end. He suffers, and witnesses suffering, but all he can manage is ridicule. He does not turn to a pitiable existentialism as does the hopeless Thaletes (Gardner's sendup of Sartre),[4] nor to a bitter, vengeful materialism as does Konon. Instead, Agathon seeks refuge in a "clowning despair . . . the total indifference to anything but the monstrous foolishness of human beings" (p. 219). He can neither affirm nor deny—only mock. Even his death is a farce, a self-parody; his final entry reads:

> Dying, I understand my panic. No worse than that of a child poised on a diving board. Hike your skirts up, Agathon, love! Point your fingers!
> Whoo*ee* am I scared!
> I must think of some last, solemn, sententious word.
> Cocklebur.
> Ox. (p. 233)

Agathon dies pronouncing the name of the man who carried him from prison. He dies also, no doubt, remembering the nobility of Dorkis, the love of Tuka, the perceptive allegiance of Peeker, the loss of his brother in the night, and the betrayal of much of life's decency. He is a man shamed in life and in death, a man who recognized evil but who did nothing to remove or change it.

"Time is a thing. . . . It bites," writes Gardner. It is the quality of man's reaction to that fact that is the measure of his existence. One can die with the beauty and heart and divinity of Dorkis, defying the blackness of Pascal's *gouffre* and make of dying a resurrection (certainly a familiar Gardner theme). Or one can crumble, let muscles slacken and head cower, and make of death a humiliation. This is the wreckage of humankind, a complete and unforgivable submission to substance and space and time. It is the turning of the human into conscienceless animal, an irredeemable reversion.

Chapter IV

Grendel

Nothing important changes.
    —"Persimmons"

Grendel, published in 1971, was Gardner's first novel to attract genuine and lasting critical acclaim. Some readers saw just enough experimentalism in it to place it (mistakenly) among the ranks of the "new fabulism" and had Gardner uncomfortably rubbing shoulders with the black humorists, while others were attracted by the book's clever attachment to the Anglo-Saxon tradition. Gardner himself attributed the novel's success to at least two factors: "One was Bill Gass's mentioning me to David Segal, who became my editor at Knopf. The other thing was the Beatles. The Beatles contributed to a fantastic thawing and breaking up of the rules. I was writing, you know, in the age of O'Hara and John Updike, all those realists, and I was putting out fantasy. At least, non-realistic fiction. These days it's called magical realism."[1] *Grendel* was Gardner's first book with the publishing house of Alfred A. Knopf, with whom he worked ever after in the publication of his fiction. This association allowed him greater latitude and greater security, and the astute editorial assistance of David Segal (of whom Gardner and many other writers have spoken so admiringly) assured Gardner of an intelligent and patient first reading. Knopf also provided Gardner with an illustrator, a tradition Gardner maintained in all of his later fiction.[2] For *Grendel,* Knopf (with Gardner's approval) contracted the talent of Emil Antonucci, who gave to each chapter head a shifting, finely-woven image of Grendel's visage (aptly enough, Antonucci also did the cover art for an edition of Collingwood's *Principles of Art,* whose influence on Gardner was demonstrated in *The Resurrection*). In short, the merger of writer and publisher was a happy one.[3]

Grendel is Gardner's reworking of the *Beowulf* epic, and it is more than a

Despite ambiguities in some key words, in Fulgentius's view of *arma* [virtue], *virum* [wisdom], and *primus* [sensuality], one easily recognizes a preoccupation of early Church writers, from Augustine to Hugh of St. Victor and Bonaventura, and of artists and poets down to the close of the Middle Ages: a concern with man's tripartite soul—rational, irascible, concupiscent—analogous to the perfect three-part divine spirit, i.e., Wisdom, Power, Goodness. (p. 230)

In *Beowulf*. . . the Fulgentian scheme of the *Aeneid* reappears intact, with one very important exception: the ending is tragic. Vergil does deal with the decline and old age of his hero. But the *Beowulf*-poet, influenced by Germanic and Christian ideas of the dreadful transience of things, carries his poem beyond the hero's moment of *felicitas* to an ambiguous victory and defeat. (p. 231)

What is central in the drama of Beowulf's expedition to Hart is the awkwardness of the situation and Beowulf's skill in handling it. He is, quite simply, a superman among very strong men—a walking icon of *arma*. His wisdom and tact make him an icon of *virum*. (p. 249)

In his battle of words he turns his knowledge against his opponent and defeats him; and in his next boast, to Wealtheow, he again shows his command of the ethic. *Virum:* in the company of his "secga gedright," he says, he resolved to do the will (or pleasure) of the Danish people. (He rules himself and knows his place as defender of order.) *Arma:* he claims himself no weaker than Grendel and in fairness renounces weapons because Grendel knows no weapons. And *primus:* he leaves the outcome—the payment, good or bad—to God's judgment. (pp. 251–52)

That is, I think, the significance of Beowulf's successive confrontations with monsters. God in his wisdom can enable a shrewd and valiant hero to overcome the enemy of rational order, Grendel. And the God who won the war with the giants can enable a man to overcome perverse power, the perverted irascibility of Grendel's dam, whose loyalty is not to Law but to an outlaw. But the pre-Revelation god of Hrothgar and Hygelac cannot overcome mutability itself, the destructive principle inherent in matter, slave to Fate—the principle traditionally represented in the figure of the dragon. (p. 257) mere retelling. Gardner takes as his narrator the monster, the benighted, fated Grendel. Gardner compresses the chronology of the original legend by neglecting the story of Grendel's dam, and only hinting at Beowulf's final battle with the dragon. The story is told in flashbacks, cinematic "cuts" by Grendel's memory to events in the monster's twelve-year harassment of the Danes. Moreover, the voice of Grendel is a blend of old and new; it speaks, in one moment, in the rolling, alliterative tones of the medieval *scop* and, in the next, in the flip, comic, sometimes cartoonish language of contemporary slang and street-talk. Grendel's discovery of his proper narrative voice is, in fact, a major developmental thread in the book. The novel, as Gardner has said, is a mix of the original *Beowulf,* William Blake, Tolkien, and Walt Disney.[4] Perhaps this bizarre variety of influences is part of the reason for the book's popularity.

There exists, of course, a more significant and serious side to *Grendel.* Among the other strains in the monster's character and thought, that of Jean-Paul Sartre, Gardner's philosophical bogy, is dominant. Gardner's long-standing feud with Sartre is well documented; in his fiction, in his criticism, and in his interview comments Gardner has consistently attacked the "whiny despair" of the existentialist position. *Grendel* as a critique of that position has been exhaustively studied by numerous previous critics,[5] as has the novel's relation with its ancient poetic source. There can be little doubt that one of Gardner's main intellectual targets is this dominant philosophical school, a philosophy that runs counter to everything Gardner urges in his writing.

There is little sense in trying to rehash or even add to all of this. What I would prefer to do is to suggest a fresh approach that takes into account both Gardner's concern with the existential "lie" and Gardner's personal history as a student and critic of the Middle Ages. By bringing to light more than Gardner's *creative* writing, I hope to fashion a new understanding of Gardner's purpose in his own reshaping of the *Beowulf* myth.

In the introduction to his *Complete Works of the Gawain-Poet,* Gardner discusses the *Gawain* poet's concept of the world and its reality, and the poet's approach to nature:

> He sees Nature at least partly in the orthodox Christian way, as a
> test of the human soul, and medieval theology and psychology
> establish the terms of the test. As we learn in the *Pearl, Purity,* and
> *Gawain* . . . man lost in the Fall the purity of his soul. In terms of
> medieval psychology, the soul is in fact three souls, the *rational*
> (loosely, "reason"), the *irascible* (loosely, "mettle" or "spirit"), and
> the *concupiscent* (loosely, "desire"). Before the Fall all three elements
> in the tripartite soul were noble; after the Fall all three were

Chapter IV

Grendel

Nothing important changes.
    —"Persimmons"

Grendel, published in 1971, was Gardner's first novel to attract genuine and lasting critical acclaim. Some readers saw just enough experimentalism in it to place it (mistakenly) among the ranks of the "new fabulism" and had Gardner uncomfortably rubbing shoulders with the black humorists, while others were attracted by the book's clever attachment to the Anglo-Saxon tradition. Gardner himself attributed the novel's success to at least two factors: "One was Bill Gass's mentioning me to David Segal, who became my editor at Knopf. The other thing was the Beatles. The Beatles contributed to a fantastic thawing and breaking up of the rules. I was writing, you know, in the age of O'Hara and John Updike, all those realists, and I was putting out fantasy. At least, non-realistic fiction. These days it's called magical realism."[1] *Grendel* was Gardner's first book with the publishing house of Alfred A. Knopf, with whom he worked ever after in the publication of his fiction. This association allowed him greater latitude and greater security, and the astute editorial assistance of David Segal (of whom Gardner and many other writers have spoken so admiringly) assured Gardner of an intelligent and patient first reading. Knopf also provided Gardner with an illustrator, a tradition Gardner maintained in all of his later fiction.[2] For *Grendel,* Knopf (with Gardner's approval) contracted the talent of Emil Antonucci, who gave to each chapter head a shifting, finely-woven image of Grendel's visage (aptly enough, Antonucci also did the cover art for an edition of Collingwood's *Principles of Art,* whose influence on Gardner was demonstrated in *The Resurrection*). In short, the merger of writer and publisher was a happy one.[3]

Grendel is Gardner's reworking of the *Beowulf* epic, and it is more than a corrupted, weighted by what Plotinus in his system called the "indeterminate"—in Christian dualistic terms the non-spiritual quality, Nature. This corruption exists partly in fact, partly in potential. The Fall dimmed the mind so that we now cannot see God; but though we are made gross by Nature, we are still born virtually innocent. Original sin makes necessary God's extension of grace, but the child who has been baptized, that is, granted grace, goes directly to heaven if it dies before sinning on its own. Thus the Fall is reenacted in every individual life. Every man comes sooner or later to his Eden.[6]

This idea of the tripartite soul originates in book 4 of Plato's *Republic*, where Socrates attempts to define the just man. It is concluded that the just person is analogous to the just city, and therefore must contain the same three properties: wisdom, courage, and temperance. The goal is unity and wholeness of the soul. The just man must bring "into tune those three parts, like the terms in the proportion of a musical scale, the highest and lowest notes and the mean between them, with all the intermediate intervals. Only when he has linked these parts together in well-tempered harmony and has made himself one man instead of many, will he be ready to go about whatever he may have to do."[7] The notion is one of spiritual harmonics and balance, a notion that was later reformed by Aristotle, who labeled the three parts "sensation, reason, and desire."[8]

From Aristotle the idea filtered down to medieval theology, where Gardner retrieved it once again, this time for use in a critical article. In a June 1977 interview, Gardner commented: "What I've done in medieval studies is try to understand poems. I did an analysis of *Beowulf* which I think is absolutely right. I think it is the first analysis of *Beowulf* to account for the whole poem. I think most people have accepted it, generally, as right. But I didn't come to it in the usual scholar's way, among medievalists at least. I came to it by trying to understand the poem, simply. Very few people do it."[9] The article Gardner is speaking of appeared in 1970 and was entitled: "Fulgentius's *Expositio Vergiliana Continentia* and the Plan of *Beowulf*: Another Approach to the Poem's Style and Structure."[10] Despite its imposing, scholarly nature, the article is underwritten by a humane, good-sensical tone that reflects Gardner's desire to "understand the poem, simply." Gardner elaborates, expands, and clarifies his earlier comments on the *Gawain*-poet, building his argument upon the concept of the triune soul. He takes as his base Fulgentius's work on Vergil and applies it to his interpretation of the Anglo-Saxon epic. The following excerpts I hope will give the reader an idea of the point Gardner is making (the bracketed translations are Gardner's own):

Despite ambiguities in some key words, in Fulgentius's view of *arma* [virtue], *virum* [wisdom], and *primus* [sensuality], one easily recognizes a preoccupation of early Church writers, from Augustine to Hugh of St. Victor and Bonaventura, and of artists and poets down to the close of the Middle Ages: a concern with man's tripartite soul—rational, irascible, concupiscent—analogous to the perfect three-part divine spirit, i.e., Wisdom, Power, Goodness. (p. 230)

In *Beowulf* . . . the Fulgentian scheme of the *Aeneid* reappears intact, with one very important exception: the ending is tragic. Vergil does deal with the decline and old age of his hero. But the *Beowulf*-poet, influenced by Germanic and Christian ideas of the dreadful transience of things, carries his poem beyond the hero's moment of *felicitas* to an ambiguous victory and defeat. (p. 231)

What is central in the drama of Beowulf's expedition to Hart is the awkwardness of the situation and Beowulf's skill in handling it. He is, quite simply, a superman among very strong men—a walking icon of *arma*. His wisdom and tact make him an icon of *virum*. (p. 249)

In his battle of words he turns his knowledge against his opponent and defeats him; and in his next boast, to Wealtheow, he again shows his command of the ethic. *Virum:* in the company of his "secga gedright," he says, he resolved to do the will (or pleasure) of the Danish people. (He rules himself and knows his place as defender of order.) *Arma:* he claims himself no weaker than Grendel and in fairness renounces weapons because Grendel knows no weapons. And *primus:* he leaves the outcome—the payment, good or bad—to God's judgment. (pp. 251–52)

That is, I think, the significance of Beowulf's successive confrontations with monsters. God in his wisdom can enable a shrewd and valiant hero to overcome the enemy of rational order, Grendel. And the God who won the war with the giants can enable a man to overcome perverse power, the perverted irascibility of Grendel's dam, whose loyalty is not to Law but to an outlaw. But the pre-Revelation god of Hrothgar and Hygelac cannot overcome mutability itself, the destructive principle inherent in matter, slave to Fate—the principle traditionally represented in the figure of the dragon. (p. 257)

For Gardner, Beowulf is a hero working against a spoiled, post-Fall trinity. His several victories and his lone defeat are emblems of man's eternal warring with the sin and contamination inherited from, and defined by, Christianity. Gardner believed the early reader (or hearer) of *Beowulf* to have understood this scheme, just as he expects the modern reader to modestly comprehend his *Grendel*.

To bring all of this back toward Gardner's own novel then, permit the inclusion of one final quotation; with good fortune, it should become clearer what sort of puzzle Gardner is constructing:

> In *Grendel* I was interested in . . . the implications of Jean-Paul
> Sartre's philosophy, and the people who followed him down to
> Marcuse and so on, and the people who went behind him. It's a
> philosophy which I think is essentially paranoid and loveless and
> faithless and egoistic and other nasty things—all of which are very
> attractive to me, although I'm also on the other side. So what I did
> in *Grendel*, I wanted to apply in modern settings some basic things
> of that poem, and one of the basic things, the essence of the poem
> is the tripartite soul, and the breakdown of reason, and man's
> desperate attempt to hang on to reason against what in the Middle
> Ages would have been treated as very simple: irascibility and
> concupiscence and the Platonic scheme. That system comes up in
> disguise after disguise and it can always be modernized; it can be
> Vishnu, Brahma, Siva, or God the Father, God the Son, God the
> Holy Ghost, or ego, superego, id—it just keeps shape-shifting. In
> fact, nobody has come along with any kind of faculty psychology to
> supplant or to adequately criticize it even.[11]

In *Grendel*, Gardner is exploring the spiritual and psychological slippage of the twentieth century. Bombarded by disaster and cataclysm, by cheapness and falsity, and by corrosive, malignant philosophy, modern man struggles to maintain some kind of rational and physical order. Man is lower than the angels ("and a damned sight more interesting") and a little above the monster; he takes three steps up and two steps down, at times rising to the heroic, at other times sinking toward the bestial.

In Gardner's own fictional design (supported by the assumptions in his critical work), Beowulf emerges as the hero, as the embodiment of the unified medieval soul. He comes as the superman and as the demigod; his mortality is spiritualized and exploded by the perfect combination of classical virtue.

In contrast stand the three configurations of corrupted virtue. There is the demeaned *arma* or irascibility of Hrothgar, whose political gains have been bought with sure brutality and ruthlessness and whose kingdom now shows cracks and sags (much like Lykourgos's Sparta). There is the fouled *primus* or concupiscence of the dragon, whose materialism has been bred in a cave and whose viciousness is thorough. And there is the blighted *virum* or irrationality of Grendel, whose anger and bloody purposefulness are the results of a flawed intellectual system. Grendel's defect is the most important because it is rationality that rules the other two faculties (as Plato tells us), and it is this "wrong reason" that has misled twentieth-century man so drastically. Grendel's distress is our distress, his embarrassment our embarrassment.

As much as anything, *Grendel* is an examination of virtue and of its chances in a sometime unvirtuous world. Gardner relies most heavily in this examination upon the Platonic formulation described above, but he also makes lesser use of the more practical and humane ethical system of Aristotle as laid out in the *Nichomachean Ethics*. Gardner desperately believes in the possibility of an ethical existence and in the survivability of the virtuous man, and in *Grendel* he tests this belief, working through the Aristotelian virtues as he constructs his idea of the virtuous soul.[12] Plato, then, supplies the thematic substance, Aristotle the structural foundation, as Gardner moves in his novel toward the appearance of Beowulf, the Aristotelian "great-souled man," the *megalopsychus*.

Grendel looks at the world and sees a race of madmen and fools, a world of pattern-weavers. They live by "lunatic theory." By imposing ritual upon their existence, they hope to impose order. It is an order that is alien to Grendel in his gloomy sense of the "deadly progression of moon and stars."[13] Grendel envisions a universe that is indifferent and uncaring and unobserving, and it makes him spiteful: "The sky ignores me, forever unimpressed. Him too I hate, the same as I hate these brainless budding trees, these brattling birds" (p. 6). He plays the role of the victim, doomed by an ancient curse, caught up in "the cold mechanics of the stars" (p. 9). Grendel shows the symptoms of being an incipient existentialist, an animal that defines meaning by his individual being. At night, Grendel peers into the abyss and, in a flash of half-hope, stares down death:

> I stand in the high wind balanced, blackening the night with my stench, gazing down to cliffs that fall away to cliffs, and once again I am aware of my potential: I could die. I cackle with rage and suck in breath.
>
> "Dark chasms!" I scream from the cliff-edge, "seize me! Seize me to your foul black bowels and crush my bones!" I am terrified at the sound of my own huge voice in the darkness. I stand there shaking from head to foot, moved to the deep-sea depths of my being, like a creature thrown into audience with thunder.

At the same time, I am secretly unfooled. The uproar is only my own shriek, and chasms are, like all things vast, inanimate. They will not snatch me in a thousand years, unless, in a lunatic fit of religion, I jump. (pp. 9–10)

Grendel can prove his being by jumping, by an act of "lunatic religion" that will extinguish his being, but chooses instead to show up the folly of such an act. It is a choice that will come round again, when the time is riper.

Grendel's budding existentialism blossoms in his first encounter with the race of man. Clamped in the crotch of a riven oak tree, Grendel confronts the universe in two of its forms. His first attacker is a bull, a symbol of blind, brute force; the bull charges, and charges once more, acting from pure instinct. Grendel sneers, though pained and bleeding, at the stupidity of it all and arrives at a recognition:

I understood that the world was nothing: a mechanical chaos of casual, brute enmity on which we stupidly impose our hopes and fears. I understood that, finally and absolutely, I alone exist. All the rest, I saw, is merely what pushes me, or what I push against. I create blindly—as blindly as all that is not myself pushes back. I create the whole universe, blink by blink.—An ugly god pitifully dying in a tree! (pp. 21–22)

In what might be a parody of Sartre's Roquentin, Grendel breaks through to what K. Clif Mason has called a "nihilistic epiphany."[14] What Grendel misses is the hidden affirmation of his vision. He is correct in thinking that we "create the whole universe, blink by blink"; he goes wrong, however, in ignoring the imaginative power of such a thought and act. Grendel's intellectual system is turned top-to-toe in that it makes of imagination a negative, not a positive force.

This position is bolstered when Grendel is approached by the king and his small band of nightriders. Grendel cannot make them out in the half-light of their torches, but they are animallike, "with dead-looking eyes and gray-white faces" (p. 23). The men are just as confused and think Grendel to be some sort of "oaktree spirit." Grendel laughs, the men cower in fear, Hrothgar hurls his ax, and Grendel howls. "And suddenly I knew I was dealing with no dull mechanical bull but with thinking creatures, pattern makers, the most dangerous things I'd ever met" (p. 27). It is a menace that is crazy and out of line with Grendel's notion of the world. The human mind fails to notice the world's meaninglessness; it goes on composing and creating, making the world anew with the movement of a finger or the tilt of the head.

Convinced of his rightness and of the madness of Hrothgar's kingdom-building, Grendel "settles his soul" on destroying the king. Grendel recalls the grim history of Hrothgar's rise and of his bloody clenching of political power. Hrothgar is a master of conquest, but he lacks a nobility to balance his acquisitiveness. His courage, or *arma,* is self-directed; he has gone beyond pride in accomplishment (an accepted Anglo-Saxon virtue) to pride in aggrandizement. He collects land and people as the dragon collects gold. His virtue is corrupted, his kingdom entropic. Grendel correctly sees the weakness built into Hrothgar's inhumanity, and pledges himself to the ruthless dismantlement of the empire purchased at so high a price. More important, he is out to destroy the order that Hrothgar, with grim majesty, represents. Grendel senses the human threat; it has a smell and a feel about it that fills him "with a wordless, obscurely murderous unrest" (p. 40).

This killing spirit is quelled, however, by the words and the harp-tunes of the *scop,* who re-creates and reshapes Hrothgar's history. He twists "together like sailors' ropes" bits and pieces of the legend, cleansing it, gilding it, crafting it into art. The Shaper alters reality and relieves man of cruel necessity. He transmutes the past like an alchemist, mixing truth with lie until a vision emerges, a vision that annihilates pain and exalts human effort. Grendel, even in his monstrousness, feels the magic of the Shaper's art:

> I crossed the moors in a queer panic, like a creature half insane. I knew the truth. . . . I remembered the ragged men fighting each other till the snow was red slush, whining in winter, the shriek of people and animals burning, the whip-slashed oxen in the mire, the scattered battle-leavings: wolf-torn corpses, falcons fat with blood. Yet I also remembered, as if it had happened, great Scyld, of whose kingdom no trace remained, and his farsighted son, of whose greater kingdom no trace remained. And the stars overhead were alive with the promise of Hrothgar's vast power, his universal peace. . . . Thus I fled, ridiculous hairy creature torn apart by poetry. (p. 44)

Grendel's image of the universe has been inverted by the Shaper's fiction. Like humankind, Grendel goes "half insane," losing reason in the rush of poetry and rhythm and sound.

Such a relinquishment of mind to emotion is a natural result of the ecstasy of art—but one must take care to make it a reflective and closely scrutinized relinquishment. In other words, one must understand the power of art to change and shift the indefinite shapes of history and memory and truth. In his "apocalyptic glee," Grendel misses the fact of the Shaper's deception and affirms the fancy. Gardner has left no doubt that the Shaper's act is virtuous: "The Shaper comes along in a meaningless, stupid kingdom and makes up a rationale. He creates the heroism, the feeling of tribal unity. He makes the people brave. And sure, it's a lie, but it's also a vision."[15] But Grendel's "seduction" (as Gardner calls it) is unfortunate and uncautious and untempered. Grendel's "glee" is aesthetic excess.

It is a lesson reinforced when Grendel is again "unmonstered" by the Shaper's voice. The poet hymns the Creation myth, and Grendel listens as he tells "of an ancient feud between two brothers which split all the world between darkness and light. And I, Grendel, was the dark side. . . . The terrible race God cursed" (p. 51). Grendel believes and is "converted" to the human-Christian logic, but his monstrous nature condemns him to be an outcast, an inheritor of the primeval doom. Grendel is damned in his inability to speak and to communicate with the humans around him; language, the fabric of the Shaper's art, is beyond him, lost in the severance of Cain from God. It is one of the gifts, however, that Grendel unwittingly works toward, and one of the gifts he ultimately achieves.

The song the Shaper sings praises the erection of Hrothgar's glorious meadhall, Hart. The poet makes of it something nearly holy, but Grendel tells it otherwise:

> The thought took seed in Hrothgar's mind. It grew. He called all his people together and told them his daring scheme. He would build a magnificent meadhall high on a hill, with a view of the western sea, a victory-seat near the giants' work, old ruined fortress from the world's first war, to stand forever as a sign of glory and justice of Hrothgar's Danes. There he would sit and give treasures out, all wealth but the lives of men and the people's land. And so his sons would do after him, and his sons' sons, to the final generation. . . . I knew very well that all he said was ridiculous, not light for their darkness but flattery, illusion, a vortex pulling them from sunlight to heat, a kind of midsummer burgeoning, waltz to the sickle. (pp. 47–48)

Hrothgar attempts magnificence but achieves only vulgarity. The hall is a symbol of his kingdom: it is crumbling even as it is sung, awaiting silently the onslaught of its destroyer. As Grendel later sings, "The wall will fall to the wind." It is another flaw in the image of Hrothgar as embodiment of *arma*. He is growing blind to his own frailty and tries to build his history on the lives and deaths of his people. He doles out little treasures but keeps the greater ones—dignity, peace, freedom—locked away securely.

As Hrothgar hoards spiritual richness, so the dragon stores up mound upon gleaming mound of material wealth. The dragon is the figure of base materialism ("My advice to you . . . is to seek out gold and sit on it"), and as such is the perfect perversion of liberality, or *primus*. He is concupiscence out of control, desire unchecked by "right reason."

Grendel's movement toward the dragon is almost Plotinian, as he sinks "away like a stone through earth and sea" to the dragon's cave. It is the descent toward matter, the lowest form of nature in Plotinus's scheme. The dragon is omniscient and godlike (though not a god): "I know what's in your mind. I know everything. That's what makes me so sick and old and tired" (p. 61). He is the god of the existentialists—bored, distant, indifferent. The dragon is horrible in his power to silence and turn to stone, as Grendel finds:

> "Be still!" he screamed. Flame shot clear to the cavemouth. "I know
> you're sorry. For right now, that is. For this one frail, foolish
> flicker-flash in the long dull fall of eternity. I'm unimpressed—No
> no! Be still!" His eye burst open like a hole, to hush me. I felt as if I
> were tumbling down into it—dropping endlessly down through a
> soundless void. He let me fall, down and down toward a black sun
> and spiders, though he knew I was beginning to die. Nothing could
> have been more disinterested: serpent to the core. (p. 61)

The dragon dismisses the art of the Shaper as illusion and the promise of free will as "piddling." He too sees man's ritualism and pattern-making as folly and hopelessness, as a desperate absurdity: "They'd map out the roads through Hell with their crackpot theories, their here-to-the-moon-and-back lists of paltry facts. Insanity—the simplest insanity ever devised!" (p. 64).

The dragon is the nihilist who denies the relationship between man and his universe. Man searches for connections, but there are none, says the dragon. "That's where the Shaper saves them. Provides an illusion of reality—puts together all their facts with a gluey whine of connectedness" (p. 65). He is a mock oracle with an apocalyptic vision.[16] "Things come and go. . . . That's the gist of it. . . . A temporary gathering of bits, a few random dust specks . . . then by chance a vast floating cloud of dust specks, an expanding universe. . . . Complexity beyond complexity, accident on accident, until—" Grendel battles with him, grows tired and closed-eyed, becomes lost in the web of logic-spinning.[17] But one thing the dragon tells Grendel stays with him:

> You improve them, my boy! . . . You stimulate them! You make
> them think and scheme. You drive them to poetry, science, religion,

all that makes them what they are for as long as they last. You are, so to speak, the brute existent by which they learn to define themselves. The exile, captivity, death they shrink from—the blunt facts of their mortality, their abandonment—that's what you make them recognize, embrace! You *are* mankind, or man's condition: inseparable as the mountain-climber and the mountain. If you withdraw, you'll instantly be replaced. Brute existents, you know, are a dime a dozen. No sentimental trash, then. If man's the irrelevance that interests you, stick with him! Scare him to glory! (pp. 72–73)

In this second takeoff on Sartre (recall Thaletes's elephant in *Agathon*), Grendel locates a specific meaning to his existence: he becomes the brute existent, the existential referent and *raison d'être*.[18]

With this new definition in hand, Grendel begins his twelve-year war on Hrothgar and his thanes. Bones crunch, blood sprays, bodies crumble, as Grendel, in a manner that is every bit as systematized as humankind's, wreaks destruction. The Shaper's song no longer comforts or inspires—it only enrages Grendel with its story of people's "blissful, swinish ignorance, their bumptious self-satisfaction, and worst of all, their *hope*" (p. 77). Grendel is a monster ecstatic in his purpose:

I felt a strange, unearthly joy. It was as if I'd made some incredible discovery, like my discovery long ago of the moonlight world beyond the mere. I was transformed. I was a new focus for the clutter of space I stood in: if the world had once imploded on the tree where I waited, trapped and full of pain, it now blasted outward, away from me, screeching terror. I had become, myself, the mama I'd searched the cliffs for once in vain. . . . I had *become* something, as if born again. I had hung between possibilities before, between the cold truths I knew and the heart-sucking conjuring tricks of the Shaper; now that was passed: I was Grendel, Ruiner of Meadhalls, Wrecker of Kings!
But also, as never before, I was alone. (pp. 79–80)

Grendel justifies his action (and his willingness to act is important) as a necessary *force:* he is now a power that may stand in opposition to any other force. His world is one of push and tug—bulls butting heads, mountains straining against mountain, humanity heaving against the universe. Grendel is done with being—he is becoming.

But his purpose isolates him and completes his exile. His tongue has failed him before, and now his heart and mind turn against whatever might have been attractive in mankind. When Unferth confronts him,

Grendel mocks his attempted heroism. He pelts him with sarcasm and apples, and degrades the small nobility that Unferth affects. Grendel is growing bitter and caustic and dragonish; his vision is becoming cloudy and his senses confused with the smell of burning skin. "The dragon-scent in the room grew stronger, as if my teasing were bringing the old beast near." Grendel abandons value and morality and pitches toward nihilism, laughing all the while at Unferth's (and Gardner's) notion of man's potential for brilliance: " 'Go ahead, scoff,' [Unferth] said, petulant. 'Except in the life of a hero, the whole world's meaningless. The hero sees value beyond what's possible. That's the *nature* of the hero. It kills him, of course, ultimately. But it makes the whole struggle of humanity worthwhile' " (p. 89). Though Unferth exaggerates a bit (there is certainly meaning to the world beyond the hero), he is basically true to Gardner's belief in the significance of the hero (a belief demonstrated, for example, in *The Wreckage of Agathon* and *Freddy's Book*). Grendel recedes further and further from the world of feeling and of rational thought. His system enshrouds him and cuts off all light; he becomes a quarreler, a bigot, an isolate. Monster now in thought as well as deed, Grendel renounces the connectedness of nature and roams solitary, friendless, uncomforted.

Grendel's blessings are few and ironic, derived from his personal law of will: "There is no limit to desire but desire's needs." He lists them:

I. My teeth are sound.
I. The roof of my cave is sound.
I. I have not committed the ultimate act of nihilism: I have not killed the queen.
I. Yet. (p. 93)

The killing of the queen is the ultimate nihilistic act because she represents everything that is dignified and hopeful in mankind. Wealtheow brings peace and mediates men's fury, and she nearly redeems the sinking Grendel. Her beauty is poetic and surpasses even the songs of the Shaper; Grendel feels her effect—"She tore me apart as once the Shaper's song had done"—and is "teased toward disbelief in the dragon's truths" (p. 108). This is the queen's glorious substance, her force—one that is equal in all ways to Grendel's brutishness. She pricks a weakness—a desire for love and caring—and it is this weakness, not Grendel's existential consistency, that changes the monster's mind. Grendel holds her, splay-legged and praying, consumed in his own monstrousness ("The smell of the dragon lay around me like sulphurous smoke"), figuring her awful death:

> I firmly committed myself to killing her, slowly, horribly. I would begin by holding her over the fire and cooking the ugly hole

between her legs. I laughed harder at that. They were all screaming now, hooting and yawling to their dead-stick gods. I would kill her, yes! I would squeeze out her feces between my fists. So much for meaning as quality of life! I would kill her and teach them reality. Grendel the truth-teacher, phantasm-tester! It was what I would be from this day forward—my commitment, my character as long as I lived—and nothing alive or dead could change my mind!

I changed my mind. It would be meaningless, killing her. As meaningless as letting her live. It would be, for me, mere pointless pleasure, an illusion of order for this one frail, foolish flicker-flash in the long dull fall of eternity. . . . I'd cured myself. (pp. 109–10)

Wealtheow is a life force, a sort of White Goddess whose energy is indestructible and irreducible. Grendel, the awesome devastator, is shown up by the queen's rich vitality. She pricks a weakness: a desire for love and caring.

Grendel has problems with Wealtheow's innocence and feminine spirit.[19] One of his soul's faculties filters the queen's spiritual nature, while another struggles with her physicality and womanness. The monster is shameless in his treatment of the queen, discovering her secrecy and violating the privacy of her flesh; and he is cowed by her ultimate and elemental will. He changes his mind because he, Grendel, "the truth-tester" cannot absorb or endure Wealtheow's own significant truth: that the world is rich and forceful and fertile. It is a truth that will be brought home once more to Grendel by the strength of Beowulf. But he is learning; his defense of cold reason shows gaps through which feeling and more rigorous thought slip.

In chapter 8, Grendel rummages again his memory and recalls the coming of Hrothulf to Hrothgar's court. Hrothulf is "the sweet scorpion," the smiling deceiver. He practices political connivery and plays the flattering nephew to the king, who is keenly aware of Hrothulf's plotting. There is a ruthlessness about young Hrothulf that echoes Grendel's own cruelty, and his meeting with old Red Horse[20] in the forest (where, of course, all of Gardner's anarchists meet and brood and plan) shows off the youth's Machiavellian nature. Hrothulf is the poet of power; he is a spider (a purposeful use by Gardner of the Blakean symbol)[21] who weaves malignant webs and sings dire songs:

> The law of the world is a winter law,
> and casual. I too can be grim:
> snatch my daylight by violent will
> and be glorified for the deed, like him. (p. 115)

Hrothulf (and Red Horse), like Grendel, denounce pattern and theory and ritual. "All systems are evil. All governments are evil. Not just a trifle evil. *Monstrously* evil" (p. 120). What they do not see, of course, is the circumscription of their own, anarchical system.

Hrothgar's kingdom, however, is ripe for the plucking. Things are in decline, slowly winding down, ungreased wheels grating and giving off small sparks. Grendel, a knowing part of the imperfect triumvirate, speaks sympathetically of the old warrior and of his present, sad state:

> Violence and shame have lined the old man's face with mysterious calm. I can hardly look at him without a welling of confused, unpleasant emotion. He sits tall and still in his carved chair, stiff arms resting on the chair-sides, his clear eyes trained on the meadhall door where I'll arrive, if I come. When someone speaks to him, he answers politely and gently, his mind far away—on murdered thanes, abandoned hopes. He's a giant. He had in his youth the strength of seven men. Not now. He has nothing left but the power of his mind—and no pleasure there: a case of knives. The civilization he meant to build has transmogrified to a forest thick with traps. . . . And then too there's his treasure-hoard. Another trap. A man plunders to build up wealth to pay his men and bring peace to the kingdom, but the hoard he builds for his safety becomes the lure of every marauder that happens to hear of it. Hrothgar, keen of mind, is out of schemes. No fault of his. There are no schemes left. And so he waits like a man chained in a cave, staring at the entrance or, sometimes, gazing with sad, absent-minded eyes at Wealtheow, chained beside him. Who is one more trap, the worst. She's young, could have served a more vigorous man. And beautiful: need not have withered her nights and wasted her body on a bony, shivering wretch. She knows all this, which increases his pain and guilt. . . . And his fear is one he cannot even be sure is generous; perhaps mere desire that his name and fame live on. (pp. 121–22)

It is a moving portrait of fallen *arma*. Hrothgar, once a figure of stamina and courage, sits like a graybeard thin with age and grief. Body, mind, and spirit have all been depleted and have left him skeletal. What once was virtuous is now bankrupt. Hrothgar had striven for honor, but now his ambition wanes. He merely wants to survive. Equally corrupt, in contrast, is the ascendant Hrothulf, who is consumed with ambition and the will to power. Hrothulf sings of fresh blood and waits for "old things to sicken and fail" (p. 115); Hrothgar dreams dreams of oak trees and dark sounds and sword flashes in the night:

A black tree with a double trunk—two trees
Grown into one—throws up its blurred branches.

The two trunks in their infinitesimal dance of growth
Have turned completely about one another, their join
A slowly twisted scar . . . that I recognize. . . .

A quick arc flashes sidewise in the air,
A heavy blade in flight. A wooden stroke:
Iron sinks in the gasping core.
          I will dream it again.[22] (p. 124)

The dream, imputed to Hrothgar by Grendel, recalls the first meeting of king and monster and the act which spurred the twelve-year-war. It is the memory and guilt of a great man in decline, and Grendel, like the Shaper, spins the gloomy history.

It is, in fact, the season of decline, winter, and "the trees are dead, and only the deepest religion can break through time and believe they'll revive" (p. 175). Spiritual belief, to Grendel, is merely another sign of man's lunacy (recall Grendel's decision not to jump into the abyss). It is angel-making in the snow, the creation of "mysterious and ominous . . . winged creatures," the fabrication of myth and fantasy. The language of the priests is old and nearly lost, curiously akin to Grendel's, and merely a convenient way of moving through the ritual: "There is no conviction in the old priests' songs; there is only showmanship" (p. 128). Even the corpses of the priests lie vexatiously on Grendel's stomach.

Grendel sports with the old men who keep the ritual and the belief. He confronts, one cold night, the white-bearded Ork, "eldest and wisest of the priests." Grendel adopts a mask of the god, becomes "The Destroyer," and reviews a blasphemous catechism with the old man. The priest unravels a long string of faith and logic and mystery, and when found blubbering by his brothers, is jeered at by some and praised by others. To Grendel, it is merely annoying. Faith, in its extremes, is embarrassing and even dangerous. Rapture and frenzy go beyond any sort of reasonable belief, and aspire to unjustified holiness. It is enough to cool even Grendel's blood-lust.

Grendel, however, is not entirely blameless. It is too easy to play games with faith and belief, to spin traps of logic and intelligence that foul the emotional metaphysic. Grendel's baiting of the priest represents the failure of wit, as Grendel alternates between buffoonery and boorishness. The mind can be made a weapon and can draw blood; it can humiliate, shame, and bring ruin if wielded with enough vicious purpose. It is the monster that acts such, the distorted reason of Grendel, and the monster is turning cold and bitter and has painful visions.[23]

> My heart moves slowly, like freezing water, and I cannot clearly
> recall the smell of blood. And yet I am restless. I would fall, if I
> could, through time and space to the dragon. I cannot. . . . I recall
> something. A void boundless as a nether sky. I hang by the twisted
> roots of an oak, looking down into immensity. Vastly far away I see
> the sun, black but shining, and slowly revolving around it there are
> spiders. But then I am in the woods again, and the snow is falling,
> and everything alive is fast asleep. It is just some dream. I move on,
> uneasy; waiting. (p. 137)

Grendel's dream is both a memory and a prefiguration. It recalls the
frightening drama of his youth and anticipates the finality of his meeting
with Beowulf. It is Beowulf who unnerves Grendel, makes him "uneasy";
Beowulf is moving upon the monster's conscience, a power destined to
collide with power. The abyss will open up once more for Grendel, and a
decision will have to be made a second time.

Winter also brings to Hrothgar's kingdom the death of the Shaper. The
empire is falling to wreckage and its history starts to pale as suddenly as
the cold cheeks of the *scop*. Art is coming to a temporary end; language
and song and poetry are dying with the Shaper, even though his appren-
tice survives him. Grendel's mind stirs with the certainty of the Shaper's
passing:

> I think of the pastness of the past: how the moment I am alive in,
> prisoned in, moves like a slowly tumbling form through darkness,
> the underground river. Not only ancient history—the mythical age
> of the brothers' feud—but my own history one second ago, has
> vanished utterly, dropped out of existence. King Scyld's great deeds
> do not exist "back there" in Time. "Back there in Time" is an illu-
> sion of language. They do not exist at all. My wickedness five years
> ago, or six, or twelve, has no existence except as now, mumbling,
> mumbling, sacrificing the slain world to the omnipotence of words,
> I strain my memory to regain it. . . . I snatch a time when I
> crouched outside the meadhall hearing the first strange hymns of
> the Shaper. Beauty! Holiness! How my heart rocked! He is dead.
> I should have captured him, teased him, tormented him, made a
> fool of him. I should have cracked his skull midsong and sent his
> blood spraying out wet through the meadhall like a shocking change
> of key. One evil deed missed is a loss for all eternity. (p. 146)

Time does *not* exist in words, in language, in song alone—it exists as
matter-of-factly as stone walls and caves. History is not an illusion of

language, but a definite presence. This, Gardner would say, is one of the great mistakes of the existentialist argument: history is not lost or locked on a page like a stored relic, but is a living, dominating force. Grendel's attempt to assign his maliciousness to the fantasy world of words is naïve and confused. His boasts of nonresponsibility are just as fraudulent as the empty hymns of the priests and the dead forms of Danish heroism. Grendel (and Sartre, for that matter) is the rational soul gone wrong; he has foundered into a corruption of truth, flourishing an invulnerability that just is not available in this world. Grendel, like mankind, is trapped or at least pushed by his past; the past can take the form of myth, or religion, or song, but it is a palpable force.

"We're on our own again. Abandoned." Grendel senses the absence of the Shaper and its effect upon the kingdom. He senses, too, the eerie expectation of an arrival. The sea groans, the dragon scent rises, and Grendel awakens with his hands upon his throat. *"Beware the fish."* It is a warning that stirs Grendel's soul in its obscurity, and makes him eager for the coming.

There is a current and an electrification that flashes through Grendel upon Beowulf's landing. Heroes, warriors, more bones for Grendel's dam: "I could feel them coming as I lay in the dark of my cave. I stirred, baffled by the strange sensation, squinting into dark corners to learn the cause. It drew me as the mind of the dragon did once. *It's coming!*" (pp. 151–52). The presence of Beowulf and his men quickens Grendel's spirit; they offer a rationale and a rejuvenation. At the same time, they are a thorn of a lost memory that picks at Grendel's side. Beowulf has the "voice of a dead thing," and "a strange face that, little by little, grew unsettling to me: it was a face . . . from a dream I had almost forgotten" (p. 154). His eyes plunge like a snake's and he has "no more beard than a fish." The vision is a mixed one, blurred with a variety of memories and shades and recollections.

More important, Beowulf is sheer physical power, "a superman among very strong men." Grendel stops and starts, his energy fading and surging:

> "Come ahead," I whispered. "Make your play. Do your worst."
> But I was less sure of myself than I pretended. Staring at his grotesquely muscled shoulders . . . I found my mind wandering. If I let myself, I could drop into a trance just looking at those shoulders. He was dangerous. And yet I was excited, suddenly alive. He talked on. I found myself not listening, merely looking at his mouth, which moved . . . independent of the words, as if the body of the stranger were a ruse, a disguise for something infinitely more terrible. (p. 155)

Grendel does not know for sure what to make of the vision before him. Beowulf both chills and livens him; his temper and bloodiness start once more to roll, and his mind retreats from the monster. His thinking again turns nihilistic: "All order, I've come to understand, is theoretical, unreal—a harmless, sensible, smiling mask men slide between the two great, dark realities, the self and the world—two snake-pits" (p. 157). He reaffirms the vision of the dragon, in all of its existentialist despair and egotism: ". . . absolute, final waste. I saw long ago the whole universe as not-my-mother, and I glimpsed my place in it, a hole. *Yet I exist,* I knew. *Then I alone exist,* I said. *It's me or it*" (p. 158). Beowulf becomes Grendel's brute existent, something that (Grendel hopes) will "scare the monster to glory."

Grendel catches himself edging toward the same madness that bites at men and even at Beowulf—"I understood at last the look in his eyes. He was insane." Beowulf is still another of Gardner's lunatic heroes. The outlines of his physical form merge with dream and memory; Grendel wanders, trying to catch the direction of things and to latch on to something sure: "The harder I stared at his gleaming shoulders, the more uncertain I was of their shape. The room was full of a heavy, unpleasant scent I couldn't place. I labor to remember something: twisted roots, an abyss . . . I lose it" (p. 164). Beowulf, in Grendel's eyes, is losing his humanness as the edges blur and become indefinite. He is becoming man and monster and dragon. And Grendel is creeping nearer and nearer the abyss.

What partly drives Grendel to this final conflict is the fury inherent in his nature. As his rationality slips further out of control, further toward the existential absurdity, he allows his emotions to take rein, and acts upon pure and instinctive rage. He approaches the clear willfulness of his mother in his delight in fresh blood and bone. He submits himself to the swift sweep of time moving toward a final darkness; he obeys, as much as bull and goat and man, the harsh "mechanics" of the moment and of his world.

In the end, Grendel falls to the eternal, grand accident. He faults trickery, but it is justice. In his pain and his fear, Grendel's eyes grow obscure and duplicitous as they try to focus on the man-creature that is tearing into Grendel's flesh:

> The eyes nail me now as his hand nails down my arm. I jump back
> without thinking. . . . Now he's out of his bed, his hand still closed
> like a dragon's jaw on mine. Nowhere on middle-earth, I realize,
> have I encountered a grip like his. My whole arm's on fire,
> incredible, searing pain—it's as if his crushing fingers are charged

like fangs with poison. I scream, facing him, grotesquely shaking hands—dear long-lost brother, kinsman-thane—and the timbered hall screams back at me. I feel the bones go, ground from their sockets, and I scream again. I am suddenly awake. The long pale dream, my history, falls away. The meadhall is alive, great cavernous belly, gold-adorned, bloodstained, howling back at me, lit by the flickering fire in the stranger's eyes. He has wings. Is it possible? And yet it's true: out of his shoulders come terrible fiery wings. I jerk my head, trying to drive out illusion. The world is what it is and always was. That's our hope, our chance. Yet even in times of catastrophe we people it with tricks. Grendel, Grendel, hold fast to what is true! (pp. 168–69)

Beowulf is transmogrified into the dragon. His fingers sting like fangs, his eyes gleam red, his tongue spits bright fire. Grendel hears the dragon's words swirling about his ears, whispers of dust and randomness. Everything in Grendel's experience, all elements of good and wrong and clear sense, melt into the blur that is Beowulf's force.[24] It is the pain that drives Grendel to his recognition, just as the pain of the bull's charge and Hrothgar's ax-blade drove him to his nihilistic conversion. Beowulf swings the monster's head toward the wall (just as Grendel earlier wished to break the Shaper) and demands a song: *"Grendel, Grendel! You make the world by whispers, second by second. Are you blind to that? Whether you make it a grave or a garden of roses is not the point. Feel the wall: is it not hard? . . . Observe the hardness, write it down in careful runes. Now sing of walls! Sing!"* (p. 171). And Grendel, driven by the undeniable reality of the wall and the pain crazing his skull, sings of walls, convinced all the time of Beowulf's madness: "You're a fucking lunatic."[25]

Beowulf goads Grendel to the madness that is art. Grendel's song is his hymn to the Shaper, whom he replaces; the world is indeed accidental and one of its finest accidents is the making of the artist.[26] Grendel unwillingly and unwittingly succeeds the Shaper as a maker of acceptable myths. He learns that creation invests the world with meaning and that it is better to make a noble lie than a depraved one. Grendel cannot negate the pain nor reclaim his arm, but he can make the affirmation of his accident. He runs from the meadhall, bellowing, moving blindly, and stands, almost dreamily, at the same, dizzying rim—and faces the same staggering choice:

I stumble again and with my one weak arm I cling to the huge twisted roots of an oak. I look down past stars to a terrifying darkness. I seem to recognize the place, but it's impossible. "Accident," I whisper. I will fall. I seem to desire the fall, and though I fight it with all my will I know in advance that I can't win. Standing baffled, quaking with fear, three feet from the edge of a nightmare cliff, I find myself, incredibly, moving toward it. I look down, down, into bottomless blackness, feeling the dark power moving in me like an ocean current, some monster inside me, deep sea wonder, dread night monarch astir in his cave, moving me slowly to my voluntary tumble into death. (p. 173)

The vision repeats itself, but this time Grendel is aware of his own mutability. History and the "dark power" of death kill Grendel, but he dies conscious of his mistake. He sees too late the miraculous power of lunatic art, lunatic religion, lunatic heroism of the soul.

Ultimately, the conflict is indeed one of souls. Beowulf is the embodiment of all that is just and heroic and possible in man. He possesses all of the Aristotelian virtues, is the perfect union of *arma, virum,* and *primus.* He is as close as man can come to godliness; he is Aristotle's *megalopsychus.* Grendel, on the other hand, is damned (however much our sympathies wish it otherwise) by the old blood that runs through him and that determines his monstrousness. He is the perverse mirror-image of Beowulf—a "great-souled monster," if you will. His mishandled reason (and his heritage) lead him to viciousness of soul, a corruption of the hero's grandeur. Gardner is playing off the two in the final chapter, allowing Grendel to at least approximate or glimpse his potential before he dies. In that last, fateful stare into the abyss, Grendel sees that art redeems, that it is imagination that separates man and monster, that life must be made ethical. *That,* says Gardner, is Grendel's "joy"; *that* is the accident we all must share.

Chapter V

The Sunlight Dialogues

Wheeling atoms, random dance,
old pictures, guard my will from chance.
Then lady, wife, old childhood wound
I'll haunt you, hunt you, down and down.
  —"Pictures From an Old Album"

The Sunlight Dialogues, published in 1972, is Gardner's largest and most complex novel. The book, which in its final form ran to 673 pages, inspired doubts even in Robert Gottlieb, Gardner's editor. Gardner told the story that Gottlieb returned the manuscript with a note advising him to "cut a third"; Gardner replied quizzically, "Which third?" And that was the end of the discussion and the revision.[1] *The Sunlight Dialogues* includes the fine illustrations of the English artist, John Napper (a close friend of Gardner and later the subject of a short story in *The King's Indian*),[2] and was, in fact, the first of Gardner's books to be fully illustrated, which accounts in part for the book's impressive originality. The novel also contains some of Gardner's own poetry (one poem having been previously published under the title, "The Ruptured Goat"), and is the source for a short-story spinoff entitled "A Little Night Music."[3] *The Sunlight Dialogues* is, in short, a rich, resourceful, and brilliant book full of magic and thought.

The Sunlight Dialogues is ultimately important, though, because it stands at the artistic and intellectual center of Gardner's work. In it Gardner attempts a philosophical and aesthetic statement that might endure as a representation of his dominant beliefs: "What I did in *The Sunlight Dialogues* was find a system, a governing metaphysical system that I believed. What I've been doing ever since is pursuing small aspects of the governing system."[4] To understand Gardner, then, one must understand this novel. *The Sunlight Dialogues* is Gardner's most expansive, most sophisticated, and most skilled intellectual declaration; in it, he ventures more, loses *and* achieves more than in any other of his fictions. Gardner lays out his universe with ingenuity and flair, and above all, brilliant sincerity, struggling with problems that, though perhaps beyond the experience of some, are common to the concern of all.

Part of the novel's impressiveness stems from its healthy infusion of philosophical and historical tradition, and its intricately layered structure. The weight of the book rests upon four metaphysical dialogues held between Batavia's Chief of Police, Fred Clumly, and the scarred and wild-eyed Sunlight Man. Each dialogue takes its direction from some thread in Babylonian intellectual, cultural, or religious history, which is highlighted by a contrasting Hebraic perspective. For the proper historical data and lore, Gardner turned to one major sourcebook, A. Leo Oppenheim's *Ancient Mesopotamia: Portrait of a Dead Civilization,* one of the most thorough studies of the Babylonian culture. Gardner's use was generous and purposeful, for among all of the other influences running through the novel—Dante, Malory, Blake, Rimbaud, the *I Ching,* and more—none is as strong and as pervasive as the strain of Babylonian legend and fact.[5]

Beyond even the novel's metaphysical connection with the Babylonian past, there is a structural connection, one that in turn fortifies the overall tone of the book. A central element in Babylonian theology was the art of divination and the telling of omens. It was believed that the gods spoke to human beings through significant actions, that omens were, one might say, the gods' language. There is also the implication that the gods, in their willingness to communicate, evinced an interest in human welfare; omens and signs, in effect, brought the gods closer to humanity. There was necessarily the demand for someone to interpret these signs, and sometimes even to become a sign in themselves:

> Mesopotamian civilization . . . admits that the deity can use man as
> a vehicle for the expression of divine intentions. In this function
> man may act on several levels; he can become the mouthpiece of the
> deity, for which purpose he enters a specific psychological state, a
> prophetic ecstasis (of several kinds), or he can receive divine revela-
> tion in his sleep, or he can allow the deity to give "signs" through
> his physical person. Such signs may be meant for the entire group
> as in the case of specific deformations or the birth of malformed
> children, or they may be meant solely for their carrier, whose
> bodily features are taken to presage his fate. . . . Furthermore, man
> is thought to carry on his own body signs which—when correctly

interpreted—refer to his fate, at time even to his own "nature." The interpretation of these signs is contained in collections called physiognomic omens by Assyriologists. The color of the hair, the shape of the nails, the size of specific parts of the body, the nature and location of moles and discolorations on the skin . . . to mention only a few—are treated more or less extensively in a number of series.[6]

It is obvious from his other works that Gardner often attributes elements of character to physical appearance and demeanor, and I think it legitimate to suggest that Gardner intends both Clumly and Taggert Hodge (the Sunlight Man) as certain types of "mouthpieces." Both men carry the marks of their specialness in their scars and small monstrosities, and it is clear that the Sunlight Man is passing through some sort of (perhaps perverse) shamanistic ecstasis. Nor is this the only connection. As will be detailed later on, Gardner (the scion of a long line of omen-believing Welshmen) makes extensive use of omens and their reading, and of prediction in *The Sunlight Dialogues*. There are oracles and mock-oracles, signs and symbols and forewarnings of all kinds, and characters are measured by their faith in the ominous.

This, then, is the substructure upon which Gardner builds the many strata of his novel. Just as part of the book's complexity is derived from its Babylonian shadings, so is another part of its charge taken from the breadth and multiplicity of its characterization and action. On its primary plane, *The Sunlight Dialogues* is concerned with the conflicts and confrontations between Police Chief Fred Clumly and his lunatic antagonist, the Sunlight Man. The book's plot is set in motion by the Sunlight Man's crazed appearance in the town of Batavia, New York, and is carried along by Clumly's efforts at first to capture and later to understand him. In this sense, the book is a metaphysical detective story, as Clumly goes after both a man and his ideas. *The Sunlight Dialogues* is in fact characterized by pursuit: the pursuit of the Sunlight Man by Clumly; the pursuit of Clumly by Will Hodge Sr; the pursuit of Kleppman by Will Hodge Jr; the pursuit of Ollie Nuper by Walter Benson-Boyle. The novel moves and is structured like a multilevel chessboard, with resolutions and endgames coming on different levels of action.

On a second plane, the novel is the tense history of the Hodge family, whose legend dominates both its members and the townspeople of Batavia. They are drawn into the action by chance relation to the Sunlight Man, but it is a relation they find impossible to deny. From the father (Arthur Taggert Hodge Sr) to the sons (Will Sr, Ben, Taggert, Art) to the grandsons (Will Jr, Ben Jr, Luke, and even Taggert's young boys), to the women and wives (Vanessa, Millie, Kathleen)—each soul linked by blood and birth to the Hodge name is at war with its past. This is the larger background that complicates and intensifies all that happens in the micro-cosm of Batavia.

Making up a third level of action and symbol are the miscellaneous characters who people Gardner's fiction, who play very strong support-ing and contrary roles, and who offer the necessary parallels to move-ments and individuals on other levels. Gardner fashions such characters as Esther Clumly, Fred's long-suffering and long-loving wife; the irksome intruder-hippie, Freeman; and the small-time, small-town, double-lived thief, Walter Benson-Boyle (who owns his own nemesis in Ollie Nuper), all of whom are lesser, but still significant counterpoints in Gardner's novel.

Finally there is the town of Batavia itself. It is a town that Gardner knows well, that (as we've seen in *The Resurrection*) has been face-lifted beyond recognition, that exquisitely represents the virtues and vices of middle America. It is the perfect setting for an exploration of character and value and belief, as Gardner has explained:

> Setting is one of the most powerful symbols you have, but mainly it serves characterization. . . . To establish powerful characters, a writer needs a landscape to help define them; so setting becomes important. Setting is also a powerful vehicle of thematic concerns; in fact, it's one of the most powerful. If you're going to talk about the decline of Western civilization or at least the possibility of that decline, you take an old place that's sort of worn out and rundown. For instance, Batavia, New York, where the Holland Land Office was . . . the beginning of a civilization . . . selling the land in this country. It was, in the beginning, a wonderful, beautiful place with the smartest indians in America around. Now it's this old, run-down town which has been urban-renewalized just about out of existence. The factories have stopped and the people are poor and sometimes crabby; the elm trees are all dead, and so are the oaks and maples. So it's a good symbol.[7]

Batavia is a town torn with swift, unexpected, and inexplicable change; it is the universe (for Gardner) in miniature, an appropriate place to work out his ideas and to evolve a system.

Beyond all else, *The Sunlight Dialogues* is a novel of ideas. Gardner here puts together his philosophical structure in its most developed form, testing his ideas against modern life as he assumes we know it. The central conflict in Gardner's mind is the pull of anarchy against the desire for order. It was a conflict inherent in Gardner's own personality: "On the one hand, I'm a real law-and-order type: Everybody should be good. And on the other hand: I want to blow up the universe."[8] What he does, plainly enough, in *The Sunlight Dialogues* is to set in open opposition representatives of each force, and allow them to work through the puzzles and obstacles of their separate ways of thinking. What they come to in the end is a compromising of each of their modes of belief.

The notion of law and order and the need for constancy of decent behavior is roundly embodied in Chief Fred Clumly. He is the watchdog of Batavian society, a microcosm that is flying apart at the seams, a world that is rushing into disorder:

> I've got worries coming out of my ears—that damned trouble with the dogs, and this plague of stealing this past two months, and now these fires, and the Force in need of men so bad it's a wonder we don't every one of us throw up our hands. Well I'll tell you something. My job is Law and Order. That's my first job, and if I can't get that one done, the rest will just have to wait. You get my meaning? If there's a law on the books, it's my job to see it's enforced. I'm *personally responsible* for every cop in my Department, and for every crook in the City of Batavia. That's my job. I'm aware as you are there are differences of opinion about some of the laws we're paid to enforce, but a cop hasn't got opinions. Don't you forget it. Some fool makes a law against planting trees and you and me will be out there, like it or not, and we'll shut down Arbor Day. (p. 23)

Clumly is a man marked by a tenacity and a fierce single-mindedness. His narrow-set eyes draw blind beads on any sort of deviance and hunt it until retrieved and brought back into line. He is, the narrator tells us, a man "as inflexible as a chunk of steel, with a heart so cold that if you touched it you'd stick as your fingers stick to iron at twenty below zero" (p. 249).

Clumly is not, however, a man without feeling and sympathy. He is surely all too human (almost to the point of caricature) in his physical appearance:

> Clumly's whole body was creased and white and completely hairless. He'd had a disease when he was in the Navy, years ago. Aside from the whiteness and the hairlessness, his only remarkable features were his large nose, which was like a mole's, and his teeth, which were strikingly white and without a flaw. The whiteness, the hairlessness, the oversized nose all gave him the look of a philosopher pale from too much reading, or a man who has slept three nights in the belly of a whale. (p. 8)

Clumly is one of Gardner's many grotesques, whose outward deformity signifies some inward distress and knottedness. He is a molelike man who burrows in on an idea and fixes upon it until it becomes clear in his mind. He is afflicted with the normal scourges of mortality. His wife Esther is a blind woman who sleeps with her glass eyes on the nightstand. They are childless, horrified at the risk of bearing a blind child. Their house is black and silent, with rats and dark water swishing in the basement. Yet Clumly, like Jonah, emerges blanched and blinking from the darkness to work his way toward a belief in the light within the darkness.

A measure of this light is brought upon Clumly by his freakish nemesis, the Sunlight Man, who is arrested by the Chief's men for splashing the word LOVE across a city street. Like Clumly, the Sunlight Man is malformed and marked. His face is burned and bearded and his eyes have a distant look that hints at madness:

> His forehead was high and domelike, scarred, wrinkled, drawn,
> right up into the hairline, and above the arc of his balding, his hair
> exploded like chaotic sunbeams around an Eastern tomb. At times
> he had (one mask among many, for stiff as the fire-blasted face was,
> he could wrench it into an infinite number of shapes) an elfish,
> impenetrable grin which suggested madness, and indeed, from all
> evidence, the man was certainly insane. But to speak of him as mad
> was like sinking to empty rhetoric. In the depths where his
> turbulent broodings moved, the solemn judgments of psychiatry,
> sociology, and the like, however sound, were frail sticks beating a
> subterranean sea. His skin, where not scarred, was like a baby's,
> though dirty, as were his clothes, and his straw-yellow beard,
> tangled and untrimmed, covered most of his face like a bush. He
> reeked as if he'd been feeding on the dead when he first came, and
> all the while he stayed he stank like a sewer. (pp. 59–60)

The Sunlight Man is the bodily figuration of fire and of its ambiguous powers of healing and destruction. He dances and raves and sings and gives off flashes of magic, and he comes to haunt poor Clumly's imagination: "This morning, a little surprised at himself, he'd checked the pistol he hadn't had out of its holster for God knew how long. His hand was shaking like an old, old man's" (p. 15). Clumly's well-ordered world is thrown akilter by the wildness of the Sunlight Man, "the strawberry eater, the skylight smasher—in a word, King Solomon's cod" (p. 54). The Sunlight Man, in an image that weaves itself through the fabric of the novel, becomes that "subterranean sea," a latent beating against the subconscious minds of Clumly, his wife Esther, and Sergeant Sangirgonio.

The Sunlight Man, however, is more than just a trickster and intelligent fool. He is a shape-shifter and a malign magician. He is the romantic anarchist who works from a grander, more expansive vision and ethic. He has a metaphysical mind and his words cut and threaten and scare: "There was a limit to teasing, a certain point, not quite predictable but nevertheless definite and final, beyond which teasing would not go. But there was no such point with the Sunlight Man: he could go on as long as the world endured. He didn't care; that was the secret. Even murderers cared, had some remotely human feeling. The Sunlight Man was as indifferent as a freight train driving a cow from its track" (p. 99). The Sunlight Man seems stripped of feeling and compassion, alive only to taunt and mock and tout the abandonment of reason. It is a rejection of everything instilled in him (in Taggert Hodge) by his father and family.

The Hodge family, a world within a world, was a family built upon law and a belief in sensible order. Arthur Taggert Hodge Sr, patriarch and senator, held implicit faith in the ability of superior men to reason their way to justice and well-being. He was a man unashamedly free in his intellect and in his humane spirit, but he recognized at the same time the limits of such freedom. The will required restraint; natural law was ineffective for the unreasonable and illogical man, for the inferior and more common man. Such political and moral conservatism was one of the legacies the congressman handed down to his sons.

The spell of the elder Hodge weighs most heavily upon Will Hodge Sr, who, like his father, pursues the ambiguities of law for a career. He is a man trapped in a "cage" of his father's design, limited by his father's own unbeatable magnificence and magnitude. Will Hodge recognizes this and determines that he will be not a builder or visionary, but a repairer and maintainer, a man who keeps things in good running condition and in good order:

> His whole life was an ingenious toggle, a belated but painstaking shoring up against last year's ruin, destructions in no way his own but his to repair. . . . Knowing he was not his father, he had long since overcome the temptation to struggle in vain to become his father. He was Hodge the immune and invulnerable, comfortable in the cage of his limitations. Or within a hair of it. For if he would have said once that he was immune to his father the Congressman's power, the power of the Image in which he, Will Hodge, had been imperfectly created, he knew better now. What the old man was unable to manage directly (and would not have wanted to manage anyhow, being a moral person) his ghost had managed indirectly: he tyrannized Hodge—if a thing so trifling was worth a big word like tyranny—through Millie his wife (or former wife), Will Jr and

Luke, his sons. Will Hodge Sr felt no indignation or regret. (p. 126)[9]

Hodge is also a man painfully concerned with justice, with responsibilities that extend beyond the limits of the law (clearly a central element of this particular subplot). His conception of the function of the law bends more easily than Clumly's literalism, yet it stops short of his brother's (the Sunlight Man's) negation of immediate, temporal duty. Will's position makes for constant suffering; he sits alone, "boiling within with grief and outrage, some latter-day Hrothgar, mighty and patient and beyond all human counsel" (p. 231), asking questions that need not be asked but that are noble for the asking. Like Clumly, Hodge recognizes a time shift that has turned the moral values of his father into an anachronism and made of God a retired observer:

> The times were wrong, not incorrupt and not out of joint but
> subtly mellowed, decayed to ambiguity: If right and wrong were as
> clear as ever, they were clear chiefly on a private scale, and though
> God was in his Heaven yet, He had somewhat altered, had become
> archetypal of a new, less awesome generation of fathers: Wisdom
> watching the world with half-averted eyes, chewing his ancient lip
> thoughtfully, mildly, venturing an occasional rueful smile. (p. 141)

Hodge watches, weighs, and judges, but does not act. It is a flaw that ultimately cripples him, just as it cripples Gardner's other Hrothgar in *Grendel*.

It is a vision, furthermore, at least partly inherited by his son, Will Jr. The product of a bitter and broken marriage, Will took with him the knifelike tongue of his mother, but escaped the arduous reasonableness of his father (and the old-style gravity of his grandfather). He represents a third generation that has been washed with the times: he specializes rather than generalizing, he prefers the broil of the city to the slow plod of the small town, and he allows a career and an obsession to rip apart his family. All of this he sees as a breaking free from the "childish clutch of the impossible," from the ideals that governed the two generations before him. His standard is paradoxical, for he defends that in which he does not believe. His grandfather's ideas "were no longer viable, his faith was as empty and dead as his estate, yet they'd left their mark on Will Hodge Jr as on all of them. The American dream turned nightmare. They were not such fools—or anyway Will Jr was no longer such a fool—as to pursue the dream, but at least, with the impossible ideal in mind, he could hate the forces that denied it" (p. 344). His motives are all askew. The law becomes a means of moral vengeance; Will chases a vice and a crime (symbolized in his personal nemesis, the swindler Kleppman) that is devoid of sense, and it changes him into an aching, ulcerous monster. He is incapable of distancing himself from the law and cannot recognize its larger significance. For Will, the law exists to preserve the shell of a dream no longer possible—and that is no kind of reasonable purpose at all.

For some in Batavia, the world is hurling itself outward, picking up terrible speed in an expanding, "accelerating demolition." Clumly, Will Hodge Sr, and Will Hodge Jr all see the universe as Einsteinian, with planets edging further and further into space, everything falling away from the center. Others, like Taggert Hodge and the Judge and perhaps Millie Hodge, sense the world's gradual wearing away and its creeping into stasis; theirs is an entropic view, a view (Gardner would say) that is less hopeful than that which sees the universe as forever active and developing. "As the planets get further and further apart," Gardner has remarked, "there's less chance of us hurting each other."[10]

To cope with this sense of disintegration and to buttress his belief in the orderly universe, Clumly insists upon a world that is connected and coherent. All things, events, and people are in some way related; things do not just happen, they are caused. It is a Whiteheadian faith in a connected, unified system. For Clumly, it is a way of getting at the truth: "It was not so much that it smelled of voodoo, for him, at least. It didn't. The Sunlight Man knew Boyle because there was some kind of connection. It was the connection, not just the convictions, you had to get hold of. A man had to *know*, understand the whole thing. No short-cuts. He had to get to the truth, the *whole* truth" (p. 225). Clumly holds firmly to a grand design and a pattern. Events are chained by cause and effect, and if you just find the proper key or starting point, everything falls into place. As he tells his skeptical sergeant: " 'Everything's always connected, Miller. There can't be order otherwise. It's all some kind of Design.' He stretched out his fingers as if holding an invisible ball. 'It's all one pattern. Find out the connections and *bam!* everything's plain!' " (p. 372). Clumly, as detective, is the rational, scientific man personified—and he reflects Gardner's own private belief in the connectedness of things.

The Sunlight Man, on the other hand, repudiates connection and avows disparateness and chance. Cause and effect are myths of the troubled and reluctant mind, as annoying as a cold sore or flatulence. In his jail cell, the Sunlight Man explains to the Slater brothers (themselves involved in an accident soon to prove fatal to another) the mechanics of a random universe:

> "You have to try to be realistic," the Sunlight Man said, whining quietly, as if speaking to himself, working out a problem in

geometry, "it was an accident, yes. You know that and I know that. Not to speak pompously, what is there in this world but accident— a long, bitter chain of accidents, from algae to reptiles to tortoises and rodents to man? By accident all our poor mothers had children, and by accident some of the children died young and the others grew up to be either policemen or outlaws. Nevertheless, where the Law is concerned . . . there can be no fiddle-faddle about Absolute Truth. They'll electrocute you if they can, and that's that." (p. 67)

There is no route to truth and the positive answer because there is no way to trace one's path back to the cause. Man tries to connect the dots, but all he gets is some jumbled and nonsensical picture that tells him nothing.

Part of the order that Clumly imposes upon his universe has its roots (strangely, for a detective) in myth and superstition and religion. If connections dot the universe like stars, and if events follow one another in some sort of logical procession, then the chance of prediction and insight is high. A man learns to believe in signs and omens and faint indications of human fate. It's the same type of quality that Clumly observes in Sergeant Sangirgonio (whom Clumly, for convenience, calls "Miller"):

Miller was superstitious. Where he got it, who could say?—some spark of true religion, maybe, in a generally indifferent Catholic childhood; or perhaps it was simply a snatch at absolute control by a soul uncommonly conscientious but imperfectly informed on the ins and outs of time and space, struggling through a labyrinthine universe full of surprises. He had the kind of superstition which runs not to avoiding black cats, walking around ladders, or carrying talismans, but to nervous presentiment and an obscure sense of the stirrings of omens and portents. (p. 218)

It is a knowledge blended of logic and hunch, and is both mental and visceral. Some people are aware of it, others obey and observe the ominous in complete unconsciousness.

A "connected universe" also implies a certain degree of personal, human responsibility. If the world works by cause and effect, then man is liable for the actions and effects he causes. It is from this sense of responsibility that springs the human ethic. Clumly's world issues no moral disclaimers or waivers—it is stringently persistent in its demand for virtuous action. Nor can a person watch after simply his own behavior, for he must at the same time make himself responsible for the actions of those around him: it is the moral responsibility of all for all. It is Clumly's "Watchdog Complex." The idea comes from his first meeting with the Sunlight Man, in "The Dialogue on Wood and Stone." The Sunlight Man tells Clumly of the Mesopotamian religious ritual, of their gods made of wood and stone, and of the severance of flesh and spirit. He tells him how the Babylonians "with everything they did asserted a fundamental co-existence, without conflict, of body and spirit, both of which were of ultimate worth. And as for the connection between body and spirit, they ignored it. It was by its very essence mysterious. They cared only that the health of one depended upon the health of the other, God knew how" (p. 318). The Babylonians supposedly solved the riddle of duality, and in doing so managed to discard the demands of responsibility—which also removed the threat of guilt (a "Jewish product, guilt," Taggert tells Clumly). Body and soul each were holy, but neither had liens upon the other.

This same separation carried over into the realm of politics, where the king ruled by the will of the gods, broad intelligence guiding the narrow. But it is a system with certain built-in problems, for

> the king rules, establishes simple laws and so on, but he judges by what we would call whim—though it isn't whim, of course: it's the whole complex of his experience and intuition as a man trained and culturally established as finally responsible. . . . It's a system which can only work when the total population is small, and the troubles are trifling. . . . But the problem is not that the system is wrong, it's that the mind of man is limited. Beyond a certain point, intuition can no more deal with the world than intellect can. We're doomed, in other words. (p. 321)

It is exactly by such whim and intuition and educated hunch that Clumly operates, and it is not until he hears it from the Sunlight Man that he realizes his own political and intellectual method. It is his first step toward metaphysical sympathy with his antagonist. Later on Clumly tells his man Kozlowski:

> I'm responsible for this town, you follow that? Responsible! It's like a king. I don't mean I'm comparing myself to a king, you understand, but it's *like* a king. If a king's laws get tangled up and his knights fail him, he's got to do the job himself. They're *his* people. He's responsible. Or take God—not that I compare myself to God, understand. If the world gets all messed up He's got to fix it however He can, that's His job. (p. 378)

Clumly takes a bit of the Babylonian and mixes it with a bit of the Arthurian and a bit of the Hebraic, and emerges with an interesting image of the benign, responsible leader.[11] Clumly affirms intuition—it is his way of working, his way of operating within Gardner's system of emotional metaphysics—and he affirms moral obligation as the only way of keeping the universe from devouring itself.

Taggert, as the Babylonian mind, curses Clumly's Judeo-Christian ethic of individual human worth, and its democracy of legal right and retribution. It is a system that cannot work in a chance universe where cases and situations vary; it is a limited system devised by a limited, ungodlike mind. Clumly accuses the Sunlight Man of not caring about people, and the wild man replies: "I care about *every single case*. You care about nothing but the *average*. I love justice, you love law. I'm Babylonian, and you, you're one of the Jews. I can't cover every single case, I have no *concern* about covering cases, so I cover by whim whatever cases fall into my lap . . . and I leave the rest to process. But you, you cover *all* the cases—by blanketing them, by blurring all human distinctions" (p. 328). It is a painful irony, for both Clumly and Taggert, that the law renders itself incapable of pursuing its own long-claimed end: justice. Taggert wants the individual free and loose and unbound by stupid, human moral restraints. He only partly acknowledges his share in the killing of the police guard and of Hodge's landlady and of Hardesty. Only as things begin to turn inward and collapse upon him does he finally recognize his part in the chaos.

Taggert is not alone in his systematic denial of the complex of relations. Will Hodge Sr, who hovers always on the rim of activity and who accepts a large share of responsibility but never moves upon that acceptance; Walter Benson, who in his neutralized silence plays a wordless accomplice to Taggert and Nick Slater in the killing of the guard ("Asleep since the day he was born," taunts Taggert); and Millie Hodge, who claims a freedom and righteousness of intellect that sanctions manipulation and exploitation of the human spirit—all follow a routine of denial and ignorance of an element of their human nature. In Taggert's case it leads to existentialism and anarchy; in Benson's it leads to quietism; in Will Jr's it leads to tokenism; and in still other cases it leads to Millie's brutal naturalism or the Judge's bitter, withdrawn pessimism.

The Sunlight Man attempts to broaden Clumly's vision further still in the second dialogue, "The Dialogue of Houses," where he explores the Babylonian enchantment with astrology and divination. Taggert assails the intellectual arrogance of modern positivistic thought, which scorns a belief so arcane and so childishly unscientific as Babylonian mysticism. There is a difference, Taggert (the magician) explains, between mere magic and divination: "Magic is man's ridiculous attempt to make the gods behave as mortals. Divination asserts man's passivity, not for spiritual fulfillment, as in the Far East, but for practical and spiritual life. After divination one acts *with* the gods. You discover the way things are flowing, and you swim in the same direction. You allow yourself to be possessed" (p. 419). In other words, the human spirit is infused with a knowledge that reaches beyond science, that absolves man of selfish, social necessity. You become, like Taggert, the god's oracle.

At the same time, one's personal fate is a matter of those same gods who give the signs and fill the oracles. The Babylonians, the Sunlight Man tells Clumly, distinguished between personal destiny (*simtu*) and the larger fate of the universe (*istaru*), "the blueprint already complete for all Time and Space." Both are inescapable, and what determines your personal end is a matter of plain luck: "There's only luck, good luck or bad, the friendly or unfriendly spirit that stood at your side when your *simtu* was designed, and stands there yet, and changes nothing. Changes only the *quality* of the thing" (p. 420). You watch for the signs, try to read their meaning, and make the best of it. The Sunlight Man takes Clumly to the center of things, explaining that

> good luck is nothing but being in shape to act with the universe when the universe says "Now!" What is personal responsibility, then? The Babylonian would say it consists, first, in stubbornly maintaining one's freedom to act—in my case, evasion of the police, you see—and, second, in jumping when the Spirit says, "Jump!" . . . You never know when the gods may speak, you never know what your luck is. You can only wait, and if they say act, act. (p. 420)

The Sunlight Man insists upon "freedom at all costs," and the essence of that freedom is the ability to act. He is totally accurate in his interpretation of human responsibility, for a person must not only acknowledge his liability, but act upon it as well. What accounts for the vital difference is the *reason* and *motive* for action.

Taggert acts "with the universe," keeping in sight the *istaru* long ago designed and declared. It is a vision that emphasizes freedom and justice. Clumly, on the other hand, elects to act for the immediate and the near— local crime, doctrines of law—thinking more of his *simtu*. Clumly's is a vision that emphasizes privilege and law (justice is the thing that "waits" while he pursues Law and Order). What Taggert desires is the opening of Clumly's vision to the grander possibilities, to the fact that the law, paradoxically, must sometimes be ignored in the service of justice. There is, it seems, a hint of hope in such a scheme, as if Gardner (in the guise of the Sunlight Man) wishes to admit to a metaphysical compromise between order and anarchy. This is why he draws the two men ever closer together, why he has Taggert teach Clumly opinions—"deadly opinions," perhaps, opinions that Clumly earlier abdicates ("a cop hasn't got opinions"). And it is also why Taggert slowly discovers the attractions and virtues of friendship and trust.

The only other person who really comes to understand Taggert's position is Luke Hodge, Will Hodge Sr's son and Taggert's nephew. Like Taggert, he is cursed with physical pain and emotional torment, with "half-daylong sieges of pain that would fill up Luke's skull, more fierce than the fiercest hangover, until he could see, hear, think of nothing but the dry fire in his brain, and at last he would faint. He'd been born unlucky: he had an enormous tolerance for pain" (p. 181). Like Taggert, Luke sees fire and feels his vision turn red; like Taggert, he is "born unlucky." He grew up a witness to the brutality of a doomed marriage, and learned of the perverse possibilities of love. He asserts his responsibility (it is an almost mystical connection) with the Slater brothers, both blasted with personal bad luck, and is the only person who is genuinely concerned with individual dignity. Of Nick Slater, Luke tells his mother: "I'd have given my life for him. That's the truth, lady. Fuck it up if you want" (p. 202). And he is sincere. Luke cares for the single, significant case, and labors in earnest for the meaningful and human (unlike his brother Will Jr, who takes on the shallow and the showy).

Luke is the only person who effectively challenges and analyzes Taggert, is the only person who can locate the "soft places in the dragon's belly" (p. 409). Luke chides him for his failure to deal with and speak seriously of his reality, and forces him to confront his viciousness. Luke recognizes Taggert's true, reshaped nature. Taggert asks him, "Suppose I say I do believe in the past? Suppose I say I once walked and talked like you?" And Luke replies: "But you don't say it. You say 'suppose.' If you said it, it would be asking me to wonder what happened, what turns a human being into a monster. It would be talking as if we were both human. You can't" (p. 409). Luke uncovers the Sunlight Man's darker side, the side that exhorts justice but promotes random death, the side that claims human ties but acts and speaks like a monster. It is the side that Taggert desperately tries to ignore, but which repeatedly and stubbornly crops up, like the memory of an old affair or an unforgotten sin.

Taggert pursues the relation between action, time, and the universe—between *istaru* and *simtu*—in the third dialogue, "The Dialogue of the Dead." Clumly and Taggert meet in a crypt, an absurdly appropriate place for a discussion of "the Mesopotamian dead." The Sunlight Man takes up the story of the Gilgamesh epic, using it as an exemplum of man's cruel paradox: the desire for glory and immortality in an all too mortal world. As Taggert says, "In Babylon . . . personal immortality is a mad goal. Death is a reality. Any struggle whatever for personal fulfillment is wrong-headed" (p. 532). The body and its transience imprisons man and at times deludes him. Youth is a ghost, nothing more. Time and space eventually close up and in on him.

Taggert asks his own question, the natural question—"Why act at all then?"—and answers it immediately: "Because action is life" (p. 533). If one fails to act, one loses the freedom and the ability to act, thus losing the essence of freedom itself. Taggert follows again with the logical question, and supplies the response:

> Once one's said it, that one must act, one must ask oneself, shall I act within the cultural order I do not believe in but with which I am engaged by ties of love or anyway ties of fellow-feeling, or shall I act within the cosmic order I *do* believe in, at least in principle, an order indifferent to man? And then again, shall I act by standing indecisive between the two orders—not striking out for the cosmic order because of my human commitment, not striking out for the cultural order because of my divine commitment? Which shall I renounce, my body—of which ethical intellect is a function—or my soul? (p. 533)

Melville would have asked, "Does one keep time by chronologicals or horologicals?" but the problem is the same.[12] Where does man owe his allegiance: to the immediate, the personal, the temporal, or to the eternal, the universal, the spiritual? It is a question that both men will soon have to confront.

Taggert brings it all very close to Clumly at the end of the dialogue, as he prefigures the future in a hypothetical vision. He draws for Clumly the setting of the fourth and final dialogue—the meeting at the towers—at which the Sunlight Man hands the gun (symbol of death and extinction and man's mortality) to Clumly and forces the decision: how do you act? Taggert, playing Clumly, answers: "If I act for the universe, I may kill you. If I act for humanity, I kill you and then myself" (p. 536). Clumly insists on a choice ("There's *always* a choice!"), but the Sunlight Man vanishes amidst smoke and trumpets, leaving Clumly to agonize. The choice, it seems, is very limited.

At least Clumly is willing to act. It is more than some characters are willing to do. Will Hodge Sr skulks about, accompanied by his own Sunlight Man in miniature, Freeman, and tries to unravel all of the strange connections. He knows his predicament: his obligation to the law and to his culture demands he lead Clumly to Taggert, reveal his identity and hand him over to the mundane justice of mankind; his obligation to the cosmos requires him to aid Taggert's escape, conceal his identity and the truth. But Hodge is so tangled up in his own ego and in the personal affronts he has suffered from those around him that he refuses to act altogether. He pries and lurks and crouches under bushes and behind automobiles, but does nothing. He has a vision that dominates his life, a vision of a father and a family, and he resigns himself to a small role in that particular drama. In doing so, he shuts out the actual drama, the drama played out in the present, in flesh and blood and brutal pain.

Just as ineffective is Walter Benson, a leader of two lives, a loser in both. He retreats into silence and bad poetry, and even when the indignities are personal—when his wife is bedded by his boarder, Ollie Nuper; when his identity becomes twisted and blurred—he makes no move to change things. His attempts to brain the lizardy Nuper are cartoonish in their failure, and are perhaps misguided in their motivation and their purpose. Like Hodge, he follows and trails his tormentor, chases him to his unhandsome death—and does nothing. He suffers through unconvincing *Angst* and rejoices in half-earned redemption; he is a man, afraid of his world, who understands and thinks very little. He screams at Nuper, with a nose clogged with cold: "You dode *care*, do you! You just dode *care*. It dode matter to you who's ride or wrong, you just win whatever way you can. You're like all of them. Irresponsible!" (p. 553). Benson's accusation echoes the earlier description of Taggert ("He didn't care"), and his emphasis upon responsibility mirrors Clumly's concern. Yet Benson still shuns his own personal responsibility. He passes through nightmares and ugly visions, but he manages to resolve it all with characteristic faintheartedness:

> Nevertheless, he felt no guilt, as far as he could tell. One can get used to anything, it came to him. In a week, a month, the whole thing would no doubt be almost drowned out of his mind. Such things happen, no doubt. He felt again the momentary sensation of nausea he'd felt that night when he first saw Ollie's body sitting white as a young girl's on the stump. *Fssss*, he thought, and— *horrible!* He closed his eyes and almost instantly he was dreaming again, walking very carefully on the glass roof of a greenhouse. Down below him, in the dim aqueous light, fronds moved back and forth slowly, like thinking creatures. It was perhaps all just as it should be; he was of two minds. *And there I will keep you forever, he thought.*
>
> > *Forever and a day,*
> > *Till the wall shall crumble to ocean,*
> > *And moulder in dark away.*
>
> His heart sped up. It was a beautiful poem. Beautiful. (p. 657)

Benson lies to himself right up to the end. Like Camus's Meursault, he tells himself that life is a matter of accommodation, that "one can get used to anything." He misuses art (and bad art at that) in sheltering and burying his guilt and his rightful liability. He is cowardly and dishonest and comes near to being as much the monster as Taggert. He is, in the words of Dante, one of "those sad souls who lived a life but lived it with no blame and with no praise."[13] Benson, "undecided in his neutrality," will be accepted by neither Heaven nor Hell, and his memory will be lost to the world.

Such a condition is particularly damning in a world where human life is so shockingly mutable. Immortality comes in just one shape: memory. All else is robbed by death and the grave. This is part of an accidental universe; violence, accident, and death are all elements that "disorder" Clumly's ordered world. If Clumly knows anything, it is his own mortality and the unimpeded drift of time, but he recognizes something redeeming even in death and its attendant rituals. Fred Clumly "enjoyed funerals. It was a sad thing to see all one's old friends and relatives slipping away, one after the other, leaving their grown sons and daughters weeping, soberly dabbing at their eyes with their neat white hankies, the grandchildren sitting on the gravestones or standing unwillingly solemn at the side of the grave while they lowered the coffin. But it was pleasant, too, in a mysterious way he couldn't and didn't really want to find words for" (p. 19). Clumly finds in a funeral a delightful sense of calm and order that, regardless of the chaos and frenzy and ugliness that may have marked a person's life, brings everything around to wholeness.

Death also provides the world with tragedy in its unjustness and its deadly ironies. Violence and accident fall by chance upon mankind, though they are often hastened by human intervention. Death might appear in a weakened heart, an unseen truck, or a bullet through a blanket; it can come even in a conscious act of will. In its strangest form, death comes as a partner to love.

For Gardner, love is the one great hope of mankind. It can restore dignity and reclaim the memory of the dead. Yet it can also generate catastrophe; even love, says Gardner, is prone to accident. There is no better example of how the varied ways of love press upon a person than Taggert Hodge. As a child, Taggert was marked with a blessedness and

> a quality of loving gentleness he'd been born with. In the first months of his life he was a sympathetic cryer, and throughout his childhood he was peacemaker to the family. In fact, like Ben, he was born to be a saint, gentle and unselfish—he even had the look of a saint: straight blond hair as soft as gossamer, dark blue eyes, long lashes, a quick, open smile—and unlike Ben, he saw what was there, not angels in pear trees but pears. "Little Sunshine," their father called him. Yet Tag had failed in the end, for all his

innocence and goodness, had been beaten by the conspiracy of events. So the Old Man might have failed, if his luck had been bad. (p. 136)

Taggert grew up in the shadow of his father, "a work of art" and "a work of love." But Taggert's *simtu* was ill-planned and worked against his inherent goodness. His wife, Kathleen Paxton, turns crazy and buries their children in a house afire, giving Taggert his unloseable scars. The Paxton family battles, in the name of "virtuous love," to keep Taggert distanced from the woman he both loves and hates; he becomes, in a sense, a victim of a love medievalized. What was once a vision that found "God was huge and unkillable and good" soon turns to fire and the memory of scorched flesh. The love that once ran through Taggert like blood is literally burned out of him, and he is made to live a life that never should have been his. Not until his sorrow—his children's graves, his brother Ben's kindness—breaks him does he turn sane again and human. His resolution to be reconciled with old man Paxton is an effort to wipe out all of the disease and bad luck of a lifetime—but before he can do it, he allows himself one visible act of love, an act that jails him and begins a bleak chain of murderous events.

There is also a nether image of love, one that is figured in selfishness and blind ego. It is a love that entraps and plays games with people, and that is viperish in its disdain for human feeling. It is a love embodied in Millie Hodge. She is the goddess Mama, the Babylonian Istar—the duplicitous and wily and murderous spirit of love. Millie thrives upon contest and challenge; she exercises her intellect and neglects her heart, a heart "painstakingly fashioned of ice" (p. 181). She recognizes her nature, is in fact proud of it: "She was a bitch. She made no bones about it. . . . Bitchiness was her strength and beauty and hope of salvation" (p. 180). Such is the woman the Sunlight Man intends to make into a saint.

Millie uses her body and her mind as tools of seduction. As a teenager, she went after Ben Hodge, the most "beautiful" of the Hodge boys in his huge and loving decency. Failing to snare Ben, Millie planned her way into marrying Will, claiming a pregnancy that did not exist and relying on Will's innocence and sympathy to carry her scheme through. It is a marriage bound for despair, despite the passion of its beginnings: "They had loved each other from the first. They clung to each other like children and wept and rutted half the night and swore they would always be faithful, and at last they slept. But days passed; seasons; and as Luke, not yet born, would one day howl above the hellfire jangle of his banjo, love grows colder" (p. 440). Millie is too smart for Will, too intelligent and too proud of her intelligence. They are at constant war with one another, both at times on the defensive. This, at least, is the way Millie sees it:

How he did it she would never know, but the truth was that by
every gesture, every glance, he made her feel worthless, brainless,
obscene. She could make a laughingstock of him, turn all his sober
arguments to the jabbering of a monkey; her very appearance made
him clownlike, bumpkinish; and yet his wordless righteousness,
more insidious than anything in the play—a righteousness without
rational foundation, indefensible and therefore mute—made a
gaudy whore of her. (pp. 438–39)

Millie had married for the family name and its traditional power, and
what happened after that was all accident.

Even the making of her sons, Luke and Will Jr, was haphazard and
random, parts of a jumbled universe. She rejects her role as Mama, origin
of life and of the world. She had been

forced into the shabby role for which she had not the faintest desire
and from which she drew, she devoutly believed, no satisfaction
(she knew what satisfaction was, knew where she would prefer to
be)—the role of God or archetypal mother or stone at the center of
the universe—because by senseless accident she had borne sons. *I
exist. No one else. You will not find me sitting around on my can like
some widow, or whining for the love of my children.* (p. 181)

Millie repudiates love and exalts self-concern and pleasure. She taunts her
husband with her affairs, stretching his limits, grinding his nerve into
dust. Their divorce is only a symbol of the hatred and selfishness that
grew cancerous and eventually destroyed what had once been right.

It is impossible, of course, for Millie to honestly love her sons. Will Jr
she ignores, and Luke she baits and prods. Like his father (thinks Millie),
Luke is childish and self-righteous, and Millie tries to remove herself from
his sickness and pain:

It was unreasonable that she should be asked to regret for his sake
what had nothing whatever to do with him, nothing even to do
with his father, little as Luke might understand that; and unreasonable that merely because she was there she should be asked, required, to endure his childish and confused vengeance for wrongs
in which she had no part. He was a baby, a twenty-two-year-old
baby: the slightest cut, the slightest affront, and home he came
howling to mother, the source of all grief. *I'm sick of it,* she thought,
but even as she thought it she knew it was rhetoric. (p. 183)

Millie is pure self-consciousness; her intellect never really allows her the
chance to feel outside of herself. She is mistaken in her judgment of Luke,

mistaken in her perception of her husband, and mistaken in her own self-appraisal.

Millie sees herself as an anarchist, as a sort of "Sunlight Woman." She rejects Will's tendency to patch and mend and repair the flaws, for it

> was not a law for her. There was something about a roof that let
> the sunlight in through a thousand chinks, or a buckled wall, a
> concrete foundation splitting open to the roots of trees. For she,
> Millie Hodge, put her money on sunshine, the restless power of the
> hay pushing outward, and slow, invincible roots. All her life she'd
> been breaking down roofs and walls—intransigent gray Presby-
> terian stone, the brittle beams of dry legalism, vows and rules
> and meticulous codes—exploding them as a white shoot cracks a
> stone, though she was a woman, held down revoltingly to earth.
> (pp. 204–5)

Her sex and her rationality trap Millie. Angry with her womanhood and misled by a too-fine intellect, she destroys indiscriminately, hauling down roof *and* walls, letting in not only the sunshine but the rain and frost and darkness as well. She plots the ruin of the Hodge family, devastating its members and pulling Stony Hill into a shambles. It is for this that Tag-gert (figure of brilliant sunshine) tortures her, depriving her of pleasure and driving her toward sainthood. In a final conversation Taggert ex-plains to Millie his reasoning:

> "I have watched objectively, partly because of the accident of my
> having been cut off from intervening, and partly, I suppose,
> because of my nature. I've observed every move of your chess game
> with the Old Man, and maybe I've sympathized with both sides, at
> times. In any case, he was right, as you see, and you were wrong.
> You brought down his house, made fools of his sons, and even
> grandsons, your own sons. But law was on his side."
>
> "What are you talking about?"
>
> "Religion. . . . All the walls mankind makes can be broken
> down," he said, "but after the last wall there's still one more wall,
> the final secret, Time. You can't get out of it. The man in the back
> room, as who's-it says—sitting with head bent, silent, waiting,
> listening to the commotion in the streets: the Keeper of the Kinds.
> You and I, Millie, we were going to run naked in our separate
> woods and play guitars and prove miraculous. But outside our
> running the bluish galaxies are preparing to collapse, and inside our
> running is the space between the pieces of our atoms. And so I
> won't kill you for your destructions, or kill the police for theirs."
> (p. 623)

The two anarchists confront one another, and Taggert illuminates their vital difference. The Sunlight Man acts from madness and ultimately from love; Millie acts from hatred and an immense egotism. Millie razes but does not rebuild, and seeks justice only for herself. Both Taggert and Luke possess an integrity that motivates them to act for a certain and definable good. Taggert is a monster trying for redemption, but Millie is a lost and not-so-simple evil: "She was ugly as a witch, and could not be beautiful again. She was ugly, and the father-in-law she had too much admired was dead, his house in ruins. The war was over" (p. 624). Millie underestimates the power of both love and hate, misjudging the effect of each on the human spirit.

Almost as potent as love is the element of imagination. "Human consciousness—an overwhelming joy, a monstrous torture, the most fantastic achievement of the whole fantastic chronicle of time and space" (p. 69), says the Sunlight Man. Imagination implies an opening up to the world's possibilities, an ascension to greatness. Through imagination man approaches a breakthrough of the barriers of time and space; the limits are acknowledged, but for an instant the lines are dropped and man crosses over into that world where actions are defined by their grandness and their potential, where man is not tied down by a concern with the immediate. Imagination involves vision and a breadth of conception. The rightly imaginative man focuses more spaciously, and selects a course of action fitted to something beyond his reach.

An imagination that is not informed by love or that fails to act upon its vision simply withers and falls, unused. It is "a kind of power failure, a sickly decline into vision" (p. 576). It is the type of vision possessed by Benson, by Will Hodge Sr and Will Hodge Jr, and by Millie Hodge. Benson and Hodge Sr fail to act upon their visions; their motives are basically correct, but they stall and tug at their ears and finally do nothing. Millie and Will Hodge Jr hold visions in which the qualities of love and decency (Dante's "primal love") are absent. It is a vision hurled downward into blackness, a vision that moves away from the humane center of the universe and toward something cold and killing.

There are too in *The Sunlight Dialogues* at least four characters who possess a finer imagination and a larger vision and who, in varying ways and degrees, act upon that vision. Luke Hodge (as shown earlier) is the only person who pierces the irony and aloofness of the Sunlight Man; he is the only one whose imagination approaches the vast, partly crazed reaches of the magician's. It is Luke who is brought into the foreground, destined (like the Sunlight Man) to choose and to act. It is Luke who:

was the one who'd been put in the middle, the one who had no
choice but to understand both sides, however he fought; no choice
even when he wanted to hate them all but to understand they were
not hateable, merely human, short-sighted, limited, tired,
stupid. . . . He had said it with bitter irony in the past, but not
tonight: *In the beginning was the Word and the Word was Luke.* . . .
From the beginning he had been the one marked—by brute
situation as much as by any gift of his—to understand them all; and
finally—he could say it now without a self-deprecatory curl of the
lip, for he knew at last, knew he had never hated any of them, the
hatred was mere self-defense, the howling of a child not yet ready
to put on his destiny like an old wool coat—finally, he knew, he
was the one who'd been marked. His luck. (pp. 636–37)

Such is Luke's *simtu*, his personal fate, but he moves on from that fate to
an action—one that is in line with the *istaru* and destiny of his world. His
attempt at killing the Sunlight Man—his uncle—is his work of vision;
even though it fails in its immediate purpose, it ultimately does destroy
Taggert, for it turns the magician toward admission and toward a quick,
and perhaps unfair, judgment. Luke hears the whisper—"It's time, it's
time"—and jumps.

Esther Clumly too hears whispers, but they are the voice of her soul in
an "endless dialogue" in the dark. Esther grasps a vision that is bitterly
ironic in her physical blindness. Cursed with sightlessness, she begins in
authentic despair and progresses to hope and cause: "Her life was a fall
from light to darkness and a brainless hope for light that would never
come, but she had at least this: she knew that her hope was brainless, she
could refuse to be deluded, refuse to hope" (p. 227). Esther is confused
by her knowledge and by her love; in an attempt to protect her husband,
she inadvertently hastens his fall. Her life is an apology, a constant beg-
ging for forgiveness of sins she never commits. Yet in her anguish, she
comes to a vision that is strikingly clear:[14]

> Then Esther Clumly went down to her bed and lay there, with all
> her clothes on, even her shoes, nose pointing at the ceiling, arms at
> her sides, inert and absurd as . . . She furrowed her forehead, trying
> to think what it was that she looked like, lying there, and suddenly
> she knew, and the insight was almost pleasing because it was so
> right. "Like a chicken," she said, and sobbed. "In this house of
> tragedy, lying here like a horrible, stiff chicken." (p. 544)

In the moment of her vision, Esther is spiritually bound to her husband.
Her grotesque fancy is the match to Fred's own earlier perception (p. 16),

and the two imaginations merge into one. Fred and Esther Clumly are two loving monstrosities, paired off however strangely, fated to live out a marriage bred from a hint of regret and a bounty of love.

Esther's thoughts of suicide are spurred by her love for her husband, and not from any self-serving pity. She reproves herself for her inability to act, reasoning like a nihilist:

> That was what she'd learned, a startling and terrible but also exhilarating discovery that brought with it a sudden sense of vaulting joy, of freedom—an escape into wilderness and boundless time: she could kill herself if she pleased, she had realized, standing at the open window dreaming of it; because the pain was hers, not her husband's, whatever pain of his own he might feel. The decision was hers, and if she chose against it for his sake, she did it voluntarily, as his equal. (p. 647)

Esther searches for a way to proclaim her own freedom and at the same time to share her life with her husband. Her suicide, she believes, would accomplish both, freeing her from material demands and releasing Fred from the burden of her blind pitiableness. Yet she rejects the existential absurdity of suicide (as do many of Gardner's characters) and instead acts heroically, if not a bit drunkenly. She defends her husband's honor, being *"more brave than was intended,"* acting with laudable Gardneresque lunacy.

Esther also shares a vision of fire (pp. 275, 276) with the Sunlight Man, though for Esther it is merely an indication of a sympathetic imagination. For Taggert, it is a symbol of his past, an ineradicable memory that has turned him bitter and furious and that has distorted his once-grand vision. Fire crackles in his ears and leaps from lines in the sidewalk, appearing in moments of ugliness and death. It is the fire that consumed his sons, that drove his wife to complete madness, and that now is licking up the remains of Taggert's own sanity.

It is with fire too that Taggert obliterates the remnants of the Hodge legend, sending the barns and buildings and silos of Stony Hill Farm up in ashes. Taggert's vision and imagination are turned monstrous by a monstrous past. He cannot make the move toward humanity, cannot quite grasp the meaning of his father's "secret," the same secret that Luke perceived and described: *"The Old Man knew the secret, that was all. He knew how to see into all of them, feel out their hearts inside his own, love them and hate them and forgive them: he understood that nothing devoutly believed is mere error, though it may only be half-truth, and so he could give them what they needed"* (p. 640). Not until Luke acts "with the gods" is Taggert shocked into awareness. He turns away from escape and relinquishes his ghost-hold on existential freedom, and as the fire flashes one final time, as accident precludes design, Taggert is himself destroyed, a sacrifice to order and human instinct, a man killed "for violent kindness."

Significantly, the former symbol of that same desire for order, Fred Clumly, is himself a man of imagination and vision—though, over time, his vision changes and is shaped anew. Clumly, as has been mentioned before, is a man who works on intuition, a player of hunches. When logic fails, Clumly falls back upon imagination and emotion, lives by an intuitive morality and an emotional metaphysic.

Clumly has watched his belief in law and order slowly shift shape in his meetings with the Sunlight Man, to the point where he no longer knows for sure what he believes. He has lost his job; he is no longer a badge and a uniform: "He had promoted himself. He was now Chief Investigator of the Dead" (p. 606). He goes to his final meeting with the Sunlight Man prepared to grab the gun, to wield death, to act upon his belief in order. But Clumly acts for justice and *istaru* instead. "You're free," Clumly tells Taggert. "I'm outside my jurisdiction" (p. 634). Taggert is beyond Clumly's—or the law's—reach; physically and spiritually, Taggert represents an element not yet classified, something outside of immediate, temporal experience. Clumly is acting upon the larger possibilities, using an expanded vision—he is finally "jumping" at the right time. Taggert leaves, physically free; Stony Hill burns, the Hodge memory a charred timber, a vision filled with fire; and Clumly heads toward the Grange Hall, a man troubled by a hunch.

Clumly knows that something is coming, that something is going to happen. He knows what the Sunlight Man himself knows: "He's run out of time," (p. 662), has come up against the final wall. Clumly's vision suddenly penetrates time and space, and for a moment he is the seer:

> It seemed to him that he did know, had gotten that close to inside the man's head—or if he didn't know would anyway recognize after he saw it that it was right, exactly as it had to be. He concentrated, trying to see what it was that he knew was going to happen; and though it was ridiculous, like straining to remember the future, it seemed to him he almost had it, but it wouldn't come quite clear. The yellow light inside the Grange looked for an instant like fire. (p. 662)

For this one second, Clumly jumps within the Sunlight Man and finally comprehends his complex and ambiguous nature.[15] Clumly sees the fire, sees the pistol's blast and the evil and horrid memory that plagues Taggert Hodge. It is a vast leap of imagination.

Moreover, Clumly's hunch proves true. As he stands at the dais, he is handed the news of the Sunlight Man's death, and it jolts him: "He was grieved, he was grieved deeply, crying out in his mind 'My God, my God! The injustice of it!' and the word *injustice* (printed like a headline in his mind) had a power over him even greater than the thing itself, as is the way of words, and tears brimmed over and fell on his cheeks and his throat tightened to a whimper" (p. 668). Clumly feels the tragedy of Taggert's death, senses the loss of a friend, and sees the disparity between what is and what should have been. He shifts the focus of his vision from law and order to the qualities of justice, teaching the lesson of the Sunlight Man. He tells his audience:

> I can say this: I'm proud of my boys that tracked him down, insofar as they did, and I wouldn't have it otherwise. They have a public trust, your police department, and I'm as proud of those boys as I could be of my own sons, if I had any. I know they did the best they could to see true justice triumphed, and justice *did* triumph, and we can be proud that we live in this great free country where that can happen. Yes! But also justice didn't triumph, in a way, of course. I can't explain that if you don't see it in your heart, it's just the way it is, maybe always was and always will be. (p. 670)

Justice requires imagination and a capacity for vision, Clumly tells them. Beyond the homily and the simplistic gestures of democracy, there must be a wish and a conception of an alternative system. Clumly echoes the Sunlight Man as he sums up: "We have to stay awake, as best we can, and be ready to obey the laws as best as we're able to see them. That's it. That's the whole thing" (p. 672). There must be the willingness to act according to instinct and contrary to custom, to see the law *beyond* the law. Systems fail, Gardner teaches, exceptions must be made, imagination and love must drive upward to a better vision.

And this is what happens, in the end, to Clumly. He proves the oracle who prophesies at the funeral: "*Uno stormo d'uccelli. . . . Voli di colombi. . . . La morte. . . . Disanimata*" (p. 380–81). As Fred finishes his speech and sits down, the shock and emotion and sense of tragic loss pervade the audience, spreading in a silence—a transcendent silence— which

> grew and struggled with itself and then, finally, strained into sound, first a spatter and then a great rumbling of the room, and he could feel the floor shivering like the walls of a hive and it seemed as if the place was coming down rattling around his ears but then he knew he was wrong, it was bearing him up like music or like a storm of pigeons, lifting him up like some powerful, terrible wave

of sound and things in their motions hurtling him up to where
the light was brighter than sun-filled clouds, disanimated and holy.
(p. 673)

The stillness, the light, the ascension—all are characteristic of that Gardneresque transmutation that comes in the artistic moment. Clumly ascends, in a rush of wings, into pure vision and spirit, into *disanimata*. He
escapes, if only for a moment, the ties of reality and soars into the world
imaginable. He sees, as Gardner sees, the possibilities of a universe directed by a vision that is infused with love and emotion and art, a universe
that makes allowances for good and evil, a universe that tries frantically
not to shut down or fall apart. It is the universe made moral.

Chapter VI

Nickel Mountain

I claim what plain experience declares,
That Love requires long years of diligence.
   —"The Stranger in the Grove"

By the time *Nickel Mountain* appeared in 1973, it had already passed through two decades of revision and alteration. The novel, as Gardner has stated many times, was begun when Gardner was nineteen, picked up again in 1958, and finally published fifteen years later, with illustrations by Thomas O'Donohue. It is the oldest in composition of his published novels, and perhaps the one that demanded the most of his time: "I spent longer on it than on any of my other books. The main thing I did was strip, strip, strip."[1] He has also said that it is his "most rounded and complete novel,"[2] though he afterward complained about certain problems with the book's style: "I knew it was a problem when I was doing the last draft. The style is just slightly whiny and babyish. It would come to me that that was the problem with the book and I would think that and then work on something else instead. When it came out, I realized I'd forgotten to put in the new transmission."[3] It is interesting to note that ever since a portion of the novel was printed in the *Quarterly Review of Literature* in 1963, and on through the several other excerpts appearing up until 1973, no significant changes were made in *Nickel Mountain.*[4] This might indicate less revision than Gardner claims, or at least certainly fewer years spent in whittling down the final product.

This publication, in parts, of *Nickel Mountain* also points to the frankly episodic structure of the novel. Each of the book's eight chapters shifts the narrative focus, moving skittishly from main character to main character. People appear and disappear for the sake of convenience and argument; Gardner uses them to make a point, deepen a character, and then lets them drift out of sight of the reader. Time progresses and is continuous, but the lines of vision change.

The fact that Gardner took *Nickel Mountain* "out of the drawer" in 1958 makes sense when one recalls that in the same year Gardner finished his Ph.D. dissertation-novel, "The Old Men." The two novels share setting, character, and mood and comprise, as I have said, the "Catskill set." It would not be surprising if Gardner was working on both novels at the same time, or that "The Old Men" actually grew out of the *Nickel Mountain* manuscript. The two novels work well as companion pieces, though the economy of *Nickel Mountain* would suggest a definite shift in style and scope from the windiness of "The Old Men."

Gardner did make the point of labeling *Nickel Mountain* a "pastoral novel," and he has given half a reason for doing so: "When I called *Nickel Mountain* a pastoral, it was only to call attention to certain qualities of the work that the reader might not get otherwise. But I don't think it is necessary."[5] Gardner purposely removes his fiction from the city, transporting it to the Catskills and to the farming country of upstate, northeast New York, because he is after a specific image. *Nickel Mountain* is Gardner's version of the American pastoral; it is what has happened to "the Garden" in the twentieth century. The novel is haunted and infused with a certain philosophical and religious animism—there is a spirit in the land and in nature that is both stubborn and giving, in the maples and tamaracks that gather in the forbidding darkness of the woods, in the birds and wildlife that are oracular and ominous, and in the sun, snow, and thunderstorms that alter the human soul as much as they change the landscape. The entire range of natural phenomena is invested with spirit, a spirit that may be either malignant or benign and that works consciously in either way.

One's place in this natural scheme, says Gardner, determines to some extent one's way of thinking. A person working a farm, whose concept of nature comes through plowing and seeding and harvesting, is going to view the world differently from someone for whom nature is an escape from serpentine streets blacked out by skyscrapers and exhaust. Gardner is talking about the geographical determination of values—political, religious, philosophical; he is out to show (among other things) "the New York City Democrats that the 'upstate apple-knockers' are every bit as politically and morally astute" as their more sophisticated urban counterparts.[6] Virtue and prejudice are shared by both camps, Republican and Democrat, believer and cynic alike. The problem comes when one group or region claims a corner on the truth. It is the same dilemma that will concern Gardner in *October Light,* where he explores the strengths and weaknesses of the flint-spined New England tradition and contrasts the urban and agrarian myths.

In *Nickel Mountain* Gardner's protagonist, Henry Soames, stands out as large and as unmissable as the mountains that dwarf his diner. He carries his three-hundred pounds like a cross or a coffin or any other sure-fire symbol of a man who is going to die: " 'They give me a year to live, Mr. Kuzitski,' Henry would say. 'I had one heart attack already.' His tone never quite went with the words, but the old man could no doubt see that Henry was a frightened man. 'I get dizzy spells,' Henry would say."[7] It is as if having lived too long in the shadow of Nickel Mountain (a name that at once implies worthlessness and power), Henry has grown too much like the mountain, has become *its* shadow, *its* image, *its* analogue.

Henry is a man troubled by shapes and dreams, all amorphous and not-quite-definable. He sees "vague images" and ominous figures traced in the snow against the black edge of the woods, but cannot articulate these visions. His imagination is trapped inside a fleshy and leaden consciousness, and when he tries to pinpoint and explain what he knows, he turns hideous and obscene and Grendel-like:

> He would grow excited, gradually, and his words would come faster, and something that rarely showed in him at other times would show in him now: a streak of crazy violence. Like a drunken man, he would clutch his fists against his chest and his voice would get louder and higher in pitch, and sometimes he'd stop pacing to pound the counter or a tabletop, or he'd lift a sugar dispenser and hold it tight in his hand as if thinking of throwing it. . . . Henry must have seen the hopelessness of trying to put what he meant into words, whatever it was, if anything, that he meant. He would check himself, straining to face death bravely, gallantly. But he was a weak man and childish, especially late at night, and all at once he would catch the old man's arm and would cling to him, not shouting now but hissing at him like a snake. His eyes would bulge, and tears would run down to the stubble on his fat jowl. (pp. 5–6)

Henry is a tortured, bifurcated man: he is monster and lover, superego and id, ugliness and beauty. He is isolated, a man who values his solitude too highly and who has lost the ability to communicate. His feelings outmatch his powers of expression, exploding from him like a man's body in a child's communion suit. His violence and rage are emblems of his inner monstrousness. He is another in a long line of Gardner's human monsters: "Sometimes I use, for instance in Henry Soames in *Nickel Mountain,* a monstrous kind of body which contains monstrous emotions, but he's holding it in and the thing, finally, of course is that he really is a monster and he's holding it in, and that makes him human. But constantly he does what he knows is right, whatever the power of his emotions."[8] Henry cannot shape the language to the feeling; it is as if somewhere between the imagination and the tongue there is a break-down, a net that catches his thoughts and images in flight: "The words came out every which way, jumbled poetry that almost took wing but then pulled down into garble and grunt" (p. 35). He is Gardner's Grendel asking, in a strange and unintelligible voice, for love at the meadhall.

Part of the problem is Henry's boundless capacity for feeling. It is an element of his character, inbred, "the weak, sentimental Soames in his blood" (p. 28). With his father's mammoth physical presence there came, almost genetically, a proclivity for emotion and passive impotence. Henry's father "was as simple and harmless all his life as a great, fat girl. It was the floundering harmlessness, no doubt, that Henry's mother had hated in him" (p. 20). This is the image in which Henry was created and from which he half-heartedly struggles to escape. He grows ever more like his father, filling his suit and his hat and his memory all too perfectly. He recalls the pain and embarrassment his father suffered from wife and friends and strangers, and finds it a harsh fate for someone who simply (and simplistically) wanted to make of life a kind and gentle history.

Behind Henry's passion (and behind his father's reticent fumbling) rolls an ecstatic wave of human sentiment. Perhaps Henry is crazy, per-haps just shaved down into distraught exhaustion, or perhaps just drunk: "Not drunk from whiskey, but drunk from something else, maybe. Drunk from the huge, stupid Love of Man that moved through his mind on its heels, empty and meaningless as fog, a Love of Man that came down in the end to wanting the whole damn world to itself" (p. 31). Henry despises man's inability to dissolve into compassion and sympathy; this is not to say that Henry denies reason—he all too much wants to frame his emotions in logic—but that he denies its tyranny over feeling. Soames affirms the acts of love, but he does not completely understand the me-chanics of such acts. He has difficulty separating feeling from action, emotion from expression, again falling into a confused and sometimes violent kind of speech. In terms of Gardner's emotional metaphysics, Henry suffers from a surfeit of emotion that warps his behavior and that overshadows his reliable intuitive sense.

This is pointed up most clearly in his relationship with Callie Wells, a sixteen-year-old country girl who comes under Henry's charge and em-ploy. She arrives (appropriately enough in this pastoral novel) in the spring, unlocking the mountain winter like the sun: "The girl appeared as if by magic, like a crocus where yesterday there'd been snow" (p. 7). Virginal freshness and fertility cling to Callie; she is the Spring Nymph come to the Mountain Ogre, an offer of regeneration to a tired old man and his world. She is half-child, half-woman, trapped (it seems to Henry) between "the beautiful and the sad" (p. 7), vulnerable to both the good and the tragic.

Henry at first assumes the role of father and protector, forcibly distancing himself from whatever else the girl might be besides make-believe daughter. Boiling up inside of Henry, however, is an emotion that turns him dark and ugly, and an urge that somehow eludes his definition of love: "In his dreams that night the Soames in his blood rose again and again like a gray-black monster out of a midnight ocean: He dreamed of himself in bed with her, misusing her again and again violently and in ungodly ways. Then, disgusted with himself, his chest burning, he found himself half-sitting on his bed with sunlight in his room and the sound of birds" (p. 37). In his dreams, Henry turns (like Sam Ghoki in "The Old Men") from father to incestuous seducer—and then, in a startling shift of image, to his *own* father, the near-dead tun of a man "sitting asleep like a boulder with his hands folded over the head of his cane, his unlaced shoes toeing inward. Chippies could walk on his shoulders without waking him" (p. 112). The almost beatific vision of his father is contrasted with this emergent brutal and pornographic aspect of Henry's soul that carries with it the memory of a whiskied whore and a hot day in a wormy hotel where,

> with only a candle burning, throwing huge shadows on the heat-buckled brown-paper wall, they had talked about loneliness and devotion and God knew what, and he had held her in his fat arms trying to tell her of the bursting piece of sentimental stupidity inside him that had longed for something or other all his life. Her hands playing on his back had been warm, vaguely like the big drops of rain that came in August. He'd told her by God he would marry her—he didn't even know her name—and she'd laughed her head off, not even drawing back, still rubbing against him, working him up. And at last in a kind of terror he had struck out at the damn drunken idiot, the stupid animal love in her raw hands and lips. What he had done, exactly, was hard to remember, or how she'd taken it. He'd hit her in the face when the climax came, that much he would never forget. That and the dry summer heat and the fact that now sometimes sitting in just his trousers, waiting, he could hear her moaning on his bed. The sound was distinct: so clear that he sometimes thought, in a moment of panic, that he'd lost his mind. (pp. 43–44)

Henry's love (or what he mistakes for love) is so formless and so outrageous that he is at first perplexed, and then murderous. He is struggling, as one critic has written, "with passionate, explosive Billy Buddian feelings,"[9] and as with Billy, they might well destroy him in their blighted violence. This, Gardner would say, is part of the monstrousness that exists within the souls of all men.

What makes things even more complex and puzzling for Soames is the ineluctable fact of his growing old and his increasing proximity to death. Henry tries to explain to Willard Freund, a youthful dreamer and eventual seducer of Callie, about visions and the illimitable, but he senses the futility of it:

> Henry had sighed, helpless, sitting in the back room with Willard the night the boy had told him of his father's plans. He'd felt old. He hadn't stopped to think about it, the feeling of having outgrown time and space altogether, falling into the boundless, where all contradictions stood resolved. He had listened as if from infinitely far away, and it had come down to this: That night he had given up hope for Willard, had quit denying the inevitable doom that swallows up all young men's schemes, and in the self-same motion of the mind he had gone on hoping. (p. 14)

As Henry draws nearer to extinction, he somehow escapes the ties of time and space, as though thinking about death and the worldly release were enough to suspend him above or away from it all. These are times when Henry strays into the mystical and sublime, into a world of imagination and spirit and incorruptibility (the world of the half-lunatic, of Ginger Ghoki and James Chandler).

He is constantly drawn back, however, by the howls and demands of the world that runs by his gas pumps and fills his diner. When Callie becomes pregnant, he immediately acts upon his emotion and upon the moral hunch he feels is right. He goes first to George Loomis, a man upon whom the world has done some of its most unhandsome work, a man who had

> more troubles in his almost thirty years than any other ten men in all the Catskills—he'd gotten one ankle crushed in Korea so that he had to wear a steel brace around one of his iron-toed boots, and people said he'd broken his heart on a Japanese whore so that now he secretly hated women; and when he'd come home, as if that wasn't enough, he'd found his mother dying and the farm gone back to burdocks and Queen Anne's lace. But there wasn't a sign of his troubles on his face, at least not right now. (p. 23)

George has had all of the bad luck of Job, without the promise (known or withheld) of restitution. Henry asks him to marry Callie, to legitimize the baby and purify the mother, but George has been alone for too long in the darkness of Crow Mountain. He refuses Henry's offer (callously, but with good intentions, laced with money), and makes the first in a series of denials that exclude him from the human circle. George does, though, bring Henry around to the fact he has ignored or shunned all along: that Henry himself loves Callie—and the realization sends him off into a strong but nonfatal heart attack. Such is the shock to a man cursed with "more heart than he knew how to spend."

Henry is an ultimately moral man. He shares Gardner's notion of an emotional metaphysic and relies on a heart that ironically is physically ailing but morally healthy and true. Like Clumly in *The Sunlight Dialogues,* Henry relies on intuition and hunches, and this time his hunch tells him to marry the girl. Henry cannot *explain* the action in all of its mixed-up folly and nobility, but as Gardner consistently shows us, heroism generally is such an inexplicable confusion. His act is a sacrifice of love and an attempt to correct a sin, and Callie understands that, as she tries to sort out the maze of feelings that have beset *her*.

She has been rudely and swiftly stripped of her teenage innocence and bliss, and cast into a world that is large and brooding and serious. She has scarcely had time to calmly consider Henry's action, to decide whether it is expedient, propitious, or loving, but her immediate response is a sort of mellow satisfaction, sanely emotional: "Callie had glanced up at him sideways and had seen again, as if it were a new discovery, how much she truly admired him, comical as he might seem to some, and she'd felt awe that he should be going through all this for her" (pp. 63–64). Callie's love is reserved and cool and vaguely touched with a sigh of relief. She does not totally understand Henry, despises in fact his frightful efforts at explanation, but somehow respects the virtue of his deed and is certainly glad-hearted for it all.

Upon reflection, however, Callie hits upon the fact that pains her most: the loss of youth and the chance of youthful love. Her admiration quickly turns to hate and fear: "Panic filled her chest. *It's a mistake,* she thought. *I don't love him.* He was ugly" (p. 70). She cannot balance the contradictions of Henry and his behavior, and cannot justify her own acceptance and submission: "Her marrying Henry Soames was almost vicious, an act of pure selfishness: she was pregnant, and he—obese and weak, flaccid in his vast, sentimental compassion—he had merely been available" (p. 71). It is difficult to tell where the truth lies. The doubts are natural, part of a rush to marriage, and though Callie believes she can learn to love Henry, she insists that love played no part in bringing her to him as his wife. The wedding, with all of its complex ritual and symbolism, takes on the features of a funeral for Callie:

They would join her celebration of the ancient forms—the ride to
the church with her mother's oldest brother, the lighting of the
symbolic candles, the pure white runner now walked on, stained,
her father's words, signifying to all the world (she understood now
for the first time, in alarm) that she had lost forever what she'd
never realized she had. There would come the magical exchange of
rings, the lifting of the veil, the kiss, and then Aunt Anna would
play that organ maniacally, tromping the pedals, not caring how
many of the notes she missed, for Callie (poor Callie, whom we all
knew well) had died before her time and had been lifted to Glory—
and the rice would rain down . . . rice and confetti raining down
like seeds out of heaven . . . and then the symbolic biting of the
cake, the emptying of the fragile glass. . . . They would join her in
all this, yet could no more help her, support her, defend her than if
they were standing on the stern of a ship drawing steadily away
from her, and she (in the fine old beaded and embroidered white
gown, the veil falling softly from the circlet on her forehead), she,
Callie, on a small boat solemn as a catafalque of silver, falling away
toward night. (p. 79)

Callie is a medieval legend, at first rescued from shame and blemish, later
ironically and tragically doomed to an improvident death-in-life. She can
neither accept the heroism of Henry's action nor rationalize her own
willingness to partake of a life that tastes sourly of ashes.

The marriage, like the wedding ceremony, is a chilling contrast in
lightness and stone. Callie, an ascendant spirit transmogrified, is all light
and essence and weightlessness; she is separate from the dark wood of the
church pews and the heavy flesh of those whose eyes follow her down the
aisle. For a moment she is released from the limits of time and space (as
Henry is, when his thoughts edge near death), and allowed the liberty she
never knew in the material world. The walls speak, the windows whisper
in her ear: she feels the animated universe, hears in one instant the sound
of soul conversing with soul, but it is fleeting, for

suddenly the room was real again, full of organ music, the lead
mullions of the stained glass window as solid as earth, the rich
colors deep and heavy as stone, even the professional simper of the
Preacher solidly real, as heavy and solid as iron chains and as heavy
as the golden burning bodies and faces of the people around her—
the people she knew and those she didn't. Only she herself was
weightless, and in a moment she too would be real again. *Go slow,*
said the room. *Be patient,* said the trees. She could feel the weight
coming, a murderous solidity, hunting her. (pp. 83–84)

Callie is the descending angel, falling now back into reality. Reality is solid and heavy, like her mountainous husband. Reality's bulk is ambiguous: it is hard and certain, yet it is also mysteriously threatening and "murderous." Callie feels suddenly the massiveness of adulthood, the massiveness of Henry's half-monstrous nature, and the massiveness of a girl suddenly warped into womanhood.

It is a reality, furthermore, that immediately deals harshly with Callie. Winter comes once more, freezing the ground as firmly as the locked insides of Callie's body. It is an ominous time for a birth, the snow stretching to the "edge of the woods," a vague presentiment to Henry of an unwanted homecoming; it is from the woods that Willard will return, from the woods that a memory, which should be closed out but which persists, will come to rile and infuriate Henry and drive him to mad violence.

Willard Freund, of course, is already present in the child that racks Callie's body. As the pain mounts and drives through her with all the purity of light, Callie turns ferocious and hateful. She purposely lets herself drift further and further away from her husband: he becomes a "stranger," and she treats him with silence and bitter disregard, until finally, when the agony cuts her like cold knives, Callie screams at Henry, witchlike: *"I hate you. It doesn't matter. I hate you. I love somebody else"* (p. 114). The truth of Callie's curse is ambiguous and unclear; it is doubtful that Callie could actually have loved Willard Freund, could not have seen beyond his insensitive and imperious ego. It is simply enough that the possibility exists. Out in the woods, where memory lives and guilt makes its way in the darkness between the trees, there is always the chance of a remembrance coming true. The woods have a way of letting loose their secrets, and Henry tries to listen, an ear open to the animistic universe:

> Voices mumbled around him, unintelligible, and he leaned forward in his chair. He saw without surprise that there were birds flying above the woods, thousands of them, gliding silently like owls, but talking, mumbling words like human beings. They flew through steam from the trees, or fog, or smoke maybe. Sometimes he could see only the smoke and the birds, as though the woods had disappeared or slipped from his mind, and then he could see the woods again, gray, moving closer. A sound of wind or fire blurred the voices and stirred the smoke into slow torsion, obliterating the birds, the bridge and the willow tree, the pines. When he saw the man coming across the yard, Henry jumped up. (p. 122)

But it is not Willard (or the memory of Willard) that emerges, and for the moment the memory dissolves and the crisis passes away. Willard had failed to appear when the pain arrived, had failed to share in the suffering and wretchedness, and in that absence his memory dies for Henry: "You had to be there, and Willard Freund hadn't been, and now there was no place left for him, no love, no hate—not in his father's house even. Willard would see. No place but the woods" (p. 123). No place but the black consciousness of his own guilt and his own recollection. Willard is one ghost that has, at least for the present, been put to rest.

In truth, Willard is not the only spirit that moves uneasily. Up there, living on that "tomb" of a mountain, George Loomis passes away a life almost too cruel for the living. He is a man nearly beaten and consumed by his own existence, giving up limbs and vitality to the machines that supposedly work for him. He lives alone, in a house lighted by the gray glare of a television, and cluttered with "things." He is a collector and a hoarder and an unbendable materialist—a latter-day dragon to Henry's Grendel. The little joy he extracts from an otherwise pitiless life comes from the clocks and the silver and the old magazines that litter his floors and shelves. "What do you use them for?" George is asked, and he replies: " '*Use* them for? Sometimes I go in and touch them,' and he winked. But it was true. It was the richest pleasure in his life, just picking them up, knowing they were his, safe from the destroyers who cut the woodcuts from great old editions like his illustrated Goethe, or saw down hand-crafted Kentucky pistols and weld on modern sights" (p. 130). George finds something reassuring in the mass and stability of "things." There is a permanence about them that mocks the weak fragility of an arm or a leg.

But in their own way, George's treasures are every bit as vulnerable to destruction as his body, and this fact wears him down. His things are valuable, and value attracts thieves and murderers: "He carried the idea of murder on Nickel Mountain like a weight on his chest" (p. 136). The thought becomes an obsession and ignites within him a lunatic fear and suspicion. Crouched in the damp grass, afraid of entering his own house, George recalls the first inkling of his personal frailty, and its cosmic implications. It was in Korea, on a dark hillside:

> He'd kept on walking, that night, cautious, but not giving in to the feeling that there were rifles trained on him; and then suddenly, crazily, he was staring into lights, and McBrearty was falling back against him, dead already, and he felt the hit, and the next minute he was coughing blood and couldn't breathe and knew for certain he was dying, thinking (he would never forget): *Now I'll find out if this horseshit about heaven's really true.* But he'd lived, and now he was no kid anymore, he knew what he couldn't have imagined then: If they wanted to kill him, they could do it—he was mortal.

Everything on earth was destructible, old books, guns, clocks, even bookholders of bronze. (p. 138)

Human beings, like their material creations, are mortal and transient and destructible. No one is better proof of that than George Loomis. It becomes the essence of his existence, but to deal with that fact he collects about him matter, not people and their affections. He lives in fear and in loneliness, shamefully freighted with "the hollowness of his life" (p. 141). He must somehow deal with the past and with the way life has acted upon him; he must learn, as so many of Gardner's characters must learn, of the healing properties of the community, learn that the past must be shared and carried collectively.

The only person who approximates genuine evil in the novel is Simon Bale, the deluded and half-crazed Jehovah's Witness. He is a moral bigot, intolerant and unmovable in his dogmatism, who consigns nine-tenths of the world to perdition "for pride, for covetousness, for forgetting the Sabbath, for believing the devil to be dead" (p. 146). (Gardner himself suspects the devil is still alive, but in a more medieval and emblematic sense.) Simon is even considered capable of setting the very fire that destroyed his wife. He is a dangerous and frightening man who, like George, lives alone: "Simon Bale had no friends. He was not only an idealist but an ascetic as well, both by conviction and by temperament, and the death of his wife . . . meant the end of all ordinary contact with humanity—or would have except for Henry Soames" (p. 150). Henry shelters Simon, takes him in when no one else will have him, introduces, in effect, the Devil into the Garden. No matter that Simon is on the edge of "warped" lunacy and monstrousness; Henry disregards George's warning: "A man that thinks he's righteous is deadly, you know it. He takes credit for things he's got nothing to do with—accidents like his living where he happens to live and knowing exactly the people he knows. He thinks he's Jesus H. Christ and it makes him arrogant" (p. 192). George here speaks for Gardner: righteousness dooms Simon just as it dooms Agathon and just as it nearly dooms James and Sally Page in *October Light*. And it almost dooms Henry, as well.

Henry, too, disregards the anger and opposition of his wife, who senses the threatening perniciousness of Simon. He is a serpent, a "rattlesnake behind glass" that insinuates itself between Henry and Callie, divides them and sets themselves upon one another. Against all of his better reason, but with visions of Paradise and skyfuls of angels, Henry assumes responsibility for the burial of Simon's wife, signing the papers with a dread and a wish: "Henry thought again of Callie and, worse, of Callie's mother, and he shut his eyes for a quick, dead serious prayer to whatever might be up there to watch over fools and children" (p. 170). It is a responsibility that no one, including Simon, will accept; but Henry, either in his goodness or self-righteousness or pure meanness, accepts the charge. He recognizes how easily one can "turn into an animal" and stop being human. To be human is to be responsible and to act—and also to feel the consequences and fears of that act.

> Those fifteen people in New York City might be right in the end, but you had to act, and beyond that you had to assert that they were wrong, wrong for all time, whatever the truth might be. And it was the same even if you only *thought* you saw an old man being stabbed: You ran to the center of the illusion and you jumped the illusory man with the knife, and if it was empty, sunlit sidewalk you hit, too bad, you had to put up with the laughter, and nevertheless do it again the next time and again and again and again. So Simon. It wasn't true that the world was about to end or that sinners were going to torment, but all the same he was right to go out with his crackpot pamphlets: Henry Soames would try to persuade him, but he wasn't going to stop him—except in the diner, because the diner, at least, was still his own.
>
> And yet he felt no quiet. The truth was that there was something Henry was afraid of, something as undefined in his mind as the substance of his child's nightmares, but real, for all its ghostliness: some possibility that became increasingly troublesome. (p. 200)

Henry affirms the need to become involved, to get caught up in the "buzzing, blooming confusion," to act.

What nags at Henry is the suspicion that he might be promoting the darkest of evils, regardless of the purity of his motives. Is George right, Henry asks himself: Is it self-righteousness that will do Simon in, that will scare Henry's young son to witlessness, and that will pervert Henry's "natural feeling for justice to a sick kind of pity"? How far, asks Gardner, does one's responsibility extend? You may let in the Devil, admit that he is working outside of nature, but how much havoc do you allow him to wreak in the Garden?

Henry is forced to that endpoint. His son Jimmy crouches in his bedroom, pointing into the darkness, screaming, *"It's the devil!"* And there in the hallway stands the loathsome figure of Simon Bale, creator of demons and nightmares. In that one instant, Henry sees the damage Simon has wrought upon his son, sees how he has twisted and wrenched his imagination, and Henry moves beyond the point of tolerance and forbearance, to the point of killing:

"You!" Henry yelled, and it came out as much like awe as like rage. His rage came slowly . . . but when it hit it was like a mountain falling. He might have killed him if he could have done it (so Henry Soames would say later, dead calm, at the coroner's inquiry), but he couldn't even hit him because he was holding Jimmy in his arms; he could only advance on him, howling in his fury, feeling his neck puffing up and throbbing. The room around him was red and his lips felt thick. Simon was whispering, "Forgive, forgive," again and again and smiling as if his brain had stopped running . . . and suddenly he turned and bolted down the stairs. Henry shrieked, driving, as the man reached the top. He did not seem to step down but to leap, looking over his shoulder with a fierce grin, as though he thought he could fly, and Henry rushed toward him in alarm and hate or was rushing toward him already by that time. . . . He saw him hit halfway down and tumble and fly out in all directions, reaching. At the bottom he lay still a minute, upside down, his arms flung out and one knee bent, the light from the kitchen door like a halo on his murderous face, and then his body jerked, and quickly Henry turned his back so that Jimmy wouldn't see. (pp. 207–8)

Innocence—or at least what is left of innocence—must somehow be preserved and protected from the perverse. Simon is crushed by accident; perhaps it is his fate, perhaps it is his time and destiny to die—but he *had* to die. Even the superficial halo cannot hide the gnarled, "murderous face."

Yet it is part of a moral human nature to suffer, even when what stirs one to suffering is pure accident or inevitability. Henry, after Simon's death, goes on a mindless and deadly eating binge, killing himself in his anguish: "Perhaps partly because of the heat—weather unheard of in the Catskills, a sure sign of witchcraft at work, or miracles brooding—the nervous eating that had troubled Henry Soames all his life slipped out of control, became a mindless external power against which it was impossible for him even to struggle, a consuming passion in the old sense, a devil (but blind, indifferent as a spider) in his guts" (p. 211). As if in bizarre recompense for the loss of Simon Bale—an act in which he had little part—Henry unleashes all of the guilt and the monstrosity of his nature, losing his reason, dumbly and slowly taking himself toward suicide. Suddenly Henry enters the existential slide that Gardner strikes at again and again. The heart is momentarily "warped" by despair, and (in John Barth's phrase) one is lured by the "charm of the abyss." Monsters like Grendel and humans like Dale Corby in "The Old Men" and Richard

Page in *October Light,* humans who have had too much of the world and who fail their heart (the heart, says Gardner, never emotionally fails humans) fall to the fury of the black chaos and to suicide. Redemption comes too late for some; for Henry it comes through his wife.

Henry's behavior shakes Callie from her countrified, pastoral idea of reality and forces her to a true and testable action: "This was real, not a matter of poetry but a study for her country rules—the rules that a child should have a father, that a wife should have a husband, and that a man trying to kill himself should be stopped" (p. 213). Callie is still in the process of maturing; her logic and morality need aging and curing and, most important of all, proving. She is for once made to think seriously of her relationship with Henry, of what it means to her, whether it is worth preserving and just how one might go about preserving it:

> She must act, she saw (wearily and angrily, flushed and spent, past all endurance), but how she must act would not come clear. With a part of her mind she wished him dead, the whole world dead; the heat coming up to her from the grill and flooding out into the heat of the room made her want to break free into violence. And yet even now, though abstractly, now, she "loved" him, for lack of a better word. She could think about her love—still there, she knew perfectly well, but dormant, an emotion locked up, waiting for September—as she might think about a pain she'd felt long ago and would one day feel again. It was the most vital emotion she had ever felt, on one hand, but on the other, an emotion partly revolting to her: She had not seen much sign of it in her mother and father; it was an emotion they shrank from, lashed out against as they might at something obscene. She understood. But Henry . . . had accepted that feeling, had in a way made it into his identity, hugging her in his great loose arms, womanishly patting some truck driver's shoulder, bending down to kiss the forehead of their child as he slept. He *was* obscene to her, to tell the truth. His whole gross being, the very possibility of his existence at the height of a weedy, rainless summer was obscene. (pp. 213–14)

Callie is having to consider her ability and desire to love. Love, for her, is a controlled emotion, one that must be kept in check lest it turn "obscene." It is this "huge, blubbering Jesus" part of Henry that she can neither understand nor abide.

Like Henry, though, Callie is also haunted by ghosts. It is Callie who sights the specter of Simon Bale, who hears or feels him haunting the household, holding in his filmy hand some awful portent of doom and accident. Callie could see "with a part of her mind that behind the house, motionless, oblivious to the deadly heat, Simon Bale's ghost sat listening in the dark, solid as granite, hearing all they said and thought and hearing the noise still miles away of something (wind?) bearing vengeance toward them: some change, subtle and terrible. They were caught" (p. 218). She knows, with all the certainty of a wound, that *"something is coming."* It has the appearance of damnation and disaster and chaos, but carries an indefinite shape. Thinking of Simon, Callie says, "He'll destroy us." Henry replies, " 'No, he'll save us.' And instantly Callie knew, in the mind-fogging heat, that he was right" (p. 247). Callie is learning to believe; she wants to survive, to discover a faith in that which makes no sense.

The only person willing to argue with Henry and try to shake him out of his insanity is George Loomis. George possesses the explanation and tries to reason it out, turning to Callie and saying:

> It's true. He says he made a choice, the choice to go on yelling, which makes him to blame for Simon Bale's dying. But he knows that's only word games. He didn't know Simon would fall downstairs, and even if he did, it's one time in a thousand you kill yourself that way. It was an accident. Henry was the accidental instrument, a pawn, a robot labeled *Property of Chance.* That's intolerable, a man should be more than that; and that's what Henry's suffering from—not guilt. However painful it may be, in fact even if it kills him, horror's the only dignity he's got. (p. 239)

Henry is simply a mechanism in the huge complexity of chance, and it is the horror of that fact that is killing him. There is, certainly, a quantity of guilt at work, but what really gnaws at Henry is his insignificance and the notion that whether one lives or dies (and the *method* by which one lives) is of little consequence. In his own simplified way, Henry comes face-to-face with the existential dilemma. He loses his faith, is cut off (like George) from nature and from humanity.

Ironically, while George is astute enough to diagnose Henry's problem, he is partially blind to his own spiritual wound (though he goes halfway in describing it in his analysis of Henry's dilemma). It is George who has killed the Goat Lady, by accident, purest accident, unavoidable accident. The Goat Lady is as much a lunatic as Simon Bale,[10] and George's involvement in her death is a parallel to Henry's role in the death of Simon. But the ways in which they react to it are different. Henry acknowledges his supposed share in the fact, acknowledges it openly. George, however, is a man who has had the poetry of his faith crushed out from him by the blind cruelties of life, who has had so much violence (fated violence, perhaps) that it makes violent his own soul:

He sometimes believed he had known all his life that he'd end up maimed, a brace on one boot, no arm in one sleeve, and no doubt worse yet to come. Once, lately, it had occurred to him that maybe he'd given up his foot and arm voluntarily, sacrificing up pieces of his body like an old-time Delaware to ward off destructions more terrible. It had seemed an interesting idea at first, but thinking about it an instant later he'd seen it for the paltry ruse it was, mere poetry, and, like all poetry, so irrelevant and boring he wanted to smash things. (p. 222)

The memory of that night follows him, that night when he wheeled around the curve and crushed wood and bone and old flesh in a fierce bit of chance, "an accident, one in an infinite chain" (p. 255). Even though he realizes its accidental nature, however, he cannot bring himself to confess; he rejects the opportunity to admit his predicament to Callie and Henry and Old Man Judkins, and (like a doomed Hawthornian soul) forsakes the human community and condemns himself to a long, solitary guilt. He is the one lost soul of the novel, a quasi-tragic figure. Part of the human ritual, for Gardner, is a sharing of guilt—expiation as a means of rescuing one's sanity and soul. George will quietly let his world slide and run down; he perceives, but cannot act from his perceptions.

But he does somehow manage to "save" Henry and Callie. It is as if Henry sees in George's pitiable, tortured face the folly of his own guilt and sense of helplessness. Everything that is large and weak and stupid in his own moral character is mirrored in George's stolid and stubborn silence. It is a mystical salvation, all of nature taking part, all of its souls converging, in Callie's imagination, in a convocation of ghosts—the same sort of convocation that is repeated over and over in Gardner's fiction, most notably in *Mickelsson's Ghosts* and the short story, "The Art of Living." All the deaths and debts are redeemed; life, both that of the flesh and the blood and that of the ground and the rain, is renewed, the long, dry summer of guilt and worry and shame washed away in the storm that breaks from atop the mountains.

What Henry had once feared—the emergence of that dark figure from the woods—does take place, but it is as if the memory too has been wiped out with the autumn harvest and the regenerative animism of the land. Willard Freund, like Henry and like George, struggles with an image of his father; it is an image that he detests and finds unbearably shameful, and that is devoid of love and human decency. Yet he returns to the Garden, a Garden that has been made imperfect by his part in its past. He returns a cynic, convinced he was "nicked in the balls from the beginning": "He was going back to the land of his innocence, the sunlit garden where all those years he had believed, in spite of everything, in parental love, the goodness and innocent virtue of girls, or at any rate of certain girls, the possibility of unselfish friendship. He was going back knowing it was perhaps all bullshit, and, for all his fear that it might be bullshit, he was going back to find it still there, and holy" (p. 273). Freund's cynicism and cold mockery stalls his ability to love. He misunderstands both Henry and Callie, misunderstands and underestimates (like Millie Hodge in *The Sunlight Dialogues*) their genius for loving.

What partially changes Willard's attitude is accident, in this case an accident that kills one man and miraculously misses taking Freund's own life. As accidents haunt so many characters in this novel, Freund's mischance comes to trouble and torment his mind, stirring up new waves of guilt and doubt (a combination of accident and the insufferable moral ugliness of his father). He treats Callie as a near-stranger and flees from Henry's illogical and loving acceptance. Yet the overpowering craziness of it all—the forgiveness of past sins, the welcoming into the present— startles him into a realization of the authentic, though lunatic, nature of love. He confronts a part of his past in Callie and their son, and is taken in by the mountainous magnanimity of Henry—incomprehensible to Willard, but instructive.

All that is left for Henry is to come to terms with the "facticity" of death and "the grave." He and his young son are a contrast in time and experience. Jimmy is fresh, inquisitive, wondering, and ignorant of life's mortal ways. Henry is a man bound soon to die, a reality he does not try to deny. The thought, in fact, frees him from this world and sends him outside of time, into the spirit and memory of his father:

> He watched the boy's face and for an instant he felt himself slipping away again into that sense that he stood outside time, involved and yet dispassionate, like a man looking at far-off mountains, or like Henry Soames' father sitting motionless and huge on a broad stump, watching chipmunks or listening to the brook move down through the glen, rattling away forever, down and down. Or as Henry himself sat nowadays, more and more, thinking thoughts that had never before occurred to him, surprised and bemused at the way things fit together. (pp. 295–96)

He comes to the wise vision of his father, the vision of gentleness and almost Franciscan beatitude.

Henry Soames is a man whose world has changed, and whose life has been resurrected. He has been lifted up and turned around by his wife, Callie—the regenerative, restorative, pastoral force.[11] He comes to see that it is but "a long train of trivial accidents, affirmed by one, that made a man's life what it happened to become" (p. 300). He works out his existence on a second or third plane, perceives things as they are outside of time and space, and then brings that rarified vision back down to earth:

> He'd grown mystical, or, as Callie said, odd. He had no words for his thoughts; the very separateness of words was contrary to what he seemed to know. It began, perhaps, with his thought of what marrying Callie had done to him; if she'd made him into her own image it was nevertheless her own image discovered—for the first time to her as well as to him—in *him:* Henry Soames as he might, through her, become. Once he had fairly tested it, he knew beyond any shadow of doubt that the new life she had shaped was his own, it fit him the way his father's old coat had one day, to his surprise, fit him, and from that moment on he didn't just wear the new life, he owned it. He felt like a man who'd been born again, made into something entirely new, and the idea that such a thing could happen had startled him, and he'd seized on it, turning it over and over in his mind the way you turn over a hundred-dollar bill. But the new life he'd found in himself had no settled meaning yet: It was all a-shimmer and vague, like a dream. It lacked the solid reality that would come when he'd lived it long enough to know it had something in common with the old. . . . With the passing of time he became in reality what he was, his vision not something apart from the world but the world itself transmuted. (p. 301)

Henry comes around, at last, (in his father's words) to "the holiness of things and the idea of magical change" (p. 302). Reality and one's life within that reality can be transfigured by the animal force of love. Henry sees the spirit that quickens all of creation; it is a fog, a darkness that blankets the woods and whirls the birds in frenzied flight, and that alters everything it touches. It provides a separate angle of vision from which to screen and judge the workings of existence. Henry, at the end, comes to an almost religious understanding of the mystical satisfaction and the assuaging tranquility of faith and love. The final tableau of the brittle, ancient parents and their "resurrected" son marks one final play upon the belief in the primacy of spirit and of love. The old man is right: people fail, grow "dead and rotten." But what remains untouched is the memory and the love held for that memory. The soul fortifies love, carries it beyond the reach of death and material corruption, crystallizes it for an eternity.

   This is as close as John Gardner ever comes to a theological statement in his fiction. He affirms the need for a moral order in the world, and accepts the possibility of a religious aesthetic that might infuse the proper moral spirit, but he abhors the rigid dogmatism and narrow bigotry that accompany the institution, or that *are* the institution. He longs for the wonder and the mystery and the miracle of the pre-Christian myth. Gardner's world, the world of *Nickel Mountain,* is an animistic world through which the spirit runs, enlivening and ennobling every element of human existence. The novel is Gardner's paean to the Garden and what modern men and women have made of it.

Chapter VII

The King's Indian: Stories and Tales

He put his faith in his hands, and in his students' hands,
flooring the ancient abyss with art till he forgot it
was there.
        —"Nicholas Vergette, 1923–1974"

Short story collections are often random affairs, chance bits of writing
thrown together with no plan or reason other than to paste up something
large enough to sell. Such is not the case, however, with *The King's
Indian: Stories and Tales* (1974). It is a complex construction—blue-
printed, developed, designed—meant by Gardner to stand for many
things. The several stories (nearly all published earlier)[1] are composed
and grouped along definite lines of thought; they stand capably enough
alone, but when brought together, even the most striking tours de force
blend submissively into a large and more impressive whole. Each of the
three sections study and drive home a point, yet all are welded skillfully
into a coherent collection that, when finished, strikes the reader with the
consolidated force of a novel.

One of the aims of *The King's Indian* is to highlight the strange and
largely unrecognized landscape of southern Illinois. The collection was
written and published during Gardner's tenure at Southern Illinois University, and the book forms, in a way, a group of one that might join the
Batavia and the Catskill groupings. (Actually, one might also include the
short story "The Joy of the Just," in *The Art of Living,* which is also set in
southern Illinois.) Gardner, even in the largely fantastical stories of the
book's middle section, used the area around Carbondale as a setting and
an evocation: "If I was going to write a book about Southern Illinois,
which in fact I did in *The King's Indian,* that's another, completely different feeling. There it's as if human beings had never landed; the human

beings—the natives, anyway—seem more like gnomes."[2] Remember that the book's title is qualified: *Stories and Tales*. Gardner is pursuing a genre—the ghost story—with all of its magic and shadow and inexplicability; and to conjure up the necessary emotion he must also conjure up the necessary setting.

As a sort of footnote to *The King's Indian*, Gardner wrote a short piece for *Vogue* magazine entitled "Southern Illinois." The article is interesting in its restatement of the mystery and otherworldliness that Gardner was striving for in *The King's Indian*. At one point Gardner remarks of southern Illinois: "It's the only place I know that—in Merlin's old-fashioned, rather stern sense—is still magical."[3] It is this sense of part fable, part truth, part arabesque that Gardner chases in his collection. Moreover, there are things characteristic of this region of the country that Gardner employs in several of his stories (whether or not they are admittedly set in southern Illinois), characteristics that he expounds upon in this article. When Gardner writes the following, one automatically thinks back to "The Ravages of Spring":

> You get a good early spring, hopefully one without a late, killing frost that will knock out the peach and apple crops; the hickories, oaks, and maples leaf out . . . a hundred varieties of flowering bushes; and you get your small basin of loam plowed up. Then, out of nowhere, one afternoon, comes a yellow-green sky and a dark mass of clouds moving in from the southwest, maybe a shaft of black that will prove a tornado—sometimes two or three of them are visible at once—and the whole world goes silent. The birds, the horses, even the crickets stop to listen.
>
> On rare occasions, when the storm is in no hurry, the first thing you hear is the creeks breaking. Flash floods strike faster than a stranger would believe. . . . You hear the rain coming then and, if a tornado's behind it, the approach of a sound like a hundred old-fashioned railroad engines. It's time to go down cellar, though it may not be much help if the twister decides to hit head on. (p. 157)

Later on, Gardner recalls: "The region's had its violent people, too— riverboat murderers, in the days when the Ohio and the Mississippi were big business; union men and scabs who killed for the dubious pleasure of digging coal; moonshiners and bootleggers, racists, comic but deadly small-time racketeers" (p. 157). This is the southern Illinois of the nineteenth century, the southern Illinois that Jonathan Upchurch lights out for in "The King's Indian." Finally, writing of the southern Illinois of today, Gardner says: "Though they listen to the radio and watch TV, they still, some of them, say magic spells, sing ancient songs about iron men (knights), and examine strangers with a wary eye" (p. 157). From this southern Illinois spring the gap-toothed madwoman of "The Ravages of Spring," the knights and witches of "The Temptation of St. Ivo" and "Tales of Queen Louisa," and the murmuring congregation of "Pastoral Care." It is the ghostly breeding ground of Gardner's crazed cast of characters, a land where the outlandish seems everyday and where people learn the marvel of surprise.

The King's Indian serves another and more important purpose: it is Gardner's testament to art. At its very center the book is an examination of artistic theory and practice. Gardner has explained that

> The whole book is a study in aesthetics—aesthetics I think in the only sense that really counts, as it expresses people through a theory of beauty. Aesthetics can never be completely abstract, it has to be derived from the physical expression of a theory in people's feelings and lives, so that to study it you make up characters and you show what happens if they shape their world by this aesthetic standard or by that one—this idea of the sublime or that one—and hopefully what you come to is true art, which everybody can share in. It puts all artistic approaches in perspective. The true story teller, like Jonathan Upchurch, in "The King's Indian," is a model for all artists—intuition in the service of King Reason—therefore the eternal artist, God on earth. So basically it's a book about aesthetics, a subhead under metaphysics. It *is* my book about aesthetics.[4]

The King's Indian is, in fact, a tangible monument (and memorial) erected by Gardner with the aid of artists—visual and literary, solicited and drafted, dead and living—allied to a specific aesthetic tradition. It is Gardner's tribute to the infinitude of art, a purpose he outlines with all the clarity of a chiseled inscription, when he self-consciously interrupts the mad narrator of "The King's Indian" to comment:

> This house we're in is a strange one, reader—house or old trunk or circus tent—and it's one I hope you find congenial, sufficiently gewgawed and cluttered but not unduly snug. Take my word, in any case, that I haven't built it as a cynical trick, one more bad joke of exhausted art. The sculptor-turned-painter that I mentioned before is an actual artist, with a name I could name, and what I said of him is true. And you are real, reader, and so am I, John Gardner the man that, with the help of Poe and Melville and many another man, wrote this book. And this book, this book is no child's top either—though I write, more than usual, filled with doubts. Not a

toy but a queer, cranky monument, a collage: a celebration of all literature and life; an environmental sculpture, a funeral crypt.[5]

Gardner hunches at his desk, writing with the shadows of Poe, Melville, Twain, Coleridge, Lewis Carroll, Kafka, and Italo Calvino peering over his shoulder, whispering advice, offering gentle, nudging criticism. Moreover, Gardner enlists the support of his artist-friends in the design and construction of his work; they provide him with color and theory and inspiration. The illustrations for *The King's Indian* are done by Gardner's good friend, Herbert L. Fink, Professor of Art at Southern Illinois University. The subject of one story, "John Napper Sailing through the Universe," was the illustrator of Gardner's *The Sunlight Dialogues* and a friend first met at Southern Illinois University. Finally, *The King's Indian* is dedicated to Nicholas Vergette, sculptor and close friend of Gardner, who died of cancer in 1974. If, indeed, the book is any sort of memorial, it is a memorial to the life of Vergette; not only is the book dedicated to him, but he is also twice mentioned (though never by name) in the title story (note the comment in the quotation above). Furthermore, in 1973 Gardner authored an article on the theory and work of Vergette, and six months later was forced to add a sad postscript to that article in an elegy to Vergette, who died on 21 February 1974 (the poem was read by Gardner at Vergette's funeral).[6] *The King's Indian* then is a reunion of sorts; the close, the distant, the dead are all convoked—as Gardner's own characters so often convoke past and present shades—once more for a joint statement on the condition of things and for a reaffirmation of the timelessness of art. Art, they all seem to say, is the only human creation that eludes the limits of time and space and manages to endure.

Finally, while it is clear that a portion of the collection is concerned with the function of art and its ethical nature, it should be noted that *The King's Indian* is also a discussion of Gardner's favorite pair of metaphysical opposites: anarchy and order. The book is constructed in such a way that Gardner first examines the social, moral, and philosophical implications of the contrasting impulses toward order and anarchy, and their relation to the artistic effort. This is done in the five stories contained in book 1, "The Midnight Reader." Gardner follows this with a study of the artistic imagination itself—what it is made of, how it functions, and how it orders and disorders the world. This is the focus of book 2, "Tales of Queen Louisa." In book 3, "The King's Indian: A Tale," Gardner self-consciously combines both themes, telling a story (or tale) that reveals the creative process at work and that shows the obstacles and choices with which the serious artist is faced. Character, narrator, and author all become involved in the same problem, that of matching imagination to reality.[7]

In "Pastoral Care," the opening story in "The Midnight Reader," the narrator (all five stories in book 1 are narrated in the first person) is a Carbondale minister enjoying the cool freedom of the neo-orthodoxy. The Reverend Pick delights in his objectivity and his self-conscious intelligence; he literally "picks" apart the antiquated institution that has overgrown into "*The Church*." "The institutional church is not the church at all, I say to them, but a foul encrustation, a birthday party for a man who's left town and forgotten to leave us a forwarding address" (p. 4). He is skeptical of his own role as spiritual shepherd, unsure of where he is leading his charges, encouraged only by the shared folly of pastor and herd: "If I weren't ridiculous—balanced (*vanitas*) on my pulpit stool—I might easily grow scornful, indifferent to these people. And if my pitiful flock were not confused and unhappy, they would joyfully go out into the world and leave my church empty. We need each other. I give them a vision they only half understand, a vision vaguely exciting, though alarming" (pp. 7–8). Pick is so critical of himself and so aware of the silliness of the pumped-up human ego, that he is unable to really *feel* the uncertainty of his congregation. The relationship between preacher and parish is a symbiotic one in which both parties feed off of the other's despair and mockery.

From his pulpit, Pick attacks the futility of system-building and its inbred perniciousness. Christianity is the image of a man, he tells a despondent believer, and of a vision: "I could have told her—I hinted at it—that that was the point of Christianity. All systems fail: psychologies, sociologies, philosophies, rituals. To believe in any firm system whatever, even Foreign Missions, is to be left—like Adam biting into the apple—with a taste of blowing ashes. Flexibility is all, the Christian's ability to respond, get up again, die if necessary, because everything is finally all right. We follow not a system but a man, I could have said" (p. 9). All systems, in their claims to inclusiveness and surety, are defective. It is intellectual arrogance to believe that man can solve all of his own problems merely by erecting a scaffold and a skeleton of old and weary ideas. What nags at Pick is his failure to calm the soul (his and others'); doubt is necessary, but there must first be some belief strong enough to withstand the doubting.

When Pick interviews the young stranger—"Beyond all doubt a maniac, or else stoned. Or Christ come down to check on me" (p. 11)—he finds himself pressed to self-examination. The young man is a bomber, a lunatic, an acclaimed anarchist; yet, like the Manichean universe, he is innocent and blessed as well: "Still gazing at me, benign, inhuman, he backs away through the outer office. At the far door he gives me a peace sign and suddenly—amazingly—smiles. He has a beautiful smile. His eyes are like Brahma's. He vanishes" (p. 23). The stranger is Christ-like, Pick sees, in his ability to sanctify and also to destroy. He persuades Pick that anarchy, when politically and (it seems) morally justified, is correct. Tradition should not be deified, but should be challenged, and should perhaps be destroyed. Pick is led by the man's argument to a sermon on the parable of the fig tree, a parable which Pick reads as an anarchist tract on a dead institution: "The prophet's tree of Judah started well. . . . Only with time did it lose vitality and purpose. That happens, you know, with human institutions. . . . Any institution, life-style, program, can be vital at its inception but become, in time, an obstacle, a sickness" (p. 27). To the usual reading of the statement, "Render unto Caesar what is Caesar's," Pick adds: "The saying admits of a more radical interpretation: If Caesar usurps the rule of God, decrees that immorality is moral, then resist him; blow up the Pentagon" (p. 28). What Pick does not realize is that he advocates the very thing he condemns: the seizing of godhood by the ungodly, the Promethean theft.

It is too late for Pick to recant, however, or to at least mollify the harshness of his words. The intruder has heard and has acted upon Pick's advice. The police station goes up in flames, torn apart by a bomber's imprecise morality, and the connection is made: *"Bomber linked to local minister"* (p. 29). Pick flees his church, escapes into the wilderness, overwhelmed by an insight arrived too late: "It has to do with responsibility, the dangerous freedom my pulpit grants. I told them what was true, or what I believe to be true (we are forgiven in advance for nonomniscience), and what it was necessary for them to hear. If I'd known he was listening I would not have spoken in quite the same way. I didn't know; but any effect my sermon had is nevertheless my fault" (p. 29). Pick simultaneously acknowledges his responsibility and admits his guilt, but it is not enough. Almost in the same breath comes the news of the destruction of his own church, a fact that sends him whirling toward despair and nihilism: "It does *not* matter. The truth explodes out of the night and the sound of wheels. The world is dying—pollution, old, unimportant wars, the grandiose talk of politicians, the whisper of lovers in cheap motels. The sentence of death is merely language, a pause between silences" (p. 32). Pick loses his faith and adopts the unreliable anarchy and pessimism of a different generation.

It requires another accident, every bit as enormous and tragic as the bombings, to shake Pick from his resignation, and when the hot and iron-heavy train blasts the young hippie girl halfway to infinity, he is recalled to proper reason. He dons once more the mask of consoler and sustainer of souls, loses his self-consciousness and confesses his helplessness: "I am no one, for the moment; a disembodied voice; God's minister.

The wildman stumbles, drops to one knee, groaning, gushing tears. Cautiously, I touch his shoulder. 'Trust me,' I say. (The fall is endless. All systems fail.) I force myself to continue. I have no choice" (p. 34). It is the "miraculous resurrection" that Gardner has spoken of. Pick is retrieved, brought back from the deathfulness of lost belief and egotism, by a chance but compelling act of faith. Pick learns the usefulness of what one might call "applied faith." It is the sort of faith that is left after an eternity of puzzling and pain and reversal; it is a faith that, though perhaps temporary and imperfect, succeeds in easing the pain (personal and universal) provoked by a world that at times appears too evil for belief. It is a Gardneresque retreat to orthodoxy, to emotional metaphysics, and to the virtues beyond the institution.

In "The Ravages of Spring" there appears another sort of skeptic, a doctor who approaches life with a cocked eye and a scorn for the absolute: "What I chiefly know about absolute values is that they do not necessarily aid the digestion, but frequently impair it" (p. 35). He possesses a wry and irreverent vision—"Life, I've often been inclined to believe, is preposterous" (p. 35)—that finds untrustworthy both the positivism of scientific discovery and the "Platonistic predilection for Eternity as opposed to Present Time." He is a man eminently commonsensical, and thus a fit narrator (despite his protests) for "a tale at first glance more fit for the author of 'The Raven' " (this is the first of Gardner's several references to Poe).

The doctor is swept up in one of those fierce southern Illinois tornados, and is led by his horse (a horse named Shakespeare?!) to the windy tower of Dr. John Hunter, an extraordinary and bizarre man who "had . . . no ordinary face. Enormous gazelle eyes as pale as glass, an uptilted nose above protruding, crooked teeth, and skin very nearly as ashen as dried-out clay. It was not necessarily an alarming face . . . but it was, emphatically, a kind of face you'd not expect to see twice on one planet" (p. 49). Hunter is a scientist—to be exact, a once-authentic, now long-dead geneticist.[8] The poor doctor takes this as conclusive evidence that Hunter is "dangerously mad," but his observation is only half-correct. The doctor's normal, pragmatic system begins to fail him when faced with something beyond ordinary human experience. Gardner asks: How does the scientist deal with what comes from beyond the scientific? How does the mind put back together what the mind has laid asunder? For this is what Hunter proposes. He tells the doctor, "All the world . . . went stark, raving mad in the second century, when the Gnostics separated body and mind" (p. 52). Hunter tests the physical world and finds it wanting, so he goes outside of that world, outside of time and space, by defying the limits of the body and its cellular death. Both Hunter and his cackling, hand-wringing wife are clones, genetic duplicates. In one stroke science smashes the power of creation and reduces fate to a joke and a relic by "crushing the mad poets' idea of Soul" (p. 52).

The pragmatist doctor insists upon natural order and the reason of things; he knows Hunter is a madman, a lunatic cracked by the power of his knowledge. Yet when the tornado hits and the tower is swept away like pieces of kindling on a beach, the doctor can barely distrust his eyes as Hunter slips from his grasp and flies toward death:

> [I] seized his legs, trying to drag him to safety—to the house, perhaps. Part of it held fast. But I felt his death tremor, his violent jerking as he fought his way to a better world—and I released him in horror. In purple-green light I watched him cringe one last time, and jerk, and die. Then, not exactly with amazement, with—what?—I watched the dying body separate. It became several small creatures, pink, blue, green. (All this was surely not real, mere nightmare; but for certain reasons which will soon be evident, it is necessary that I record all I saw or thought I saw, on the chance that something in all this may give some hint of what actually took place.) I studied the creatures, so it seemed—I could hold four or five in my two cupped hands—and then I apparently lost consciousness. (p. 58)

Despite his Hawthornian disclaimers, the doctor is troubled by the reality of his nightmare—a reality brought directly and undeniably home when he goes to the well, tracking the cries swallowed beneath the ground, and finds "three small, wet, bawling children—boys. They were all of them red-headed, buck-toothed, and pale as ghosts" (p. 59). All, in other words, identical John Hunters! They are the pink and blue and green sparkles given off by Hunter in his death throe, cells carried into life by science in all of its audacity.

All three, however, are outside of nature; all three suffer matching illnesses, infirmities (as the doctor realizes) that reach beyond pure physical pain: "It was the souls of those three lost children that were unquiet, not their bodies, but I had no medicine for the human soul" (pp. 60, 65). It is a mock resurrection, one that cruelly mirrors the doctor's own barely surviving faith in the sense of existence. When one of the children succumbs to the superstition of the old mad farmwoman, the doctor falls back upon the science and the faith that *he* knows, and waits for fate to decide:

> My mind was full of wind, reeling and shrieking, but the whole world outside was calm, waiting without hope or plan, with the vast and sorrowful gentleness of a deathly sick horse.

> Then, very slowly, I lowered my hands toward the children.
> Their fingers closed around my wrists—fingers weirdly unawkward
> for their age—and when I'd gotten my hands around their backs
> and raised them to my chest, they clung to my ears, my glasses, my
> nostrils, as if no tornado on earth would shake them free. When the
> leering old woman reached out to them, joyful, they shrank, sucked
> in air, and screamed. They were out of the woods. (p. 68)

The children emerge from a strange sort of life-death-life sequence into a world suddenly changed and transmogrified, though still ruled by a whimsical Nature. It is a world still odd and full of mysteries—the world of southern Illinois—a world admitting of things contrary to order, a world that burlesques even the best of systems.

The world in "The Temptation of St. Ivo" is a younger one, the world of medieval monks and temptors. Brother Ivo is an artist, an illustrator of Biblical texts—an excellent one, the best—but he is humble and well aware of his human, Fred Clumly–like condition: "I am old. Fifty. My weight's in my miserable belly. My arms and legs are like a sickly old woman's, as white as potato sprouts under the cassock, and as flabby, as jiggly, as buttocks" (p. 70). Ivo's universe is ordered about the monastery and God's irreducible law that turns the world into a pattern, as intricate but as related as one of his drawings:

> The scheme of providence demands of us all that each man humbly
> perform his part, sing his own line in the terrestrial hymn, as the
> planets are singing, unheard, above us, and with charity forgive
> those to left and right when they falter. That may sound pompous,
> simpleminded, but it's true, or anyway I hope it's true. A man can
> go mad, discarding all tradition, reasoning out for himself the
> precise details of celestial and terrestrial law. I've been there. Live
> by rule, as all Nature does, illuminating the divine limits exactly as
> ink fills invisible lines. . . . We are merely instruments, and he who
> denies his condition will suffer. The world is a river, and he who
> resists the pressure of Time and Space will be overwhelmed by it.
> (p. 70)

Ivo's is the mind of the medieval cleric: ordered, devout, without questions. But it is not the mind of an artist, for it lacks imagination and the willingness to "resist the pressures of Time and Space."

This is why he hates Brother Nicholas: "Long-nosed, eagle-eyed, his flowing hair more black than a raven's . . . whispering, brazenly defying the rule" (p. 70). Nicholas is the third of Gardner's anarchists, a "devil" who teases Ivo toward violence and violation: "He willfully, pointlessly strikes out at me. He scorns all rule, defies all order for mere anarchy's sake" (p. 73). Nicholas challenges Ivo's graybearded concept of order and obedience; he dares Ivo to exercise his will and discover what lies beyond the monastery walls, filling his ears with black whispers: *"Brother Ivo, your rules are absurd! The order of the world is an accident. We can change it in an instant, simply by opening our throats and speaking"* (p. 75). Nicholas emphasizes the freedom of will and the grand possibilities of choice. He reduces it, in fact, to a matter of personal responsibility for Ivo by forcing him to a decision: *"Brother Ivo, I've decided to murder the Phoenix. I've discovered where it lives. . . . You don't believe in the Phoenix, Brother Ivo? I give you my word, you're the only man who can save the beast. . . . Do not be too hasty in judging my project, Brother Ivo. Many notable authors have spoken of the Phoenix, and holy men among them. . . . Despite all that, you deny the bird's existence. Very well! But it exists, nonetheless, and I have found it, and I mean to murder it. Prevent me if you can!"* (pp. 75–76) Brother Nicholas is out to destroy the Phoenix—its mythology and symbolism. The Phoenix is the emblem of God's order and design, and the emblem of Ivo's delicate workmanship, all interwoven, as Ivo realizes: "I remember when he looked at the Phoenix with which he makes fun of me now. A design as perfect—I give thanks to God—as anything I've done" (p. 77). It is also the symbol of the resurrected Christ, the promise and the hope: "And in the feathers of the bird, ingeniously, almost invisibly woven, the characters RESURREXIT" (p. 77). It drives Ivo to prayer and to an overblown consciousness of his sin, and bolsters his belief in the laxity of his "order" (the pun is unmistakable in Gardner, as unmistakably purposeful as his naming of Nicholas).

The matter is complicated by Nicholas's own claims on art; like Ivo he illuminates (another pun) the Biblical texts, and Ivo begins to wonder whether it is his own duty to save his brother-artist: "A man cannot be a master artist if he lies to himself, settles for illusions. . . . What if I, a fellow artist, was his soul's last human hope? What selfishness, then— what spiritual cowardice—that I refused him what he asked, a companionable voice!" (p. 78). Ivo must choose, as Nicholas once must have chosen: Do I keep silent, maintain my vows, obey the doctrine; or do I purposely speak out, break all pledges, and perhaps save a soul while contravening all tradition? Just how far should one extend the limits of human freedom?

> I can say this: He whispers to me of freedom. He tells me he's freed himself of all restraints—religions, philosophies, political systems. He tells me he means to so use up life that when death comes it will find in him nothing but shriveled dregs. . . . *You understand*

this, he whispers. *You're a man of keen intelligence, though afraid of life.* . . . "You're wrong," I would tell him. Not wrong in mere doctrine. Even if there were, as he claims, no Heaven or Hell, he would be wrong. A terrifying error. . . . Having broken down my defenses . . . he'll press on, break down my further defenses—teach me gluttony, lechery, sloth, despair. He'll hammer till I'm totally free, totally abandoned. . . . And so I cling to my creed, my rules, my traditions. If God is just, despairing man's cry will be answered. If not, what hope for any of us? So I reason it through for the hundredth time, and am no more satisfied than ever. Like a man hopelessly lost in a wilderness, I search the darkening sky, the pitchdark woods for some sign, and there is none. (p. 79)

Ivo is another human being coming to terms with the notion of existential freedom. If the skies are deserted, what difference does it make whether one opts for compliance or rebellion?

This is the question Ivo poses to his confessor. Ivo cries, "Rules are my only hope against his nihilism," and the confessor answers: "True, if it's nihilism. On the other hand, as you've suggested, if all his acts are a devious plea for help—if his terror in an abandoned universe is as great as your own this moment—then surely you'd be right to break the rule. It would be the act of a saint, a soul whose purity is beyond the rules that protect and keep the rest of us" (p. 82). The fact that it is Brother Nicholas behind the confessional curtain does not change the essence of the challenge or the promise. It is *action* which will drive Ivo to saint-hood (just as Taggert Hodge wishes to make a saint of Millie, and makes one of Luke); it is evil, in all of its tortuous ambiguity, that tugs ordinary man to something blessed. Remember, it is *St.* Ivo—and he wins his sainthood by seeking to save the Phoenix, by *breaking,* not following, holy law.[9]

So he ventures into the forest (as we already know, the Gardneresque haunt of sinners and anarchists), anxious and crushed with despair: "I abandon hope. I have lost Brother Nicholas, though I'm by no means confident that he has lost me. . . . I am afraid, sick unto death with fear. I have no faith that the universe is good, as I have thought. Yet I am here. I have no choice" (p. 87). It is the exact situation that the Reverend Pick finds himself in, and that which all men and women tested by a possibly empty universe find themselves confronting. Nor is he alone in the forest. As tradition would have it, there is a knight, Gardner's archetypal symbol of virtue and hope (crazy-headed or not), pursuing the "nerve-wracking business of knight-errantry."[10] Together they try to outface the darkness and the silence, faith and nobility allied against an indefinable evil:

"There's something in there," he whispers, and closes his visor. We peer into the darkness. It seems to me that I see Brother Nicholas standing motionless in the blackness of the forest eaves. He stares straight at us, smiling his mysterious, scornful smile.

Nothing means anything, the figure whispers.

Faster than lightning, the dagger has flown from the gauntleted hand. We do not hear it strike, consumed by moss, dead trees, the darkness at the heart of things. *Nothing means anything*, the forest whispers. The knight is trembling. The face still seems to smile at us. But it is not a face, we know now—some trick of light—and the voice is not the Devil's voice but some heavy old animal in its lair, unable to sleep because of age.

"Mistake," my defender whispers. (p. 89)

Perhaps there is something in there, perhaps not. What matters is our willingness to break free of an aged and rickety system, and at least peer into the forest, even if it means breaking a few of the old rules. Gardner is not counseling anarchy here, but a sort of virtuous antinomianism which has as its base an authentic and tested ethic. By going to the forest, Ivo both exercises his will and liberates his imagination; he joins belief (his own religious tradition) with vision (the knightly perseverance) and emerges with an aesthetic and a canonization.

This idea of the forsaken universe is taken up once more in "The Warden," a Kafkaesque, Borgesian tale set somewhere in the vastness of a nowhere land. The universe becomes a prison, and "the Warden has given up every attempt to operate the prison by the ancient regulations. Conditions grow monstrous, yet no one can bring them to the Warden's attention" (p. 90). Vortrab, the chief guard, can no longer draw any sort of response from behind the Warden's door; he can only knock and listen to the pacing that stretches on into the night. It is an absurd place where guards game and laze about and prisoners are held for no crime or reason. In the bowels of the prison lies an old, blind, sticklike man, a professor (or so he's called by Heller, the man who knows him best) who speaks oracularly upon mind and matter:

There are gradations of matter of which man knows nothing, the grosser impelling the finer, the finer pervading the grosser. . . . The ultimate, unparticled matter not only permeates all things but impels all things, and thus *is* all things within itself. This matter is God. . . . There are two bodies, the rudimental and the complete, corresponding with the two conditions of the worm and the butterfly. What we call "death" is the painful metamorphosis. Our present incarnation is progressive, preparatory, temporary. Our future is perfected, ultimate, immortal. The ultimate life is the full design. . . . Only in the rudimental life is there any experience of pain, for pain is the product of impediments afforded by number, complexity, and substantiality. That is not to say that the rudimental life is bad, however painful in a given case. All things, after all, are good or bad only by comparison. To be happy at any one point we must have suffered at the same. Never to suffer would be never to have been blessed. But in the inorganic life, pain cannot be; thus the necessity for the organic. (pp. 96–97)

There is no immateriality, says the Professor, only successively finer degrees of matter. All—in life and in death—is body, flesh, and bones. Cells do not die and give way to spirit, but are refined into a purer form. Moreover, pain is a necessary part of material existence; it defines our lives and gives reason to our happiness. The idea is nearly Sufic in its progression through finer (more spiritual?) levels of matter,[11] and the Professor seems to be in a transition stage, somewhere beyond pain and suffering, entering the complete and "inorganic" body.

Such thoughts naturally breed uneasiness and stir sleeping ghosts. Vortrab attempts to deny the Professor's metaphysics, but the ideas (and the haunting, strangely southern Illinois landscape) tug at his reluctant imagination and pull him toward vision: "I had a feeling of standing outside myself, as if time and space had stopped and in one more second would be extinguished. As quickly as the queer impression came it passed, faded back into shadow like a fish. And for some reason impossible to name, I was left with a feeling of indescribable, senseless horror, a terrible emptiness, as if I'd penetrated something, broken past the walls of my consciousness and discovered . . . what?" (p. 99) In the instant that Vortrab releases his hold on consciousness and on material, worldly demands, he jumps outside of the bounds of time and space. It is exactly what happens to Fred Clumly and to Henry Soames and to so many of Gardner's characters: the sudden discovery of the power of the imagination.

Yet Vortrab is not a man given to such fancies, suppressing imagination instead of encouraging it. Those who let their thoughts run free, those who are characters of imagination, Vortrab brands as crazy and wrong-headed. It is a trait he cannot understand in his own father, "a foolish old man, but one with all his sensibilities refined by landscape painting" (a hint at the story to follow, a fore-image of John Napper?). The old man insists (perversely, Vortrab contends) upon confusing the Professor with the long-dead Josef Mallin, imaginatively resurrecting the anarchist, "a nihilist, destroyer of churches, murderer of medical doctors" (note the echoes of earlier Gardner anarchists in book 1) from an ugly and bloody past:

The period of Mallin's imprisonment . . . was a terrible strain on all of us. He was a brilliant devil, black-haired and handsome and deadly as a snake, so cunning at bribing or persuading the guards that at last the Warden himself took charge of holding him. It was shortly after his death that the Warden began that interminable pacing in his chamber. Mallin's execution, I might add, was unpleasant. His crimes were the worst of the three main kinds of which the laws speak, so that, after the decapitation, his head was thrown to the sawdust in the village square, to be eaten by dogs, as the law requires. (p. 101)

The father understands the effect of the dead upon the living. He sees, through lunatic eyes, the psychic connection between Mallin and the Warden: "The minute the axe comes down on Joe Mallin, the Warden's life will go fsst!" (p. 102). He knows why the Warden paces behind his door, unresponsive, obsessed. He knows of the existence of ghosts, of the life that runs on beyond reason. As Gardner has maintained, the father is an artist and a creator who has experienced the madness which is art: "I admit . . . that I've never seen a ghost myself, that I know of. . . . But I know a little something of states of entrancement. Sometimes when you're painting, a kind of spell comes over you, and you know—you positively *know*—that there's no chance of erring with the picture at hand. You're nailed directly to the universe, and the same force that moves in the elm tree is moving your brush" (p. 102). The father haunts his own son just as Mallin haunts the Warden. He echoes the Professor's very words, conjures up the emotions that strike at Vortrab, and pierces his consciousness with the violence of a fist through glass.

What is more, the old man is the only person who understands what motivated Mallin and his wanton, anarchical viciousness: "The unpleasant facts of life, [Mallin] claims, charge the human soul with longing. They drive a man to make up a world that's better than ours. But that better world is mere illusion, says Mallin; and illusion, being false, a mere cowardly lie, is as foul as actuality. So he goes at the universe with dynamite sticks.—It's a natural mistake" (p. 114). The anarchist is merely the artist who finds illusion contemptible. The artist creates a better world, content with his counterfeit; the anarchist finds all worlds—real and painted—absurd and abhorrent, and so destroys. Josef Mallin is the bomber in "Pastoral Care," the mad geneticist of "The Ravages of Spring," and the long-down-the-line descendant of Brother Nicholas in "The Temptation of St. Ivo." He is Gardner's fictional anarchist-clone. One can either choose, says Gardner, to play the artist and create, improve, and believe in the value of this life; or one can choose to deny the worth of this world and set at its foundations with hand, bomb, pen, or brush, bent upon bringing it all to the ground.

Even Heller can sense the oddity and ultimate preposterousness of it all. When Vortrab finally lets on that he has not seen the Warden in months, Heller laughs and asks, "Why, then . . . what makes you think he's there?" (p. 110). He admits to his abandonment and to the fact that no one is in charge. There is no one to order the burial of the Professor, who has finally passed from the organic to the inorganic life, yet Heller takes charge, telling Vortrab: "My people . . . have a long history of dealing with absurd situations. Leave everything to me" (p. 112). Heller knows something of the folly of a world divided between mind and matter, spirit and flesh. He has heard the Professor's talk for too long not to have invested some of his faith in the crepuscular; at the Professor's funeral, when all the ghosts convene (eleven dark-cloaked Jews, the Warden with a forehead shot away, and somewhere, I am sure, the spirit of Josef Mallin), Heller tries to persuade the empirically minded Vortrab of the possibility of a ghost race, dead spirits returning angry to a world that insisted upon the reality of "sticks and stones." Vortrab holds fast to his stubborn realism—or he holds at least until he sees the vision of the Warden, a dead man haunted to the point of suicide. Such things change a person: "I no longer bother to deny that I am frightened, hopelessly baffled, but neither do I pretend to believe that sooner or later he will answer my knock. I need rest, a change of air, time to sort out my thoughts" (p. 119).

So there they sit, Vortrab and Heller, guarding a prison that grows more absurd with each day. When a peddler tries to pawn off a book (a ghostly pirate of Sartre's *Being and Nothingness*)[12] attacking humanity's puny attempt to deal with the world's duality, Vortrab runs him off with his walking stick and muses:

> [Heller] thinks I'm mad, of course. Each new regulation I bring "from the Warden," each new pardon or death sentence, increases his despair. I understand his feelings. I do what I can for him. "If Order has value, you and I are the only hope!" I whisper. He nods, mechanically, stroking his beard.
>
> I worry about him. Late at night, when he should be asleep, I hear Heller pacing, occasionally pausing, deep in thought. (p. 119)

The pacing goes on. What Mallin was to the Warden, so the Professor seems to become to Heller. Only Vortrab, the unimaginative one, fails to see what is happening, fails to see the futility of the illusion (it is an unartistic illusion). It is as if Heller knows that he is doomed; he knows nothing will change, that Vortrab and all the other "stubborn realists"

will continue to insist upon a confused and inflexible kind of order that
fits upon this world like an old uniform on a man grown well-bellied. It is
the kind of order that kills art and makes it a ghost and a memory.

Not until we reach "John Napper Sailing through the Universe" does
Gardner offer us a complete picture of how the artistic imagination makes
its way through a disordered and deadly universe. Napper, as a painter,
has made the journey from negation to affirmation, has made it with a
genuine sense of suffering and cost. It is evident in his work. The "old"
John Napper, as Gardner discovers, is blanketed in shadow and bleak
denial:

> From out of the closet and under the bed we dragged some old
> John Napper paintings. They were a shock: dark, furious,
> intellectual, full of scorn and something suicidal. Mostly black with
> struggles of light, losing. He'd been through all the movements,
> through all the tricks, and he thoroughly understood what he was
> doing—a third-generation master painter. Understood everything,
> it seemed to me, but why he kept fighting instead of slitting his
> wrists. No sense of the clownish in the universal sorrow. No sense
> of dressing up, putting on gray spats, for the funeral. (p. 124)

This is the pretransitional Napper, the Napper (like the Professor) still
going through the necessary suffering and living the rudimental life. He
has yet to begin to "sail."

The transitional work of Napper reveals a change of attitude and aesthetic: he has gone Romantic. Of one such midway work, Gardner
writes: "It had Turner things in it—illusions of movement, sultriness,
light seen through cloud, the faintest suggestion of a ship, trouble. The
universe was churning" (p. 30). The world has suddenly become less
morose and more hopeful. The key is in the agonizingly slow breakthrough of light; it is the symbol of faith working its way out of the black
morass of nihilism and hands-in-the-air acquiescence. The world broods
one moment, smiles the next; the trick is to catch the brief reflection
between the changes.

Not until Napper grows completely lunatic, "full of joy, mad Irish,"
does he move on to that world of pure imagination where happiness is a
blend of pain and release from pain. It is there on his canvases where, as
Gardner sees,

> at the center of all that joyful movement that shadows away toward
> not quite joyful—the face hangs perfectly motionless, holy. . . .
> He'd gone to the pit, in those Paris paintings, fighting for his life,
> squeezing the blood from his turnip of a world to hunt out the

> secret life in it, and there was none there. He'd hounded light—not
> just visual light—straining every muscle of body and mind to get
> down to what was real, what was absolute; beauty not as someone
> else had seen it but beauty he could honestly find himself, and what
> he'd gotten was a picture of the coal pocket. (p. 133)

That vision of light must come after one works his way through the darkness. It is an earned vision, says Gardner, one that signals a metamorphosis (as the Professor called it). An untested faith is naïve and shallow and washes out in the first storm. Neither must one stop at an unchallenged despair; as Napper has learned, art consists of a struggling—intellectual, emotional, physical—with the darkest elements of existence. In the end, also like Napper, you may not actually come upon the light, but you will find something there that is worthwhile. It drives you to madness, an excess of imagination and feeling that leads you to "see the best in everything." The artist creates the world *ex nihilo* (not, as Hunter says in "The Ravages of Spring," "*Nihilo ex nihilo*"); it is an imposing responsibility, one that can take a man to drink or to anarchy, or even to a redefined belief in the light at the "world's dark center." What Gardner deplores is the denial of imagination in the pursuit of order; if anyone is crazy, it's the person who labors to maintain a system that is colorless and broken down and beyond its time.

This is part of the lesson of book 2, "Tales of Queen Louisa." The stories in this section (and the story "Trumpeter," published elsewhere) are fantasies, fairy tales that are more akin to Gardner's children's stories than to his other adult fiction. Furthermore, Gardner does not mean for us to take them *too* seriously; we should first enjoy them, and *then* think about them. We should approach them with all the capacity for belief and wonder of a child, but also with the adult consciousness of their "made-upness." If we are going to accept the world as it is, says Gardner, we must accept as well its mystery and improbability and fancy. We must use, in other words, the imagination that many of us abandoned when we grew solemnly out of childhood.

In the first story, "Queen Louisa," we are introduced to the mad queen—mad beyond reasonable doubt, a person who shifts between woman, lizard, and toad with all the facility of an unfettered imagination. She dismisses the shadowy worries that afflict her by providing them with nothing to stick to; she is the symbol of a consciousness that is basically artistic and full of bright vision and light. She is a woman who works by intuition—"These hunches of hers were infallible"—and by a graced lunacy.

When the kingdom (momentarily without its king) is threatened,

Queen Louisa rides out to meet the destroyer-witch who haunts an abandoned mystery. What she finds is that

> the garden's stone walls were encased in ice, as was every tree and
> shrub and leftover flower stalk. But in the center of the garden
> there was a glorious rosebush in triumphant bloom, such bloom as
> would hardly be natural on even the warmest summer day. And
> beside the bush there was a horrible ugly old witchlike person who
> was trying to cut down the rosebush with an axe. With every swipe
> she took, the trunk of the bush grew wider and stronger, and the
> roses bloomed more brightly. At the feet of the ugly witchlike
> person, an old red hound lay whimpering and whining. (p. 145)

The rose bush is an emblem of virtue and regenerative good; random
attempts at evil inadvertently breed beauty, and are powerless against a
healthy imagination. The witch is an anarchist and an existentialist:

> The witchlike person laughed. "You see, my ancient enemy," she
> cried, "your whole life has been a terrible mistake! The forces of
> evil do exist! Ha ha!" Words cannot describe the unearthly horror
> of that final "Ha ha!" She raised the axe in one hand and brandished
> it. "We're cosmic accidents!" cried the witchlike person. "Life is
> gratuitous, it has no meaning till we make one up by our intensity.
> That is why these gentle monks have joined me in seeking to wreak
> havoc on the kingdom. Not for personal gain. Ha ha! Ha ha! But to
> end the boredom! To end all those mornings of waking up vaguely
> irritable! Ha ha!" She sidled toward the queen. "I have seduced
> your husband. What do you think of that? I have filled him with the
> feeling that life *is* meaningful, if only because it can be thrown
> away." (pp. 146, 151)

When the knights rush in to slaughter the witch and her wolves, Louisa
halts everything with a loud "Stop!"—and all *is* stopped, though not
explained, because she is the queen and that is all that matters. What she
does not tell them is that the whole scene was a creation and an artifice:
"She'd admit, in all fairness, that perhaps the rosebush *was* cut down,
since she was insane and could never know anything for sure, and perhaps
the whole story was taking place in a hotel in Philadelphia" (p. 151).

Louisa (and Gardner) are playing fairy tale tricks (the sort of tricks
Gardner devises in *In the Suicide Mountains,* his adultish children's tale),
tricks that turn a dog into a king and a pack of wolves into a band of
monks and a witch into a lady-of-waiting. The story comes close to
self-conscious, self-parodying fiction, with Gardner perhaps even drawing himself in at the very end: "The boy beside the coachman said: 'Isn't

this a marvelous tale to be in?' The coachman, who was silver-haired and wise, gave his nephew a wink. 'You barely made it, laddie!' " (p. 152). Queen Louisa has the artist's mentality which rests upon a benign madness—the sort of madness evident earlier in John Napper. She can forgive malevolence and rebellious youth because her mind makes significant leaps of reason. She need not make all of the connections, touch all of the logical points of progression: the gaps she fills in with imagination.

She is a vivid contrast to her husband, King Gregor—or *Bold* King Gregor "as he liked to call himself and as he'd tentatively suggested from time to time that he might not unfittingly be called, but it had never caught on"—who is reasonable and rational and overburdened with the responsibilities of state. He is pestered and pricked with madness and folly (thus the title, "King Gregor and the Fool"), and it is affecting his work—which is unfortunate, since

> he dearly loved his work, and he was good at it. That was why he spent too much time at it, as the Fool kept pointing out, and tended to neglect his family. No doubt it was true that it was because of his neglect that Mad Queen Louisa spent more and more of her time these days as an enormous toad, though in her natural shape she was the most beautiful queen in the world. And presumably it was why his daughter—if it was true that, as Queen Louisa insisted, he had a daughter—had run away from home and only recently returned, having gotten herself into trouble and having no one to turn to. (p. 153)

Gregor is an orderly man surrounded by chaos. He finds life "baffling," a conglomeration of idiot ways, and his one wish is "to introduce, in his own small way, some trifling note of sense" into a kingdom that is rapidly splitting into silliness and skinny-dipping.

The poor man cannot even fight a proper war. The field is a mess, ranks are broken like disparate parts of a jigsaw puzzle, and bodies are hewn apart with no sense of medieval, chivalric propriety. To make matters worse (or perhaps for a moment better), Queen Louisa decides to visit her husband and see exactly what it is a king does during his day. In anticipation of the Queen's appearance, Gregor and his foe, Just King John, hastily reorder the field, realigning scattered troops and dragging corpses and horseflesh into the cover of the woods. When Louisa approaches, the signals are given and the armies quicken:

> And now like earthshaking thunder or the rumble of a vast, dark flood came the deafening rumble of the horses' hooves as the armies came plunging with bright lances lifted to strike at each other's

throats. Horses neighed, demonic, stretching their powerful legs for more speed, and the quarter-ton lances came gracefully dropping from nearly upright position toward the deadly straight-on position of the hit. Violently, bravely, down the field they came roaring, their flags wildly whipping, and suddenly, louder than a mountain exploding, Queen Louisa yelled: "*Stop!*"

The horses skidded in alarm. The lances dropped past hit position and stabbed into the ground and lifted up the knights like pole vaulters and left them hanging straight up, kicking wildly and trying to let go.

"What have you done?" King Gregor screamed.

Queen Louisa said with a baffled look, her white fingers trembling, "Listen, they could have *killed* each other!"

"That's the *idea!*" King Gregor screamed.

"Grotesque!" cried King John, and beat the ground with his fists.

Queen Louisa tipped her head, seemed to think about it. Slowly, she turned her lovely face to examine her husband's face, which was contorted with rage and awful humiliation.

"Gregor," she said, "you people are all crazy." (p. 165)

Louisa knows evil and stupidity when she sees it, and in her beautiful insanity she can stop it with a word (remember the rosebush and the witch). Even her ally, the Fool, senses the ludicrousness of the kingly business of killing, and circulates a couplet that fairly giggles:

> You think I'm small because I'm lazy;
> But big brave knights get killed. That's crazy!?

It sends King Gregor over the edge, demanding the Fool's head. When the Fool claims biblical origin for the poem, Gregor calls in King John (sleepy-eyed and in nightcap) to rule upon the issue (John is known to be a biblical scholar). And Just King John for once lives up to his name, siding with the lunatic element in pronouncing: "Yes! . . . The passage is distinctly Biblical. Loosely." John's decision restores a bit of order and peace to the kingdom and sanctions Louisa's sweet, solving madness. Gregor is a decent and high-minded man, but he is caught up in the transition of systems and institutions, and he causes disasters. Louisa tries to turn the world humane by affirming life and art—and you *have* to be a little crazy to do that.

Only a crazy woman would pluck a peasant stranger-woman and call her her daughter, which in the story "Muriel" we discover did happen. Muriel is a sane girl who, by an act of chance insanity, sees her life and circumstances changed in an instant. Gone are the poverty and humility and the wan existence—but "the best thing about suddenly having been turned into a princess was that Muriel escaped all those tiresome and ultimately dangerous ideas that her friends imagined it was necessary to maintain" (p. 171). These are the ideas that turn pennilessness into a religion and interpret power as a purely repressive, political fact. As Muriel insightfully tells her peasant friends, describing Queen Louisa: "She's a very fine person, in whichever shape. She organizes great charity balls and calls off wars and heaven knows what. She's majestic, really. I believe she's a kind of saint" (p. 181). Such ideas become dangerous when they are organized and lead toward anarchy, which is something with which Muriel (*née* Tanya) is familiar.

She has been to the forest, and as anyone who reads Gardner knows, "no one ever came to the great, dark forest but rapists and anarchists and outlaws." She has met—been abducted by, in fact—the grim, murderous Vrokror, anarchist-pirate. Yet he has a certain sympathetic appeal that Muriel finds winning: "No man on earth was ever more beautiful and tragic, though certainly he was possessed by the Devil" (p. 187). He is "angry and malevolent" but he has "suffered more anguish than have most men of eighty." He is a man turned sadly wrong by misfortune and the accidents of life, and even the possibility of Muriel's love cannot save him at the moment: "Tanya . . . within our lifetime I will destroy all governments, all ideas of station. Peasantry I will make an obscure, archaic word. . . . I have penetrated the grotesque stupidity of things as they are" (pp. 187–88).

What is most pernicious about Vrokror's way of thinking is its ability to trap the old peasant friends of Muriel, turning their heads toward revolution and destruction. The confrontation between king and rebel is inevitable; mayhem prevails, the peasants lie battered and bleeding, and Vrokror escapes (for a purpose, we find later). Only Queen Louisa can put it all back together again, as once more by a vast act of imagination she brings everyone back into the fold, turning peasants into royalty, shepherds and milkmaidens into princes and princesses. No one dies, though all suffer, and Louisa is not about to let anyone off without a lesson:

> "People with tiresome and dangerous ideas should be switched,"
> she said, and sent out for a willow switch. She did the switching
> herself. Everyone but Muriel and King Gregor was switched, even
> Madame Logre, though she loudly protested.
> "I never did a thing!" cried Madame Logre, and wholeheartedly
> believed it.
> "That," said Queen Louisa, "is the most tiresome and ultimately
> dangerous idea of all!" (pp. 193–94)

Vrokror is left hissing on a mountainside, the useless anarchist in a magical kingdom. As Louisa says, "All error begins . . . with soreheads" (p. 194). If you're going to be an anarchist, recommend Louisa and John Gardner, you had best be a "joyful anarchist," one who sees the possibilities that exist for a positive disorder. It is always better to build than to tear down—it makes people happier.

Gardner concluded this section with a story entitled "Trumpeter," which was published separately in *Esquire* in December 1976, and later included in *The Art of Living and Other Stories*. Trumpeter is Queen Louisa's dog, a silent observer and reasoner of the ways of the Queen and her kingdom. Trumpeter knows that the original princess has died, that Muriel-Tanya is a substitute offered by Louisa's fine distraction, yet he also understands the sort of blurred reason behind the Queen's actions, understands "that in making them her children, as perhaps they were indeed, since the life of a dog is but a heartbeat, so to speak, in the long span of man, the queen had brought happiness to a kingdom that had suffered, before that, grave troubles—peasants against royalty, 'madness against madness,' as the minstrel said: an obscure saying; but Trumpeter, in his heart, understood it."[13] This "madness against madness" is at the heart of the "Tales of Queen Louisa"—the idea of proper and improper forms of madness; the one makes you an anarchist, the other makes you an artist. (Note how in this wonderful kingdom, even the dog can intuit, can feel "in his heart," the rightness of things.)

All that is left to perfect the kingdom is the marrying of Muriel, and Louisa (after opening up the treasury to pirates and thieves, thus eliminating greed and want and cutpursery) delivers her masterstroke: she pairs the princess with "Vrokror the Terrible" (he, too, must have a title it seems), displaced and exiled anarchist, a man reduced to living "all alone on the top of a mountain, eating tundra plants" (p. 83). Louisa yanks Vrokror out of his isolation, matches him with the beauteous princess Muriel, and turns the kingdom into a stylized bit of lawlessness, a crystal vase: "The palace was full of light—beyond the windows, thick darkness. Nothing was wrong; nothing could go wrong. It was a balanced kingdom, the only kingdom in the world where art reigned supreme" (p. 87). Louisa is the consummate artist. She is physical light and vision; her lunacy is sublime and inspired, and touched with an humane intuition that urges her toward sainthood (Muriel's earlier judgment is exactly on the mark). She draws together opposites, synthesizes, and comes up with the ideal measure of compromise and hope. She is the Gardner aesthetic personified: the transforming, transmogrifying, light-bearing artist.

In "The King's Indian" we see the Gardner aesthetic fictionalized. Gardner borrows his framework from the masters of the nineteenth century, adopts themes and ideas from the "great tradition," and works out the complexities. He begins with the standard "boy at sea" metaphor that worked so well for Melville and for Poe, and constructs his story line around it. To tell the story he hires a Coleridgian "loon" mariner (the aged Jonathan Upchurch) who spills his tale like an expiation and who keeps his guest awake deep into the morning. There is even a hovering angel who supplies the frowns and smirks and ale, and who lets us know that it is not only the mariner who is telling the tale. It is the artistic triad of artist (Upchurch), critic (guest), and muse (angel), all exemplified and all borne into life.

The young, innocent hero, Jonathan Upchurch, is a lad struggling for an understanding of the ways and the workings of the universe. He leans toward philosophy, a self-conscious intellectual; when he finds himself adrift and hoodwinked (so the symbolism begins), he muses:

> I looked at the name, laid in gold on the bow, the Jolly Independent, and the irony made me burst out laughing. It was a self-regarding Byronic laugh, soul-tortured and metaphysical, at first. But even as I laughed a change came over me. Two things came stealing to my mind at once: the sea-dogs had sold me someone else's boat, so it was mine and not-mine, like the whole of Creation—that was one of them—and the other was that, gazing out toward the eastern horizon, feeling the motion of the waves and wind, I wanted to be there, with Plato and Plotinus, despite all my sensible talk about southern Illinois. In landlessness alone lies the highest truth, shoreless, indefinite as God! thought I. Better to perish in that howling infinite than be . . . something or other.[14]
> (p. 212)

The investigation into metaphysical freedom has begun: Just what is the nature of personal freedom? To what extent can one exercise one's freedom? What are the limits? Gardner pursues the same intellectual quarry as his nineteenth-century predecessors.

He is also concerned, like Poe and Coleridge, with the distinction between appearance and reality and with the powers of the imagination. As a youngster, Upchurch learned dramatically what the imagination can do when pushed far enough, when he witnessed the mesmeric abilities of "the infamous Dr. Flint . . . a great gray craggy Adirondack of a man" (p. 199). Flint takes his daughter Miranda, spellbound, coursing back through time, back to the ancients and the precivilized, and the trip proves nearly too much for young Jonathan:

> I began to feel something going wrong with my vision. I clung to my parents. Great gabbling birds flew all around me, purest white,

darting, dipping, plunging, screeching, their wingtips stretching
from wall to wall as they warred, all eyes, steel talons, and beaks,
with the writhing serpents on the balcony around me. I screamed. I
had seen all my life (I was then about nine) queer shadows at the
edge of my bad left eye. Fraud though Lord knows he had to be,
Flint had made them solidify a little. I was now convinced those
shadows were real as the Parthenon, and a man like Flint, if he ever
got his claws on me, could populate my world with such creatures.
I'd have none of it! . . . I became that instant a desperate man, a
fanatic. No mystic voyages for Jonathan Upchurch, says I to
myself. No fooling around with those secret realms. (pp. 200–201)

Flint's defiance of time and space is horrifying—it is the nightmare, fantasy world that exists at that outermost reach of the imagination. It is all very well that Upchurch pledges himself to pragmatism and common sense, but Fate has already written his ticket. His voyage is to be incontrovertibly mystic and terrifying and perplexing.

The ship that picks up the stranded and unconscious Jonathan, the whaling ship *Jerusalem* (again, Gardner is having his little joke), is a death ship, ill-omened and ill-crewed: "Ye've jined with a company of deadmen, ye see; deadmen pursuing a deadman down into his grave and, could be, through it" (p. 216). The mates are philosophical and suspicious, the Captain (Captain Dirge!) a laconic, gloomy man propped up by the blind lunatic Jeremiah. It is a ship meant to give lessons to a fresh, walleyed boy, and Jonathan learns an important one very early on: "A man mustn't jump to conclusions about what's real in this world and what's mere presentation" (p. 238). What appears to be true is proven false, sham, pretense. The worst thing a man can chase is absolutism, whether it be the absolute faith of Billy More (the Buddian symbol of virtue and personal salvation for Upchurch) or the absolute egotism of Captain Dirge-Flint. The world is too variable and too surprising for certainty.

But Jonathan is after the answer, and he hunts it to its weird and forbidding end. He begins a pessimist and a skeptic, a proper attitude aboard a ship like the *Jerusalem:*

I began to have an uneasy feeling—residue, perhaps, of my reading
of Boethius—that my seeming freedom on the still, dark whaler was
a grotesque illusion, that sneaking alone through hostile darkness I
was watched by indifferent, dusty eyes, a cosmic checker, a being as
mechanical as any automaton displayed in the Boston theaters. . . .
Mad as it may sound, I had to concentrate with all my might to
resist the temptation to shout or kick something over and force
them to reveal themselves. . . . It was that that dizzied me, I told

myself—made me populate the ship with a ghostly audience. Adrift in a universe grown wholly unfamiliar, I'd been suddenly ambushed by the dark vastness which suggests to the mind of a healthy man the magnificence of God and of all his Creation but suggested to me, and very powerfully, too, mere pyrotechnic pointlessness. (pp. 232–33)

Jonathan is a mind severed from experience and memory. He is afloat on a microcosm that is mad, gone crazy with the force of a lost imagination. On the *Jerusalem,* reality is created and destroyed by Flint (masquerading as the ironically blind Jeremiah), whose mind has been twisted by his creative brilliance; he goes from mere entertainment to crime to Faustian willfulness. He turns the universe into a mechanism, an "automaton" to be manipulated.

In such a world, a person has two choices: if one is dull, he falls back upon intellect (i.e., intellectual metaphysics); if he is imaginative, he relies upon intuition (i.e., emotional metaphysics)—which is what Jonathan does. When the universe becomes inexplicable, says Jonathan, when "there is more in this world than philosophy dreams of," play a hunch:

A hunch is a religious experience, an escape from mere intellect into reality, home of the soul. Put it this way: The mushroom- and root-eating savages of the South Pacific have queer experiences, learning out of conversation with lizards, or from the scent of wildflowers, answers to questions which couldn't be answered by any means that old scoundrel Locke would countenance. Time and Space become impish, now ingenious and full of wit, like Ariel, now sullen and ill-mannered, like Caliban in a funk.[15] Effect precedes cause, causes and effects which are spatially remote refuse to be sensibly separate in time. The physical world turns crepuscular. . . . All we think and believe, in short, is foolish prejudice, even if some of it happens to be true (which seems to me unlikely). Or to make it all still more altiloquent: Human consciousness, in the ordinary case, is the artificial wall we build of perceptions and *con*ceptions, a hull of words and accepted opinions that keeps out the vast, consuming sea: It shears my self from all outside business, including the body I walk in but muse on the same as I do on a three-legged dog or an axe-handle, a slippery wild Indian or king at his game of chess. A mushroom or one raw emotion (such as love) can blast that wall to smithereens. I become a kind of half-wit, a limitless shadow too stupid to work out a mortgage writ, but I am also the path of the stars, the rightful monarch of Nowhere. I become, that instant, the King's Indian: Nothing is waste, nothing unfecund. The future is

the past, the past is present to my senses. I gaze at the dark Satanic
mills, the sludge-thick streams. I shake my head. They vanish.
(pp. 241–42)

This is Gardner's clearest description of the subjective power of his emotional metaphysic. It is also perhaps his most colorful and rhetorical
expression of the state of the artistic mind. The artist, overwhelmed by
emotion and imagination, becomes the King's Indian, illustrator of the
world's mysteries, explicator of the illegible texts.

On one side of that wall are the Wolffs and Wilkinses and Flints of this
world, chained securely by their anarchy and existentialism and naturalistic pride. Their laws are crude and clawlike and encourage the animal
nature in man:

1. Distrust Reason
2. Deny Equality
3. Succeed by Lies
4. Govern by Violence
5. Oppose All Law but Biological Law (p. 299)

Order (says Wolff) is naturalistic, a Machiavellian dominance by sheer
force. Or order may be self-imposed, an anarchical and existential order
(as Wilkins proposes): "My acts add up to nothing. No Heaven, no Hell,
mere chain of events neither guilty nor glorious. . . . I vow nothing.
Nothing. There are no stable principles a man can make vows by, and
there are no predictable people, only men like myself. A whole world
crammed with cringing half-breeds unfit for the woods or the gabled
house" (p. 302–3). The world becomes mere impulse and whim; the
distinctions between rape and love, death and creation vanish with the
obliteration of the moral tradition. Or order is the quest for individual,
"absolute vision," a quest that almost invariably ends in individual and
absolute annihilation. Such is the fate of old Flint, spontaneously consumed (like his ancestors in Poe and Melville) in the flames of his own
pride and shamelessness, "the daring assertion, always mistaken, that man
is God—a high office otherwise left empty" (p. 243). These, Gardner
contends, are all the wrong answers to the right questions: "The universe
is indifferent. If you decide that the world's a shadow, then you become a
pure utilitarian, a pure materialist. If you refuse to play games, you don't
say there is a God or there isn't a God, and you leave it all open, and you
can't function as a human being without other human beings—this is the
only security we can reach."[16] Gardner says it another way in "The King's
Indian": "What we claim we desire in this vale of tears is resplendent
truth, distinct bits of certainty that ring like doubloons, but that very

claim is, like everything else in the universe, a skinner, a bamboozle, an ingenious little trick for out-sharping the card-shark gods" (p. 258). It is the Melvillean vision of "God and truth as Confidence Man."

Thus, what survives is love and human interdependence, and the ability to accept a specific amount of lunacy—personal and cosmic. Beauty sometimes turns ugly, but there is always the hope of redemption through love and imagination and art. Everything plummets and perishes but "raw emotion," which rises (like Ivo's sainthood and Louisa's found-ling family) from the world's iniquity. Miranda and Jonathan-Ferdinand reconstruct their "brave, new world" from the hopes of the old; the birds circle, the wind fills the sails, and Melville's ghost rises once more to lead them on to a different dream. Gardner's metaphorical ship of fools (a metaphor now ragged from use) sails by the barest of luck and good chance, and under the grace of the white-plumed Holy Ghost, who sagely warns: "Hang on thyself, . . . thou fucking lunatic" (p. 323). All one *can* do, indeed, is "hang on," remain humble, and save oneself through an ordained madness. It is the same lesson Gardner teaches in his poetic epic *Jason and Medeia,* in which he seems to anticipate the perfect postscript to his collection of tales and dreams. It comes with the culmination of Jason's pain and terror upon the *Argo,* the world finally comprehended:

> Or if not the gods, then this:
> the power struggling to be born, a creature larger than man,
> though made of men; not to be outfoxed, too old for us;
> terrible and final, by nature neither just nor unjust,
> but wholly demanding, so that no man made any part of that beast
> dare think of self, as I did. For if living says anything,
> it's this: We sail between nonsense and terrible absurdity—
> sail between stiff, coherent system which has nothing to do
> with the universe (the stiffness of numbers, grammatical constructions)
> and the universe, which has nothing to do with the names we give
> or seize our leverage by. Let man take his reasoning place,
> expecting nothing, since man is not the invisible player
> but the player's pawn. Seize the whole board, snatch after godhood,
> and all turns useless waste. Such is my story.[17]

It is the world made clear by art through the collaborative effort of reason and imagination. "The King's Indian"—and *The King's Indian*—are deli-cate reflections of this world in all of its magic and shadow and ambigu-ity, like a hundred revolving mirrors giving off a blur of the same image: the human being as the King's pawn, the King's Indian.

Chapter VIII

October Light

For nothing on earth is more dry-rot wasted hollow
Than righteousness.
                    —"Art, Life, and Aunt Etwell"

October Light appears to have had more "reasons" for its publication than any other of Gardner's works. As Gardner once explained: "I heard that everyone else was doing a Bicentennial book, so I thought I'd better do one, too. And then it turned out that I was the only one, besides John Jakes, who *did* write one."[1] Gardner is only half-joking. *October Light*, by necessity, had to be published in 1976, for its subject is America—its physical and intellectual growth and proclaimed decay, its present spiritual condition, and its likely direction in the future. That Gardner was the only writer to deal seriously with the subject is, Gardner might say, an indictment of contemporary American fiction, and a mark of the general abdication from responsibility by his fellow authors.

So it is, then, that in one sense *October Light* is a celebration of America. The subject matter and the chapter-heading quotations from the founding fathers make clear one of Gardner's several intentions in the book, yet even before the appearance of *October Light* Gardner was busy laying the groundwork, making public his attitude toward the country's observance of its 200th year. In 1975, Gardner wrote an article for the *New York Times*, an article with the painfully cute and (I have to believe) editorially imposed title, "Amber (Get) Waves (Your) of (Plastic) Grain (Uncle Sam)." In this piece, Gardner revealed a hint of what he was currently up to in his yet unpublished fiction, letting slip a loosely guarded secret: "John Gardner's a *patriot!*" Not the fervid, irrational, cloudy-eyed disciple of America's infallibility, mind you; simply a person hanging on to a belief in the original principles and faiths of his country, and in the immortality of the American Dream:

> The American Dream, it seems to me, is not even slightly ill. It's escaped, soared away into the sky like an eagle, so not even a great puffy, Bicentennial can squash it. The American Dream's become a worldwide dream, which makes me so happy and flushed with partly chauvinistic pride (it was our idea) that I sneak down into my basement and wave my flag. People all over the world have decided that they have a God- or Allah- or Buddha-given right to a more or less decent existence, here on earth, right now. . . . That idea—humankind's inalienable right to life, liberty, and the pursuit of happiness—coupled with a system for protecting human rights— was and is the quintessential American Dream. The rest is greed and pompous foolishness—at worst, a cruel and sentimental myth, at best, cheap streamers in the rain.[2]

Gardner is a patriot acutely aware of America's political and philosophical history. He is, too, a patriot actively at war with quick and exploitative fervors, with movements in both ideological camps. "One is a movement to celebrate and canonize without mercy or thought all that's foul and mindless in the American heritage. (The serpent on the Right.) The other is a movement to 'demythologize' those eighteenth-century heroes who've been foully, mindlessly adored, and supplant their myth with a new myth, America as trash. (The serpent on the Left.)," as he says in the same article.

Gardner's critique in this essay of the sort of inane historical idealism that insists on a vision of "George Washington with his teeth in, Samuel Adams looking honest, Ben Franklin with his clothes on (among other crank opinions, you may recall, Ben Franklin held that it was healthful to go around bare-naked), or that huge drunken ox Ethan Allen looking sober as a church"—should strike an immediate resonance for anyone who has read *October Light*. Gardner's complaints are the complaints of James Page, like Gardner a patriot and, like Gardner, nettled by the historical lamination of America's heroes. The "bare-naked" Ben Franklin and the mountainous, yawing Ethan Allen, they argue, have been characterized out of existence. Thus, Gardner calls them up once more—as *characters*—in order to "reheroify" them, strip them of their perfections, and make them mortal. What separates Gardner (and James Page) from the "serpents on the Left" is Gardner's motive, for, as he says in the *New York Times,*

> It's right to demythologize those heroes, as long as we remember those rough, contradiction-filled idealists were, for their time and

in some ways for any time, heroes. It's right to insist that when we talk about "the good old days"—when we gaze up in awe at those Yankee demigods—we should remind ourselves that it's partly illusion: Things were not as good then, and are not as bad now, as we sentimentally maintain.

October Light is, in a small way, about heroes: how they are made, how they are destroyed, how they may be resurrected. Nowhere in his writing, with the possible exceptions of *The Wreckage of Agathon* and *Grendel,* does Gardner deal in such depth with the myth of the hero. And what he did in his article for the *New York Times* was to provide a basis for his fiction, defining his historical stance, making a personal declaration of belief in the viability and necessity of the hero, particularly as he or she plays a part in our own national past.

At nearly the same time as he was writing his article, Gardner was busy settling into life in New England. Teaching in Bennington, Vermont, and living in nearby Cambridge, New York, Gardner found himself in a world radically different from that to which he had grown accustomed in southern Illinois. And the move played a role in the formation of *October Light,* a book conceived in Illinois but brought to light, after much alteration, in Vermont: "I was working on it before I lived in Vermont, but I changed it completely. I had it originally set in southern Illinois, and then I realized I loved the idea of putting it in Vermont because of its association with the revolutionary war. I really loved that I got Vermont into the thing. It really changed everything. I had to rewrite completely."[3] The novel is so obviously a study of the New England tradition, fraught as it is with conservative truth and prejudice, with stiff-necked pride and open generosity; it is a reflection, once again, of Gardner's concern with the geographical implication of values, a concern earlier displayed most prominently in *The Old Men, Nickel Mountain,* and in certain stories in *The King's Indian.* In *October Light* Gardner tests these values—against themselves, against others—and shows their validities and their failures.[4] Without the New England setting, without the longstanding and relatively unchanged moral history of the region, *October Light* could never have been written as it was, might well have been instead the story of an Illinois corn farmer, the story of Jonathan Upchurch in the twentieth century.

Perhaps the most important influence on the novel, however, came from the work Gardner was pursuing at the time in aesthetics. Within a year after the publication of *October Light,* Gardner also brought out several essays that examined the craft of fiction writing and the state of the art in America in the 1970s.[5] These later appeared in *On Moral Fiction,*

Gardner's lively and controversial test-by-fire of most of America's contemporary writers. What I am suggesting is that *October Light* was written
"under the influence" of *On Moral Fiction,* that the novel is a fictional
companion piece to the criticism. All that Gardner later says in *On Moral
Fiction* is imaginatively drawn out in *October Light,* with characters and
structure issuing oblique and direct statements that are eventually echoed
in the essays. When Sally Abbott, reading her paperback, lapses out of
consciousness and into "an alternative reality more charged than mere
life, more ghostly yet nearer,"[6] she is being offered as proof of Gardner's
(and Aristotle's) argument for the reality of a "vivid and continuous
dream," a condition Gardner describes in *On Moral Fiction:*

> Words conjure emotionally charged images in the reader's mind,
> and when the words are put together in the proper way, with the
> proper rhythms—long and short sounds, smooth or ragged,
> tranquil or rambunctious—we have the queer experience of falling
> through the print on the page into something like a dream, an
> imaginary world so real and convincing that when we happen to be
> jerked out of it by a call from the kitchen or a knock at the door, we
> stare for an instant in befuddlement at the familiar room where we
> sat down, half an hour ago, with our book.[7]

Sally Page is Gardner's reply to the linguistic puritanism of William Gass.
And later, when Sally peers into a waking dream and recognizes the
characters of her book (*OL,* pp. 391, 395–96), it seems a fictional re-
creation of a similar vision experienced by Gardner and defined in *On
Moral Fiction* (p. 202) as a sort of creative entrancement. When Ed Thomas finishes his "song" to the seasons and to the land, and we hear James
Page's heartfelt response (through dentureless gums): "Ith true. . . . Like
a good window-thash . . . or horth" (*OL,* p. 418), we remember it when
we run across Gardner quoting Chekhov in *On Moral Fiction:* "Art tells
the truth" (p. 150). Finally, when Sally, James, and his daughter Ginny
Hicks all muse on the virtues and dangers of television, we know they are
prefiguring Gardner's own attack upon the medium in his book of
criticism.[8]

Where the connection is most evident, however, is in the structure of
October Light, in the inclusion and function of the inner novel, *The Smugglers of Lost Souls' Rock.*[9] It is a harsh, hip, violating sort of novel; that is to
say, it runs counter to all traditional moral and aesthetic rules, plays havoc
with reasonable expectations, and indulges itself in manipulative games
with the reader. For Gardner, it is an example of immoral fiction, or
fiction that cheats and deceives—in short, the very sort of fiction he
condemns in *On Moral Fiction.* Art, says Gardner, is "a tragic game," one

that mirrors the seriousness and irreversibility of life. Yet the inner novel mocks life's tragedy, turns art into an R. Crumb comic book, makes of ideas and emotions pulseless abstractions. It is "the Devil's visions . . . all dazzle and no lift, mere counterfeit escape, the lightness of a puffball . . . the lightness of a fart, a tale without substance, escape from the world of hard troubles and grief in a spaceship" (*OL,* p. 12).

We are never able to take any part of the inner novel seriously simply because, in the most Aristotelian sense, it is a comedy. Its concerns are narrow and insignificant, its plot mere mechanics, and its characters walking shadows. The inner novel rehashes existential and nihilistic metaphysics, never really working out solutions or alternatives; it is black comedy at its meanest and most sterile. It runs along, heedless of Gardner's warning in *On Moral Fiction* against "the reduction of plot to pure argument or of fictional characters and relationships to bloodless embodiments of ideas" (p. 9). Such books, argues Gardner, allow and encourage confusion. They make whimsical, unearned statements, they joke about suicide and the finality of death, and skew a person's moral standard. The repeated salvations of Peter Wagner, the shamefully convenient spaceship-*deus ex machina* ending are embarrassing, but not harmless intellectual simplicities. Sally Page, the person most affected by the novel, is alert to the book's perniciousness. She sees that it is "base, unwholesome. That nonsense, especially about suicide proving a man's 'good sense.' People might say such stupid, irresponsible writing did no harm, but you could bet your bottom dollar, no one who'd experienced the tragedy of the suicide of someone near and dear would ever in this world dream of saying such a thing" (*OL,* p. 19). There are precious few second chances in life, as Sally knows from the very real suicide of her nephew, Richard Page.[10] There is an emotional wrongness about the book, a notion that is intuited by Sally, but that is partly explainable (for Gardner) by formal aesthetics: "It's the total effect of an action that's moral or immoral, Aristotle pointed out. In other words, it's the *energeia*—the actualization of the potential which exists in character and situation—that gives us the poet's fix on good and evil; that is, dramatically demonstrates the moral laws, and the possibility of tragic waste, in the universe" (*OMF,* p. 23). The characters in *The Smugglers of Lost Souls' Rock* are cartoon figures, talking in balloons, lacking genuine feeling and depth, no more than quick sketches from the artist's pen. We read along, smiling at their slyness, finding their insouciance amusing, perhaps realizing all the time that there is no reason for their witticisms to be taken seriously.[11]

BUT!, Gardner exclaims, clamoring to be heard, the problem is that such art does affect life, does frequently turn a head or two, change a right-thinking mind. Sally Page is an earnest and thoughtful reader, yet her personality is subtly warped by the novel's influence. She steals lines from the book's characters, becomes foolishly self-conscious, loses her ability to reason independently. Her attitudes change; she turns spiteful and vengeful and murderous, weaving violent plots against her brother. She veers toward immorality, as the lines between real life and the tawdry imitation offered up in the inner novel start to cross. Therein lies the danger of improper and counterfeit art, says Gardner. Once artists cease to affirm life's value, once they jump outside the great tradition, once they commit themselves to despair, they forfeit their claim on integrity and purpose and become a species of moral outlaw. They turn from instruction to seduction, forgetting about the inherent truthfulness of art. They lose track of how life actually works, make huge jumps and generalizations, miss the fact that the world functions by process.

It is this emphasis upon process, in fact, which so largely characterizes Gardner's *October Light*. In *On Moral Fiction* Gardner states that "life is all conjunctions, one damn thing after another, cows *and* wars *and* chewing gum *and* mountains; art—the best, most important art—is all subordination: guilt *because of* sin *because of* pain" (p. 6). This is a fairly brief but accurate description of the workings of Gardner's novel. The author observes the vast gathering of chance and circumstance that makes up mortal existence and organizes it, orders it, gives it a sense of cause and effect. In *October Light* Gardner deals specifically with the thorny problem of human guilt, its roots and its effects, tracing its sinuous process as it moves through the lives of its characters.

Gardner centers his study upon two old and crabbed Vermonters, James Page and his sister, Sally Page Abbott, both as stubborn and self-righteous as the New England tradition would have them. Out of this stubbornness springs their feud, a war between flesh and value and intellect. "A battle of the bowels," James calls it, and it certainly is that; but it also is wrapped up in the conflict of moral belief and political outlook. James is a solid and stolid Republican, frugal with word and dollar, conservative, a tortuous blend of moralist and pragmatist. He is also an imaginative man; his life is speckled with visions and dreams, a product of a former, much older time: "The old man had been born in an age of spirits, and lived in it yet, though practically alone there, and filled with doubts" (p. 9). He is a man who believes in heroes and the reality of historical myth. He is a patriot and, in part, a poet, for as Gardner writes in *On Moral Fiction:*

> What the warrior-hero does on the battlefield, especially if he is half-god, like Achilles, shows ordinary men what the gods love. . . . Every hero's proper function is to provide a noble image for men to

be inspired and guided by in their own actions. . . . And whereas
the hero's function . . . is to set the standard in action, the business
of the poet (or "memory" or "epic song," and also the business of
arts other than poetry) is to celebrate the work of the hero, pass the
image on, keep the heroic model of behavior fresh, generation on
generation. (pp. 28–29)

Gardner says as much here about heroes as about art. One thing that is
clear, though, is that James Page is an artist in the oldest sense, a *scop*
passing on the tradition and the legend, keeping tenuously alive the myths
of Ethan Allen and Ben Franklin and Sam Adams (recall Gardner's talk of
these "Yankee demigods" in his *New York Times* article). James Page—and
the novel—are Gardner's attempts to revivify America's long-moribund
heroes. This, Gardner writes, "is what true art is about—preservation of
the world of gods and men." And their heroes.

James is not a frivolous man. He is a thinker and a brooder, an animal as
convinced of his rightness as an old farm dog, yet

it wasn't mere myth or mere history-as-myth—exalted figures to stir
the imagination, teach the poor weighted-down spirit to vault—it
wasn't mere New England vinegar and piss that made the old man
fierce. Though he was wrong in some matters, an objective
observer would be forced to admit—cracked as old pottery, no
question about it—it was true that he had, off and on, real,
first-class opinions. He knew the world dark and dangerous. (p. 10)

He knows the existence of evil as well as good, knows that life is
essentially tragic, that there are forces out there just itching "to undo
him, both him and his ghosts" (p. 13). Humanity, Gardner implies, is a
carrier: memories, ideas, pains, all are borne by men and women until
death decidedly splits them into pieces. James carries a legacy of death:
one son dead in a fall, a second son dead by a suicide, a wife worn away
by cancer, and an uncle gone (like his son) by suicide. These long
strings of tragedies weigh a man down, bend him round; James's pain is
physical and metaphysical, both types brought on by a symbolic "lock-
ing up" of his parts. He uses in fact portions of his past as a defense,
hailing the superstition of his dead Uncle Ira, combining it with a
common-sense faith in the universe:

He did not of course, when he stopped to think, believe in elves
or believe that bees can talk with fairies or pigs with wind, or that
bears are visitors from another world; did not believe in Jack Frost
or even, with his whole heart and mind, Resurrection. Though he
muttered spells from time to time—though for luck he spit left or

made a circle to the right, and carried with him everywhere he went a small stick (a stick of ash) and a rattlesnake's skull, protection against changelings—in even these he did not, when he considered carefully, believe. He believed in the most limited natural magic, the battle of spirit up through matter, season after season; and he believed that his ghosts, insofar as they were real or had the power of things real, were allies in the grim, universal war. (pp. 13–14)

What James knows—and what so many of the other characters know—is that the world is fragile, that the wonderful so easily and so often slips into the painful. For James, in fact, such slippage has been too frequent: "*His* world, he knew for pretty sure, was beyond fragility. Smashed." (p. 14).

His sister, on the other hand, is a woman not yet so crushed by the world's ponderousness, though the memory of her husband and of his odd death trails her constantly. She is, to James's mind, a "cotton-headed fool who confessed, herself, that she had faith in people, though she was eighty years old and ought to know better" (p. 6). Sally is progressive, somewhat liberal, something of a feminist (a secondary concern of Gardner's in the novel), and worst of all a Democrat—just a step away from a latter-day New England witch. She is a woman more alive in the present than in the past, though like all of us she cannot completely escape her history.

Both James and Sally are haunted and shaped by things that have gone before them, by deaths and memories of deaths, and by particular attitudes toward those memories. James remembers his son Richard as his "chief disappointment" and as "a lad born for hanging," and holds him responsible for his younger son's death. Richard was weak and cowardly and soft-willed, too shy to survive the New England winter, the world's cruel ways, and his father's thoughtless hounding. To Sally (and to Richard's sister, Virginia), the boy was a beautiful victim, a saint:

> Poor Richard! He could have been a glorious boy, if James had just let him *be*. Besides handsome, he'd been wonderfully quick, and charming—though never around James, which was a pity. James might have liked him better if he'd allowed himself to know him. Everyone liked Richard. Little Ginny had downright worshipped him, which was why she'd renamed her adopted boy Richard. . . . No wonder if James had been upset, of course. He'd never admit it this side of the grave, but everyone knew he'd detested that boy. Blamed him for his second son's death among other things—it had been Richard left the ladder against the roof of the barn. (Richard blamed himself even more for it. Horace had once tried to talk to

him about it, hoping to set him straight; but no chance, the chance of a hankie in a hurricane. Richard had treasured his guilt, as Horace told her. It was the one thing his father had taught him and he'd got down pat.) But it was long before the death of little Ethan that the trouble had started. It was as if James had taken a dislike to the boy when he was still a little mite in his cradle. "Don't be a cry-baby!" James was always saying. (pp. 134–35)

What killed Richard, and what dogs so many of the characters in *October Light,* is a grand complex of sin and pain and guilt, of memories and models true and twisted.

Eating at the soul of James Page is the image of his crazed Uncle Ira, the most important person in James's life. As noted already, James totes in his pocket the magical relics of his uncle's superstitions; but he also carries his uncle's example, his emotional and moral figure, which has shaped so significantly James's own character. Actually, it is his sister Sally who understands the situation best, as she too recalls the memory of this odd and distant man:

In her mind's eye she saw silent, gray-bearded uncle Ira, a small, solid creature with animal eyes, an axe on one shoulder, on the other a gun. He stood for her memory as for a photograph, a picture in what would by this time be some discoloring old album, his snowshoes brown against the yellow, dead snow. He came out of the past like a creature from the woods, his reluctance and strangeness absolute, hostile; and beside him now stood her brother James in a lumberman's cap, long coat and snowshoes—James who had loved him, in a way even worshipped him, unless perhaps, as her husband had suspected, it was an unwitting trick James had played on himself, twisting fear of the man to intense admiration as little Dickey sometimes did (so it seemed to the old woman) struggling to pacify this older James. (p. 25)

Sally's husband is on the mark with his opinion: James did indeed so much fear the man, with his gruff, stonelike ways, that he transformed that fear into awe and then into an ideal. Ira's image pervades the novel, exerting his bestial influence on everyone. As we have seen, he had his greatest effect on James, who grew up in the man's presence; James had been, like Richard, a withdrawn, meek, voiceless child until Ira came along to change him: "He was a *strange* man, Uncle Ira. Not exactly human—he even smelled like an animal—as if his mother'd been brought low by a bear" (p. 136). This bearlike image lopes through the book, darting in and out, firing our awareness at the almost physical scent and weight of its existence. Ira is the central symbol of the irrepressible past.

Ira is even the indirect cause of Horace Abbott's death, a man killed by the sudden and frightful emergence of the past. Richard's assumption of old Ira's identity—the bear-smelling overcoat, the axe cradled upon the shoulder—is an ironic and tragic flouting of all that has gone into ruining his life. His appearance at Horace's door, like a sentient ghost, horrifies the man into an early death, his heart proving too weak for such a violent jogging of the memory. And it is this second coming of Ira that remains the insoluble mystery to Sally and James:

> She knew that in a moment she would turn and see Horace in his chair, his mouth forming an *O* as if of slight surprise, and she would cry out and run to him. . . . Every line in the room was as sharp as a razor cut—books, glass-topped table, hat-rack by the door—and for an instant it seemed there was a smell, exaggerated by memory but elusive as ever. Someone had been there, someone from her past, perhaps her childhood. All this she had told the police, later, going over it and over it in meticulous detail. "What did it smell like?" "I don't know. The woods," she said. "Decaying leaves. Like a zoo." (p. 104)

Ira is James's hero, Sally's ghost, and Richard's curse. He is part of each one's past, a past that is locked away, dark, mysterious, and baffling.

When people fail to understand their past, loaded as it is with sin and worry and anger, it simply increases the chance for suffering. As James knows (via Estelle Parks and Professor Kodama), the world is "very fragile" and delicate. Such fragility lends itself to tragedy and to accident (a theme examined once before by Gardner in *The Sunlight Dialogues*); people die, or come close to death, through acts of pure whim, as if there were no such thing as "natural cause." Thus, Richard scares Horace to death and James scares Ed Thomas to a likely death; Sally nearly kills Ginny and James nearly shocks Sally out of life; and Ira and Richard take their own lives, as if unwilling to leave their mortality to chance. So much is inexplicable in this universe, so much is seemingly without reason, that a life without suffering is inconceivable. It is the horrible dual nature of the world, "life's monstrosity and beauty" (p. 370). It is the lesson of Schopenhauer, offered in *October Light* by Lane Walker and Rafe Hernandez (minister and priest, respectively), of the necessity of suffering, of its ability to intensify these spells of happiness and well-being.

Such a universe, moreover, requires a vision and a moral system that are worth living for. You can see the world aright, says Gardner, as do Estelle Parks and Horace Abbott—as complex, mixed of tragedy and goodness, ultimately serious—and build your vision upon art and a willingness to lay no blame, simply to understand. Or you can live as inflexibly as a railroad tie, as do James and Sally—act from hatred and jealousy, allow your heart to lock up cold as a Vermont stream in winter, fight way beyond the point of reason and to the verge of disaster—and refuse the comfort of community and family and ignore the curative effect of love.

What happens is that James sets up illogical and improper models, misunderstanding his own worship of his Uncle Ira, and forcing that misunderstanding upon his own son. In a sense, James was ironically and sadly correct: Richard *was* a lad born for hanging, because James never allowed him to develop differently. This idea of modeling is central to the novel, as Gardner has declared: "Every character in *October Light* is either a model or the *victim* of a model or trying to break his way free of a model."[12] Ira is a model for James, and thus a model for Richard, who is a victim of that model. Horace is something of a model for Sally (as, unfortunately, are the characters of her trash novel), though she lacks his incisiveness and broad compassion. Ginny idolizes her brother, loves her father, and sadly is a stranger to her mother. Even little Dickey, the young son of Lewis and Ginny, is laboring beneath the model of his grandfather, learning about strength and myth and stalwart moral stiffness.

The tragedy comes with the breakdown of such models, with their inherent corruption or their ultimate failure. As Gardner has explained:

> We are born imperfect. Nobody is capable of taking care of all the troubles in the world, and you inevitably feel unwhole. But there's something more. When you're a child, you think of yourself as perfect, as total. And then you check yourself inside and you find that when you tell a lie, you're called a liar. So what you have is this image of yourself, and then as you live you betray that image over and over and over, until you develop a second image of yourself. And this image is with you all your life. There are two shadows: one is the shadow of perfection, that keeps haunting you, and the other is the shadow of the tempter, telling you, if I'm not perfect I'm a monster. In your daily life what you try to do is keep a balance, but what happens is that the possibility that you are flawed keeps upsetting that balance, keeps nagging you into an unforgiveable sort of guilt.[13]

Guilt. For Gardner it is "the eighth, and most deadly, sin,"[14] and perhaps the sin most characteristic of our age. Moral and political circumstances have brought us to a state of perpetual guilt in which we stand around confused and forlorn, scratching our heads, at once proud and ashamed of our values. How we arrived at such a condition is the subject not only of *October Light* but also a good portion of *On Moral Fiction*, where Gardner more clearly spells out what it is he is trying to do in his fiction.

Gardner argues in that book that the twentieth-century world has lost
its ability and its willingness to discriminate between the good and the
bad, the moral and the immoral, that in our rush to a sort of intellectual
democracy we have abandoned the traditional ethical standard-setters—
religion and individual moral opinion:

> If we agree, at least tentatively, that art does instruct, and if we
> agree that not all instruction is equally valid . . . then our quarrel
> with the moralist position on art comes down to this: we cannot
> wholeheartedly accept the secular version of the theory because
> we're unconvinced that no man's intuition of truth can be proved
> better than another's. We are aware that our devotion to individual
> freedom, our anxiously optimistic praise of pluralistic society, since
> other societies are always unjust—hence our carefully nurtured
> willingness to sit still for almost anything—may tend toward the
> suicidal; but when we ask whom we should trust, we find
> ourselves, predictably, in the position Yeats described: "The best
> lack all conviction, while the worst / Are filled with passionate
> intensity." In the name of democracy, justice, and compassion, we
> abandon our right to believe, to debate, and to hunt down truth.
> (*OMF,* pp. 41–42)

Our world has become so open, so tolerant of disparate and untested
opinion that to make a moral choice has become immoral. Bad art mingles
with good, bastardizing truth and obliterating features that were once
well-pronounced. The age grows more and more perplexed by what it
reads and hears and sees, until obvious moral distinctions cannot and will
not be made. As a result,

> what we generally get in our books and films is bad instruction:
> escapist models or else moral evasiveness, or, worse, cynical attacks
> on traditional values such as honesty, love of country, marital
> fidelity, work, and moral courage. This is not to imply that such
> values are absolutes, too holy to attack. But it is dangerous to raise
> a generation that smiles at such values, or has never heard of them,
> or dismisses them with indignation, as if they were not relative
> goods but were absolute evils. (*OMF,* p. 42)

Moral relativism sets in and there is a sort of ethical levelling which
eliminates the need for personal judgment. This is turn presents another,
equally serious problem, the

> age-old dilemma of the democratic optimist: distinguishing, as
> theologians put it, between the sinner and the sin or, in secular

language, distinguishing individual dignity and worth from the individual's value (or lack of it) to the group. If we cannot make out what guilt is, virtue is academic. Few would deny that our humanness is enriched by our increasingly sophisticated notions of guilt and of society's part in the guilt of individuals; but if the moral artist is to function at all, he must guard against taking on more guilt than he deserves, treating himself and his society as guilty on principle. If everyone everywhere is guilty—and that seems to be our persuasion—then no models of goodness, for life or art, exist; moral art is a lie. (*OMF,* p. 44)

Art in such a case turns acid and cynical, convincing mankind of its worthlessness. Art, in other words, turns into *The Smugglers of Lost Souls' Rock.*

Gardner goes on to distinguish between two varieties of guilt, one natural and the other less so. That the world is sorrowful, Gardner does not deny: "Life's potential for turning tragic is a fact of our existence" (*OMF,* p. 45), says Gardner, and we cannot attempt the Romantic evasion of that fact. When tragedies are accidental, we suffer, question the logic of the universe, and watch as our world turns darker. When we start laying *blame* for such tragedies upon ourselves, when we accept responsibility for such sad mischance, we also assume, says Gardner, tragic guilt. We enhance the tragedy of the event by a subjective imposition of cause upon ourselves.

But Gardner goes on to consider what has happened in the modern world, where Romanticism has been rejected and replaced:

Even where guilt has been defined out of existence, positive virtue sits uneasy. We notice three main attacks, those associated with the names of Freud, Sartre, and Wittgenstein. Whereas the inescapable sorrow and bitterness of life—the fact that we die, that even children die—had for centuries been explained in the Western world as punishment for a fairly specific crime, the crime of Adam, or original sin, we learned from these three men a new kind of guilt—not really new, perhaps, but certainly never before so pervasive—the kind we call "free floating." This new kind of guilt, more terrible than the other, springs from the fact that, though one has done nothing particularly wrong, one cannot, by one's very nature, do anything of particular worth. It is the guilt of the metaphysically abandoned animal who, conceiving ideals beyond his nature, can only eat his heart out, self-condemned. (*OMF,* p. 46)

Truth, beauty, goodness all become unreachable, are excised from our heritage. We lose, in fact, a healthy portion of our heritage; we are asked to conveniently forget our history, forget the achievement in thought, forget in effect all human connection. Civilization is immobilized. It ceases to advance—turns, instead, static and doubt-filled and sterile. We stand shaking, thrust suddenly into the center of the universe, exiled and "serpentized." We become sin itself.

This is the world that Gardner explores in *October Light*. There is hardly a main character in the novel who does not suffer some one form of guilt or another, who does not feel that dull picking at the heart that disrupts and destroys a life. No one, not even the youngest, is exempt. Young Dickey's innocence is no defense at all; he has already learned of sin and its consequences, and he nurtures his own small bit of blame. Dickey cowers in half-understood fear of his grandfather's shadow (as did his Uncle Richard), and it is Dickey who tells on his grandfather and brings the family's wrath down upon James's head; but more important, it is Dickey (or so Dickey painfully reasons) who began it *all*—it was Dickey who rescued Sally's novel from the pigpen where James had first tossed it. Ironically enough, no one but Dickey sees the implication of his remark: "It's because of that book" (p. 359). It is *The Smugglers of Lost Souls' Rock* that urges Sally to violence and perversity—bad art pressing its influence upon life. Had the book remained where Gardner no doubt believes it belonged, the feud perhaps would have ended long ago, good sense prevailing. In his own simple and childlike way, Dickey states Gardner's own aesthetic position; unfortunately, it also draws Dickey into the intricate web of guilt and weak feeling that has trapped the rest of his family, almost as if he has inherited the ill fortune of his namesake.

Dickey's parents endure separate sorts of guilt. They suffer from an understanding of the world, a world partly simplified and refined through honest emotion. Virginia feels the guilt of sudden recognition; in an instant she sees the almost tragic waste of her father's life highlighted in his impassioned outcry against the shoddiness and obscenity of his world. Love and understanding, for Virginia, become one:

> Ginny stared at him, shocked, her heart going out to him. She'd never more than glimpsed the anger and helplessness now suddenly made plain. Even Dickey understood, standing by the wall with a guilty look, as if everything were his fault. As for Lewis, she realized glancing at him now that he'd probably understood from the beginning. She could only stand with her mouth open. Staring at the tremor in her father's cheek, watching him go past her, angry as a bot and close to tears, saw from inside him what it was like to

be old and uncomfortable, cheated, ground down by life and sick to death of it. As if suddenly coming to, she started after him. "Dad, I'm sorry," she said. (p. 193)

Ginny's is the pain that goes along with seeing, all at once, the drawing down of a life toward death, the familiar guilt and impotence felt by a child for an aging parent. Hers is the tragic awareness of time's ruthlessness; what she has done in the past now seems small and inconsequential, certainly not adequate for the amount of love she has kept hidden away.

Ginny is also correct in her judgment of her husband Lewis, who has indeed "understood from the beginning." He has the presence of a saint (both Ginny and Sally say so, although Sally thinks him simple-minded and Nit-like), and the virtuous diligence of an artist. His way of thinking is straightforward, Vermont-like, and perhaps a bit *too* practical:

> He was rarely brought conviction by even his own most sensible reasoning. Life was slippery, right and wrong were as elusive as odors in an old abandoned barn. Lewis knew no certainties but hammers and nails, straps of leather, clocksprings. He had no patience with people's complexities—preferred the solitude of his workshop down cellar, the safe isolation of a maple grove he'd been hired to trim, or some neighbor's back yard, where he'd been hired to rake leaves—not because people were foolish, in Lewis Hicks's opinion, or because they got through life on gross and bigoted oversimplifications, though they did, he knew, but because quiet and unschooled as he might be, he could too easily see all sides and, more often than not, no hint of a solution. (p. 124)

Lewis is a paradox: he insists upon being his own man, maintaining his physical and spiritual independence, yet he is a "hired man." He seems afraid of the individual thought or opinion. He is reluctant to force a decision, preferring to remain the observer. So he stands by Sally's door scraping, sanding, painting, ruminating—and all the time feeling "more than before . . . guilty and depressed." He understands the roots of the family war, understands what drives both brother and sister, and it starts to affect his own frame of mind, bringing him to a personal conflict and to an epiphany:

> Behind the house, where the back yard sloped down to the faded red barn on its rough rock foundation—the dingy white hives of the bees just beyond—there was only one tree, an old jagged hickory, most of its leaves fallen, so they could see the full glory of the crimson sunset above the mountain and the slope of the pasture. Perversely, for all his grief, or because of his grief, Lewis Hicks did

see it, and registered that it was beautiful. He saw how the stones and grass of the pasture turned spiritual in this light, radiating power, as if charged with some old, mystic energy unnamed except in ancient Sumerian or Indian—how the forested mountains that had been a hundred colors just an hour ago . . . were now all suffused with the crimson of the sky, transmuted. Lewis Hicks saw and registered how even the old man's machinery was transformed by this stunning light, the old yellow cornchopper tilted against the silo more distinct, more itself than it would normally be, final as a tombstone. . . . He had no words for his impressions, but his misery intensified. He was wrong and wronged. Wordlessly caught at the intersecting planes of the sunset's beauty and Virginia's strange anger—strange to him even though he saw he'd been a fool, and all she'd said was right—he suddenly wished his whole life changed absolutely, wished himself free and in the same motion wished for the opposite, or the same perhaps, wished he were dead. All husbands wished that, he supposed, from time to time, same as elves and bears. And perhaps all wives. But how mysterious that not even *one* could be spared, not even he, remote from the world, in a barnyard in Vermont. Did even cattle have such pangs of unhappiness? Grasshoppers?

Dickey said, "Why's she so mad?"

Abruptly, almost without noticing it, he was better. His soul crashed inward from the sky, the sweep of mountains like ocean waves—collapsed back to time out of timelessness—and he became a small man walking, holding his son's hand, moving again through specific time and place, not a disembodied, universal cry but a sober-faced husband and father who had certain problems, certain groundless duties. (pp. 187–88)

Lewis, perhaps unconsciously, has rolled to the edge, has come as close as anyone can to that "free floating" guilt of which Gardner speaks. He is brought low by the anger and spitefulness of life, by the possibilities of love turning into hate, and for a moment takes upon himself the guilt of his kind (or at least of his generation). What pulls him back from the edge, however, is the redemptive quality of love and of common human responsibility. Nature, once obscured and miscolored by despair, becomes once more for Lewis a symbol of the world's rightness; he feels the inherent morality of things, sees the awesome transmutative power of the October light, and retreats from the pit (as Grendel cannot). Like Henry Soames in *Nickel Mountain,* Lewis experiences the almost animistic wonder of nature and for that moment exists beyond the limits of time and space.

If Lewis is the "saint rescued," then Richard Page is the "saint lost." He is a man trapped in a prophecy and a model, a man forced to a conclusion by the stern idealism of his father, James. Richard's sister, Ginny, recalls the sort of curse under which Richard lived. He was a boy who

> was always in trouble, though he never did a thing; their father just somehow had it in for him. . . . All through her childhood, it seemed to her, her father had been beating him for one thing or another. "A lad born for hanging," her father had called him, and again and again laid his belt to him, or a milkhose, or a stick. She knew pretty well what it was in him that made their father furious. He was timid—exactly as their father had been, Aunt Sally said— afraid of cows, the horses, even of the chickens; afraid of strangers; afraid of cold and of thunder; afraid of ghosts and nightmares; afraid, more than anything else, that one of them might die, or that his father might go crazy, as a man had done once down the road, and might shoot them with his gun. Perhaps if her father had been able to see . . . (p. 255)

His fears are human and natural, yet they are transformed into cowardice by his father—a man beset by his own fears. Even when Richard, for a single instance, stands firmly and challenges his father, James interprets it as the action of a moral weakling. There is simply no way Richard can escape the destiny James has molded for him; once young Ethan Page falls from the barn, and once Richard is made to assume the guilt of that death, Richard's fate is ordained. He is bound to be unlucky, to lose a woman he loves and to kill the man he perhaps loves most. It is, in fact, his pushing of Horace Abbott into death, an act of pure accident, that drives Richard to the loft and to the rope; it is the final parcel of guilt laid upon his soul, heavy and despairing enough to turn life into a misery and death into an acceptable release. It is the part of the mystery left undisclosed to Sally and James until the very end. For both of them, Richard is a memory and a reflection, differently perceived and considered.

Sally recalls the boy's purity and holy meekness and his inability to hurt (which forms the fatal irony of Richard's scaring of Horace). The barbarous and tyrannical treatment she receives from James is, for her, an image of the cruelty suffered by Richard, and she vows not to break beneath it. James's threats and curses and general oppressiveness, his blowing away of the television, his fixing of the shotgun at her door like a deadly, silent sentinel—all spark Sally's anger, reinforce her obstinate nature, and make her ripe for the shabby morality of her trash novel, which turns her stubbornness and ire into vengeance. From the book she learns to cultivate guilt in others as a means of compensating for the

cheating she has experienced in her own life—something Lewis recognizes (p. 197). Her former good judgment is twisted by the novel's
celebration of a mode of selfish, egotistic pride, forcing her to a denial of
the simple kindness of her great-nephew Dickey, who comes to her
barred door with food and sympathy. Sally turns him away, and in doing
so piles guilt upon both the boy and herself. The "victory" is more important than the injustice, and she tells herself that "if she was wrong then
very well she was wrong, she could pay in the Afterlife" (p. 230). Yet any
victory so soured with guilt, Gardner says, is truly more of a loss than a
gain. Sally treats Dickey in almost the same manner in which James
handled Richard, sticking to principle and ideal, ignoring basic human
need. She is untrue to everything she once believed, and the idea that she
might make payment later on is mere wishfulness and self-deception.

When Sally sets her death-trap for James, and when chance intervenes
once more and turns Ginny into the unintended victim, Sally's moral
accounting becomes more intense, more evasive, and more deadly. She
has very nearly killed her niece—an accidental act perhaps, but the motive
behind the act is outright vengeance. Sally has so seriously duped herself,
so deeply fallen in with the malevolent magic of her novel and with its
warped notion of human nature, that she becomes a righteous murderess.
She cannot accept guilt, only assign it:

> "If your daughter's in the hospital it's nobody put her there but
> you, James Page, same as you put old Ed Thomas in the hospital
> and would've put me in the hospital if not in my grave if I hadn't
> defended myself. You can rant and rail till the cows come home,
> and try to make me feel guilty and come clean up your mess for
> you—all the blood you spilt and the dishes you broke and I don't
> know what-all—but the situation hasn't changed one iota, or if it
> has it's for the worse." . . . Despite the image of her niece fallen and
> stock-still in the doorway—on the hall floor behind her blood-
> spattered apples, blood pouring down from Ginny's scalp as from
> a hose (but that had not frightened her, at least not unduly: there
> was always a good deal of bleeding with a scalp wound)—she must,
> she saw again, hold firm, stick tight to her principles. Days,
> months, years passed quickly when you were old, but even so,
> twenty years of life was a span worth getting decent terms for.
> She'd been cheated long enough. (pp. 371–72)

Sally quite effectively has locked herself away from the community of
humankind, turned herself into a self-serving egoist, as narrow-eyed and
irrational as her brother. What she takes for being cheated is simply an
unwitting judgment upon her own former rightheadedness: an ability to

deny herself immediate desire, a concern for friends and family, a willingness to sacrifice, a belief in values more lasting and more true.

Sally is saved, however, by an inborn faith in life. When she reaches the
end of *The Smugglers of Lost Souls' Rock* she recognizes its cheapness and
fraudulence, its own cheatfulness. What brings it so painfully home to her
is the unpredictability of death, its habit of appearing where least wanted.
She recalls her husband's death, letting it mix with the news of Ed Thomas's frailty, and the memory draws her out once more into the world.
But it must also be said that "the old woman came out of her room for
many reasons, the least of which was that, in a technical sense, at least, she
won the war. In fact, she hardly noticed the victory when it came" (p.
425). She turns again to a recollection that is cloudy and puzzling, a
recollection that possesses the key to her total unlocking. Once the past is
clarified (as much as it can be), says Gardner, the present becomes much
more liveable; and so it becomes for Sally—once all the pieces have been
provided by James.

Not until James illuminates his past does everything fall back into its
rightful place. James's past is a horrid miscellany of nightmare, myth,
earnest belief, and guilt, full of things dark and inexplicable. Instead of
grappling with that past, James elects to "lock it away," ignore it, and
make no attempt to understand it: "All life was foolishness, a witless bear
poking through the woods" (p. 14). But in James's case, that "witless
bear" refuses to be ignored; it persists in his memory, in his sight, in his
day-to-day living. It becomes the voice of his dead wife Ariah, whispering, "Oh James, James," a reminder of his mistaken willfulness. It is the
memory of his Uncle Ira, bearlike in appearance and conception. In its
clearest form, though, this bear-past comes in the memory of his son
Richard, whom James kills (or helps to kill) by insisting upon values
outdated and unsuitable to his son's personality. When Richard hangs
himself, James attempts to wipe the boy's existence from his mind—he
burns Richard's house, condemns him for the death of his younger son,
and stays away from all visual reminders of Richard's life. Yet the past
keeps coming, cropping up like death, undeniable:

> He'd had fights with his wife, he remembered vaguely, about
> money and time—and later, fights with his gloomy-hearted,
> weakling son. His chest gave a jerk as the memory ambushed him,
> his boy—or rather man, by then—hanging from the gray attic
> rafter, still as a feedsack, as if he'd never been alive. For days, even
> months, he'd been unable to believe it: a few harsh words, a quick,
> impetuous little slap—it seems the boy had been up to something,
> only God and James' wife Ariah knew what. Seemed to do with

whores. He'd refused to speak up, had called James a bastard, hence the little slap, not even hard, mere show of anger with his open hand—"little" it had seemed to James then, that is; he knew better now, for with this stony stillness, this absolute, dead-final victory, his son had avenged himself. Whatever meaning James Page had imagined he'd seen in this pitiful earthly existence he had known that instant for what it was: mere desperate assertion, mere hopeful agreement between two people who could tear up the contract in an instant. He saw the boy standing high on the haywagon, grinning under his hat, sunlight and the wind-fluttered branches of trees wheeling and sliding above his head; and then the old man saw again in his mind the absolute, drab, metaphysical stillness of rafters. He had survived it, he couldn't say how or why. Had worked, had walked on the mountain at night, prowling like a lost bear hunting for the door to the underworld; had drunk some, more than was right, for a span; had written lists of words, little scraps of thought, once a kind of prayer, setting what he had by way of heart in his Agro pocket notebook. At night, when he slept and fell off guard, he would wake up crying. His wife would be holding him. (p. 303)

James stores up his grief, deep-freezes it like the Vermont landscape in January, afraid to let it come creeping out where it might save him. The picture album remains closed, the heart stays dark, no chance of fully understanding the past. Love is an emotion that has been pressed from James's soul by a life full of pain, a life that is now drawing nearer its end, death highlighting its apparent futility. There is no room for light, the sort of light that comes in October, the sort of light that saves and regenerates, the sort of light that saves Lewis Hicks and (in other Gardner fiction) John Napper and Fred Clumly and Henry Soames, and that is denied Grendel and George Loomis (who is very much like Richard Page in his lucklessness).

Such light comes gradually, if it comes at all—a part of a natural process, the healing of wounds and the renewal of seasons. It is a part of the benevolence of guilt that it can sometimes drive a person to clarity, which is what happens to James Page. The past slowly opens up, at first in anguish, like old bones creaking up and out of a chair. Ginny's accident recalls earlier sorrows and earlier accidents, and stirs the old pains into movement: "Such guilt was coursing through the old man's veins he could hardly breathe. He felt as he'd felt when his son had killed himself, or, long years before, when he'd found his uncle Ira in the woods" (p. 404). James thinks back on his comments to Richard, holding himself responsible for the boy's death, wanting to take back his words, his carelessness, his flawed hero. James gropes for the "secret door" that would admit his son back into life.

> But there was, of course, no secret door; that was the single most important fact in the universe. Mistakes were final—the ladder against the barn, the story about the death of Uncle Ira that he shouldn't have told. He felt himself fingering the snake's head again, scraping the tip of his bobbed finger against the one remaining tooth and a brief flush of some queer emotion went through him—not anger, exactly; perhaps a brief flicker of understanding. There was a wastebasket standing by the table in the corridor ahead of them, and he drew out the snake's head and, when he came to the wastebasket, dropped it in. "Thorry," he said aloud. (p. 406)

In his casting off of the snake's head, James sheds part of his past, his guilt, and his memory of Ira. He realizes the perniciousness of his ideal, how it has sorrowed him and destroyed his son, and he apologizes—to both Ira and Richard. One has to be willing and able to express one's love the first time around, for the world's fragility and inclination to accident do not allow for a second chance; there are no boats in the dark harbor, no drunkards by the railroad track, no flying saucers to lift one away from the tragedy of this universe of ours. There is only resurrection among the living.

There is a corollary to James's truth, however, that James forgets, and which is brought clear to him by Ed Thomas in his lyrical, creative "song" of Vermont. Ed is a man put close enough to death to envision life's worth; his voice is reasonable, sane, tinged with emotion—the voice that pulls James Page back into life, gives Sally her victory, and reconciles, for a time, at least, the contraries of the universe. Ed's song is an evocation of the past and a reminder of how the earth really operates, telling James things he knew but had forgotten: of how the past works upon the present, how time cannot be halted, how progress is two-sided, how humankind and nature are both metaphorical. The land, Ed sings, moves through cycle after cycle—it is seeded, it bears, turns hard and withered, "locks up" tight under snow and frost, and then slowly and irrepressibly opens up, "unlocks," everything going wet and muddy, a preparation for seedtime once again. Like Lewis's earlier insight, Ed's song is an epiphanous awakening for both Ed Thomas and James Page. James is softening, like the land, and when it comes time to forgive Hernandez, the Mexican priest, James does so with as little grudge as possible for an old man. In a short space, James Page has learned of the intricacies and connections of art and religion, how the spirits of both tend to encourage light over dark, life over death. He offers up the second prayer of his lifetime, a prayer for the life of his daughter and for the chastisement of his lifelong error: the denial of the past and of its effect upon the present.

When Sally makes evident the great flaw in his belief and locates the real reason for Richard's suicide, the past comes flooding in, all at once, unstanchable. James recalls his wife, her voice, her whispered pleas, and at last understands it: "He saw her in her last illness reaching to touch his cheek, saying *Oh James, James,* forgiving him—and forgiving herself— though he, even when she was dying, could forgive neither one of them" (pp. 427–28). The past becomes good again, bearable, welcomed, just as "life *was* good, as poor Ed Thomas understood now more clearly than ever, now that he was dying" (p. 428). James turns symbolically to the past in the photo album, dusty with disuse and disbelief, opening the past once again, and even more of the truth washes over him. He understands Ariah's silence, her refusal to relinquish her son's secret, and the reason for that secret:

> Guilt. All this time he'd carried it, a burden that had bent his whole life double and when he caught it and held it in his two hands and opened them, there was nothing there. He'd been benighted, just as the minister said. And she too, poor Ariah, had gone to her grave full of guilt because, having told James, she blamed herself for the suicide. And the boy—James brushed away tears again, crossly—it had not been rage at his father, had not been revenge, or only a little of it was that. It had been the burden of five years' nurtured guilt at the fact that, in some foolish or maybe drunken prank—Richard had been twenty, a grown man, or so Richard would have thought, though no man of seventy-two would allow that a boy of twenty was grown—the boy had frightened his uncle to death, and, cowardly all his life (whipped all his life, threatened and hollered at and told he was a coward—James would face all of it, now that he'd come to), he had not even stayed or cried out to his aunt for help, but had been true to the image James Page had created for him to live by, or both James and Ariah and even little Ginny—they'd all been in on the conspiracy—and had fled. Benighted, the lot of them, himself worst of all. He'd prayed for punishment, and had been punished well: punished years before the prayer. (p. 430)

Good models nourish; bad models kill. Told long enough and appealingly enough that we are corrupt or lost or irresponsibly free, we come to believe it. Thus the need for true and moral art, and for true and moral values. If we are to create myths and heroes, argues Gardner, they must be life-affirming ones, not the sort that denigrate existence and make a joke of it. James is better off singing the virtues of Ethan Allen than of Ira Page; Ira showed the possibilities of the world's darker side, but "Ethan Allen had been put upon the earth like Hercules, to show an impression of things beyond it" (p. 433). We must, in short, make art work like life.

This is what James ultimately succeeds in doing. His heroes are processed through myth into truth, and become legend. He finally admits to the presence of the past, confronts it, in fact, in the figure of the bear.[15] To kill the bear would be to destroy the past, himself, and decent belief; the bear is James's mirror image—old, hoary, frightened, trying to survive—and like James it is merely "poking through the woods," sorting out the past (while it even *is* the past), making sense of the jumble of fact and circumstance that comprise life on this planet. The voice James hears (and surely he *does* hear it) is Ariah's, surfacing again, like Ira's ghosts, like the image of the bear, "*Oh James, James!*" If there is reproach in her voice, it is not the reproach of a curse or of rebuke, but of a distant and understanding blessing on a life at long last come to terms with its bitter tragedies.

James is a man rescued from his haplessness by an act of mystical recognition, the sort of thing that happened, Gardner says, to Dante. Dante had become lost in a *selva oscura*, had become mired in private and public miseries, had turned from loving to hating, and had rejected his circle of friends. Moreover, he "also contracted . . . tragic guilt. He could be something of a monster, a man who frequently returned evil for good, a vindictive neurotic who often failed to notice the pettiness, cruelty, and injustice of his own acts. But at times he did notice, and suffered greatly" (*OMF*, p. 31).

This, in essence, is also what happens to James Page: he is overwhelmed with the weight of his personal, metaphysical guilt, and turns monstrous, as do so many of Gardner's characters.[16] Also like Dante, however, James is retrieved by a virtue greater than the strength of his despair. For Dante, it was "the image, memory, interior sensation of Beatrice. She alone was still real for him, still implied meaning in the world, and beauty" (*OMF*, p. 32). For James Page, it is the thought and voice of Ariah that ultimately lead him to the unlocking and discovery of his past, and to a sloughing off of his tragic guilt and its attendant monstrousness.[17] James stumbles upon the same truth, says Gardner, that Dante and subsequent Romantics claimed; namely, that "love is a form of knowledge." Monsters are redeemed, pasts rectified, guilt explained, through an understanding that comes through loving. If you reject this knowledge, you shoot the bear; if you accept it, you purposely miss your aim. Let the past be, advises Gardner: acknowledge its existence, use it, in fact, to comprehend the bafflements of the present, but don't try to kill it or stash it away in a cedar chest. That is what causes ghosts and black visions and suicidal swoons of guilt, and makes bad art attractive.

If anything, *October Light* is Gardner's prescription for the ills of life in the twentieth century, and it is a fitting summary of his work up until now. The novel is a sort of holistic cure that combines the lessons of humane art, emotional metaphysics, and common sense into a remedy for the gloomy malaise that seems to characterize the way we half-live now.

Chapter IX

Freddy's Book

We've heard their talk before,
and we agree, or know we never will,
and gently, slyly, in we move for the kill.
                        —"Five Sonnets to Joan"

Freddy's Book (1980) proved to be one of Gardner's most puzzling and controversial works—puzzling in its structure, and controversial in its fusion, or confusion, of content and method. Gardner described *Freddy's Book* as "two novellas,"[1] a description that seems to imply a lack of structural and thematic connection between the book's two parts, "Freddy" and "Freddy's Book." The structural unity of *Freddy's Book* is certainly problematical; the second section makes no attempt to retrieve the realistic, contemporary story line of the first, instead leaving the reader cold and wondering on a mountaintop in medieval Lappland. Thematically, the two parts relate more clearly, with the second section echoing or explicating ideas that crop up in the first section.

A less noisy but perhaps more telling ado arose over Gardner's creative method in *Freddy's Book,* a method closely tied to the book's substance and subject. *Freddy's Book* is ostensibly about the distinction between history as fact and history as art. In "Freddy," Gardner explains and explores the historiographical schism between the writers of "hard history" and of "psychohistory," between history written from accepted, provable fact and history written from responsible imagination. The author of the first writes history; the author of the second writes fiction. In "Freddy's Book," Gardner offers an example of psychohistory, or more accurately, an example of psychohistory taken one creative step further. In essence, "Freddy's Book" is a historical revision, a psychohistorian's interpretation of events in sixteenth-century Sweden.

To give his fiction the tenor of history, Gardner makes use of two pieces of "hard" historical scholarship. One is Ingvar Andersson's *A History of Sweden;* the other is Michael Roberts's *The Early Vasas: A History of Sweden, 1523–1611.* Gardner's reliance upon Andersson is minimal, but his borrowings from Roberts were extensive enough to move one critic to charge Gardner with plagiarism, a charge Gardner refuted by arguing for a methodological "collage technique," a combining of fact, memory of fact, and fiction.[2] It is a method he used before in *The Wreckage of Agathon* (arguably Gardner's first work of psychohistory), *The Sunlight Dialogues,* and perhaps his *Life and Times of Chaucer.* In too many instances to mention or document, Gardner either takes directly, paraphrases, or furbishes historical detail from Roberts for use in the second section of *Freddy's Book,* where Swedish history is transformed into a study of character—personal, national, intellectual—and belief.

It is important to note here one other source for *Freddy's Book,* one that contributes more substantially to the philosophical edge of the book: Sir Thomas Browne's *Religio Medici.* The association is not so far-fetched or so distant as it at first might seem. In a 1979 interview in *The Cresset,*[3] Gardner mentioned a work in progress entitled *Rude Heads That Staresquint.* The title itself is a misquotation of a line from Browne: "vulgar heads that looke asquint on the face of truth"; and it reappears in the first section of *Freddy's Book* as "rude heads that stare asquint at the sun."[4] The fact is that *Rude Heads That Staresquint* was the working title of *Freddy's Book,* and that while Gardner subsequently changed the title of his book, he incorporated into the text this phrase from Browne. In truth, not only the line but the *sense* of the line—and of Browne's *Religio Medici*—is worked neatly into both sections of *Freddy's Book,* weaving in and out of the fabric of the piece, tracing the imaginative thread that runs between skepticism and belief, falsehood and truth.

The first section of Gardner's fiction, "Freddy," is intensely realistic in tone and form, and serves as a sort of prologue to the second section. In "Freddy," Gardner designs a bizarre meeting between two historians—Jack Winesap (surely some meaning lies behind that name!), a psychohistorian, an explicator of fairy tales, and Sven Agaard, an old-line, traditional historian, a Scandinavianist. They are obvious representations of two historiographical methodologies, but they also serve (naturally, for Gardner) as two intellectual types, two psychological and philosophical ways of thought.

Jack Winesap is hearty and convivial, a "gregarious, infinitely curious being" (p. 4) who knows enough to laugh at the silliness of his importance. He acknowledges himself "a mere poet of a historian" who adorns fact with fancy, truth with supposition, certainty with possibility. He is one of the "new school" of revisionists and psychological conjecturalists who goes beyond reconstruction to fabrication.

Sven Agaard, on the other hand, clings to the old school, is, in fact, everything that Winesap is not. Agaard is small and "doll-like," and has a tic of speech that turns his laugh into a nervous, sheeplike "baa." Moreover, he is aloof, secretive, and hermetic, a diminutive symbol of respectful but eccentric age who has all the ingredients of one of Gardner's lunatics. Agaard admits to "grave mistakes," and keeps a cap upon his "lidded wrath," a wrath that threatens to spill over, monstrous, at any moment.

Surely the oddest thing about old Agaard, though, is his son—a "monster." His son, in fact, is the means by which Agaard and Winesap come together. Remorseful, anguished, one of "the rude heads that stare asquint at the sun" (as he describes himself), Agaard invites Winesap to visit him and to meet his son. Winesap, vaguely and indefinably guilty, agrees. And a world that was real and for the most part reliable slowly takes a strange and shadowy turn.

Agaard's house (true to Gardner's intent and tendency) is a huge, spooky, forbidding structure, not at all, as Winesap tells us, his "sort of thing":

> It was a gloomy old place, chilling as a barrow . . . and the closer I got to it, the gloomier it became, also the quieter. I arrived at a kind of graveyard gate, writing over the top, formed of rusty iron letters, too many of them missing for the name of the place to be readable. I thought, inevitably, of creaky old allegories, demented gothic tales—a thought that began in amused detachment but ended somewhere else, so that a shiver went up my spine. The place really did give off the smell, or rather the *idea*, of death. (pp. 18–19)

Walls roll, doorways moan, and hallways seem locked in air as cold as the winter winds—"cavewinds"—that swirl outside. Gardner wants things mystical and suggestive; he wants a small world where cats seem to be people, where the senses turn into question marks, and where the what-might-be is clearly the what-is. Gardner figures a fantasy landscape, "a gloomy, shifting marchland beyond which lay heaven knew what" (p. 30).

What begins as a tense, polite dinner invitation turns into an open debate of historical method. Agaard chides Winesap for his study of, as he calls it, "pseudo-history," and Winesap concedes its sometime fancifulness, admitting "that psycho-history is not always a terribly serious pursuit. It's sometimes trivial, nothing more than a pleasant entertainment—

not that that's all bad" (p. 32). But to Agaard (and to some extent Gardner, who echoes here his own criticism of such modernist writers as Barth and Barthelme), it is not the entertainment value of psychohistory that is so pernicious, but its moral ineffectiveness:

> I'll tell you the trouble with trying to learn history from fairy-tales. . . . They're mindless—even the best of them!—all bullying, no intelligence, no moral profluence, ergo no real history! Static! They're exactly true to life, those dreary flats between historical upheavals. The handsome prince comes; he finds his beloved and they live happily ever after; and no one any longer speaks or sends cards to the stepsisters. . . . People like you, Professor Winesap . . . may *pity* the stepsisters, the wicked old stepmother. You may try to understand them by some theory of dream-analysis. You may even work it out that the cruel old witch who's behind it all is of use in the world, provoking those she injures toward greater benevo-lence. . . . It never occurs to you that the beautiful princess and the wicked old witch believe exactly the same thing: Anything at all, including cunning and lies, will work for the beautiful; nothing helps the ugly. (pp. 34–35)

Psychohistory, to Agaard's mind, is little more than intellectual alchemy, changing evil into good, justifying injustice as a means to justice. "If history were done properly . . . it would make us better *men*" (p. 36), says Agaard. History reveals the persistent, undying morality of things; it does not whitewash the truth, but instead highlights it, identifying evil where there is evil and good where there is good. Certainly, Agaard here is speaking for Gardner and his formulation of moral art, demanding that art and history look squarely into the face of truth (or "the sun"), even though it may blind or stun them.

The argument over technique, however, is overshadowed by the ap-pearance of Freddy, Agaard's giant-son, who is revealed almost like a circus sideshow freak. Agaard wrenches open the curtain, with a look on his face that is

> like mingled anger, fear, and triumph. There before us, half-turned away, sat a monstrous fat blushing baby of a youth, his monkish robe unbuttoned, his lower parts carefully covered with a blan-ket. . . . The skin of his face and arms and chest was pink-splotched, shiny. He was as big as some farmer's prize bull at the fair, big as a rhinoceros, a small elephant. . . . His eyes, when he turned to glance at me, just perceptibly nodding, were red-rimmed, huge be-hind the gold-rimmed glasses; his childish pink lips were drawn

back from his teeth in what I recognized only after an instant as a sheepish smile. His expression was pitifully eager, yet at the same time distrustful, alarmed, not unlike his father's when he'd met me at the door. One side of the giant's upper lip was slightly lifted, delicately trembling with what might have been disgust—perhaps disgust aimed at himself. He pretty well knew, no doubt, what a strange sight he was, there in his cell. (pp. 46–47)

Freddy is all flesh and weight and gargantuan physicality, though he possesses a voice that is "sweet, like a young singer's." " 'Out of hand,' " mutters Agaard, and one infers the almost total loss of control; things, genes, nature, all are "out of hand" in the image of Freddy.

Because of his size, and because of the natural ill-treatment he has suffered in the past, Freddy has turned reclusive and hermetic, has "made a world for himself" (p. 41). Freddy locks himself in and away from the outside world, fraught as it is with its hurts, its insults, and its indignities. His aloofness is the part of Freddy that is most like his father, almost inherited. Yet Freddy also writes books, Agaard tells Winesap, "He writes poetry . . . I don't know if it's poetry. Long things in prose, vaguely historical" (pp. 37–38). Like Winesap, Freddy is a "mere poet of a historian," a writer of psycho/pseudohistory. It is the part of Freddy that is most unlike his father, and perhaps the part that pains his father most.

There is a like-mindedness between the boy and Winesap that drives the latter to concern and anger over Agaard's lack of effort in helping his son, in bringing him out into the world. Yet he too quickly realizes the folly of turning the "giant loose in the kingdom," and even recognizes the attraction of Freddy's solitude. The least Winesap can do is offer Freddy an exchange, a magical trading of gifts, of books, of charms. Winesap lies abed, enveloped by the darkness of the night and by the rocking walls of the house, listening to the slow, deep footfalls that echo across the hallway floor toward his bedroom. The door opens; it is Freddy:

He struggled with the door, too low and narrow for him, and at last, silently, he bent down on one knee, and I made out that he was pushing something toward me through the moonlight, some inert gift or offering, the object wobbling in the frail, flecked light, moving in at me as far as his enormous arm would reach. He lowered the object and dropped it on the floor. It struck the carpet with a thump. Slowly, he drew back his hand. After that he rose, stood motionless a moment, then, without a sound, drew the door shut. I heard floorboards creak. He seemed to move more lightly now, as if it had been a great weight he'd carried, that gift he'd brought, the object lying there solemn in the moonlight,

> mysteriously still and sufficient on the dusty gray carpet—Freddy's
> book. (pp. 63–64)

So ends "Freddy." And we, like Winesap, are left to read and wonder over
Freddy's gift. Yet we must also ponder the sense of this first part of
Gardner's book, for it is clearly more than diversion and entertainment.
We know, for instance, from his *Cresset* interview that apparently
Gardner's original intention was a book about Winesap: "In a novel I'm
working on, called *Rude Heads that Staresquint,* the central character is a
psycho-historian."[5] Somewhere along the line, then, perhaps at the moment when Gardner hit upon the idea of actually writing a psychohistorical fiction himself, "Freddy" was turned into a condensed version of that
once-planned novel.

We know, too, that Gardner does not care for psychohistory: "I think
that it's amusing and fun, but it's not really worth reading a whole book
of it because psycho-history is basically unsound."[6] So that in "Freddy,"
Gardner joins a discussion of historiography with a discussion of art,
fictionalizing once again his aesthetic theory. Gardner, I suspect, actually
holds some middle ground: he scoffs at the pretensions of psychohistory
to scientific reliability, but he is drawn to its fancifulness and its willingness to occasionally guess. In "Freddy's Book," Gardner synthesizes these
two attitudes, mixes hard history with psycho/pseudohistory, and comes
up with a fiction.

Whether it is Gardner's fiction or Freddy's fiction is one of the puzzles
of this second section, and neither writer ever really allows us to overlook
his hand in it. Freddy, like his father, is a Scandinavianist; he is also a
recluse, a "monster of sorts," a bookish, eccentric person. Freddy's
knowledge of experience comes either from books or from his preher-
metic days of school, where he was harassed and humiliated into silent
rage. Just how credible a thinker and a writer can such a person be? There
are even hints (teasingly thrown in by the *other* author of "Freddy's
Book") that Freddy projects himself into a character or characters in his
own story, which purposely lures the reader into a psychohistorical reading of this psychohistorical fiction.

The fiction itself is placed in sixteenth-century Sweden. The timing is
significant. The later Middle Ages are fading; the Renaissance is ascend-
ing. It is a period of intense historical change: exploration has pried open
the Western Hemisphere like an oyster, Gutenberg has imagined and
realized the printing press, political power has begun to shift from disparate local polities to centralized nation-states, and Luther, with hammer
and nail and pen, has unleashed the Protestant Reformation upon a sleeping Europe.

In Sweden, that sleep was perhaps deeper than in most countries. Its bounds spread chaotically, with many small cities dotting the southern portion, while the northern regions rolled unchecked and relatively unexplored beyond Finland and an otherworldly Lappland. Its people were largely uneducated and unsophisticated: more or less un-Europeanized. Agriculture was rudimentary and often unsuccessful; birch-bark many times served for bread when harvests were poor. Moreover, the country was less an independent nation than a sprawling fiefdom of Denmark, which for years, through the Union of Kalmar, controlled Sweden's economic, religious, and political existence.

In short, it was a country ripe for revolution, and in 1521 the royal family of the Stures rose against the Danish crown in a fateful, brutally crushed and avenged revolt. The rebels were tortured, quartered, or burned in furious retributive justice. Death, like the pyres' smoke, hung in a pallor over Sweden.

All of this is the historical prelude to "Freddy's Book," the factual background for Freddy's psychohistory. What happens after the failed rebellion, after the Sodermalm Massacre, is Freddy's psychoreading of the Swedish record. The story is sketched in the actions of four major characters, two of whom are historical and verifiable, one of whom is a creation of the fiction, and one whose identity and existence have been argued for centuries. Gustav Eriksson Vasa (1496–1560) is one of the few survivors of the Danish slaughter, a relation to the Sture family, and a candidate for the kingship.[7] He is at the same time wary and impetuous, possessed of a slyness that under pressure gives way to a schoolboy fury and petulance. What most marks Gustav Vasa, though, is his fearlessness: "He was no more afraid of the Devil than he was of God or Death" (p. 80). Or at least he is not afraid of the Devil before he comes to know him.

Gustav is not the only Swede with a connection to the Stures. Hans Brask, Bishop of Linkoping, is a powerful, though subtle and discreet, political figure. His influence extends far beyond the jurisdiction of his see, and he is the representative force of Catholic orthodoxy in the country. Ironically enough, he bears all the markings of one of Gardner's familiar anarchists: he dresses in black, is lean and angular, with teeth that are yellow and sharp as knives, and he walks "a little mincingly" (p. 111), one of several hints toward his homosexuality. Moreover, Brask understands the Devil—or he feels he *might* understand the Devil; and for some reason, the Devil shies at the Bishop's presence or at even the mere mention of his name (p. 104).

Not quite so contemptuous of the Devil is Gustav's cousin and closest friend, Lars-Goren Bergquist, "who was afraid of nothing in the world except the Devil" (p. 67). He is, indeed, a courageous and stalwart man, "not a fool or a superstitious oaf," but a man of great, if hesitant insight: "He was also considered to be of great intelligence, for though he thought slowly, he thought clearly and soundly, so that again and again his opinions were found to be more valuable in the end than the opinions of men quicker and more dazzling" (p. 68). A man of sure and trustworthy "opinions" in Gardner's fiction is a man to be watched—and Lars-Goren is difficult to miss, for he is unusually tall ("eight feet with his shoes off"), with "long, clumsy feet . . . and long, strong hands." Lars-Goren is, in fact, a bit of a giant. He is also the creation of Freddy's imagination.

The Devil, on the other hand, seems a creation of both imagination and nature. In "Freddy's Book," he is a historical force, an intruder into the vast course of social and political events:

> At that period the Devil showed himself in Sweden at least every other day. From time to time in the history of the world, there comes some great moment, sometimes a moment which will afterward be celebrated or mourned for centuries, at other times—perhaps more often—a moment that slides by unnoticed by most of humanity, like a jagged rock below the surface of the sea, unobserved by the ship that slips past it, missing it by inches. At the time of this story, the world was teetering on the rim of such a moment. Immense forces hung in almost perfect balance: the tap of a child's finger might swing things either way. It was for this reason that the Devil made such frequent appearances. He was keeping a careful watch on how his work was progressing. (p. 68)

At times like these, when civilization is disrupted, historical circumstance is supplanted by historical manipulation. The Devil leaves nothing to chance.

Yet even the Devil knows fear, mistrust, apprehension. In his mountain home in the ice-white regions of Lappland, he

> felt . . . something or someone at his back, some threat he could never put his finger on. Sometimes, jerking around suddenly, it would seem to the Devil that he glimpsed it for an instant, but then, as he stared more fixedly, it would resolve itself into nothing of importance. . . . Instantly, whatever it was that he saw would dim and blur, for the Devil was old and, though still far stronger than all the armies in the world, he was sometimes troubled—if he stared at things too hard—by snow blindness. (p. 71)

There are chinks in the Devil's scaly armor, weaknesses that float like small mysteries throughout the book, and Gustav, Brask, and Lars-Goren spend their time and thought trying, in various ways, to unravel these mysteries. Gustav has a government to run, a "masterpiece" to create, and he cannot do so without at least coming to some sort of truce or pact with the Devil. Brask, though disdainful of him, still does not perceive the flaw in the Devil's nature, does not quite see the trick to outwitting and defeating his personal and theological nemesis. For Lars-Goren, to comprehend the Devil is to comprehend himself: if he can define his fear, he can vanquish it once and for all. The political and private worlds of each man are riddled with flux; the balance is tipping, the child's finger (as we come to see) does rap the drum's head, history does turn lunatic.

With the Devil's help (fanning, always fanning the fires of chaos), Gustav comes to the Swedish throne in 1523. His flesh has nearly been turned to steel by the violence of his rebellion, but his mind retains its wishful political logic. Gustav has "high hopes: he knew himself no fool, knew to the last detail what was wrong in Sweden and what he, as king, could do about it; knew, moreover, that he had a gift for inspiring those around him, so that surely his government must prove a masterpiece of sorts" (p. 121). Yet at the same time, Gustav recognizes the ultimate political reality of his situation, knows "that sooner or later, he must drive his friend the Devil out of Sweden" (p. 120). In some ways, Gustav's is the worst predicament of all. He sincerely desires beneficent change, but he also knows that the Devil's voice is constantly at his ear, whispering confusion and mean ambition.

There is a certain tragedy in Gustav's existence that is pointed out to him by Bishop Brask, himself a victim of his nature, his position, and his ideals. In a voice that is both scornful and self-pitying, Brask tells Gustav: " 'Betrayal of ideals is a great sin and a torment. But what you do, that's merely savage, merely bestial. Who blames a dog if he eats cow dung? We merely look away in disgust. Dogs will be dogs. But if a man eats dung, and not from madness, which makes him just an animal again, but for some considered purpose not central to his survival but pursuant to his comfort or luxury—*then* we look away with a vengeance, my friend'—he raised one stern finger—'not in disgust but in scorn!' " (p. 110). The Bishop's analysis is not entirely accurate, for he misses or is willfully blind to his kinsman's own grand vision. Gustav tries to create a political work of art in a time when all forces are regimented against him; he acts in defiance of historical circumstance and (as history itself proves him) he succeeds impressively. He is transformed into a national, historical hero.

Bishop Brask, on the other hand, has long since sacrificed his ideals to necessity and fatalistic despair. Brask is no fool; he survives plots and counterplots, the workings of true fools. But Brask is bored by it all, finds it all so "tiresome." He is trapped by the demands of his own rhetoric and style ("always the intolerable burden of style!"), and he only observes, always wryly, the actions of other men. In Brask, rhetoric takes the place of feeling, scorn the place of effort. Brask is, in fact (as Lars-Goren later realizes), "a monster . . . a man who no longer had feeling for anything except, perhaps, style" (pp. 150, 153). Brask has lost the ability to love. He is a nihilist, an exhausted, defeated, withdrawn crier of the world's meaninglessness.[8]

Fortunately, the world is not made up entirely of Hans Brasks. There are, in the world and in Gardner's fictions, those persons like Lars-Goren who characterize the qualities of faith, endurance, and the warmth of the hearth. Lars-Goren is the only major character with family, and it is to that family and to his manor that Lars-Goren retreats after Gustav's victory. Love and succor and ministration do wonderful things to a man long separated from those for whom he cares most. Lars-Goren stands with his wife, amidst the awkwardness of reunion, and

> after a moment, for the first time since he'd arrived, they kissed. The feeling of strangeness and guilt fell away; he understood by sure signs that, odd as it might seem, he was the joy of her life, as she was of his. . . . It seemed a long, long way from where the Devil schemed and plotted. Indeed, it was hard to believe in the Devil's existence, here in his own long bed, with his wife. Yet the Devil was real enough, he knew, somewhere far away—or maybe not so far away. (pp. 129–30)

Lars-Goren's castle is his refuge from the chaos of Stockholm, an emotional locus where even the Devil, though present, feels uncomfortable.

The Devil, of course, troubles Lars-Goren more than anything in or out of the world. "One had no chance against the Devil," Lars-Goren understands, but he lives "in the desperate hope of understanding the enemy and outstriding him" (p. 80). And to outdistance and understand the Devil, Lars must identify his fear, his panic at heart's center. It is not, he is sure, the fear of death: "A hundred times he'd faced death in battle and once he had very nearly died of a mysterious disease" (p. 81). No, it is not death that he is fearful of, though he knows it is only "luck" that makes it so. Nor is it the fear "of eternal damnation—hellfire, instruments of torture, and the rest—the things one saw in holy pictures or heard about in stories" (p. 82). Lars-Goren knows that God exists, exists as a vague, munificent (with both good gifts and bad) spirit. His is the God of the Lapps: "It was simply there, beneficial or harmful in about the way wolves or reindeer are, a parallel existence neither loving nor malicious, not even consciously indifferent; a force to be reckoned with, avoided or made use of, like the ghosts in one's hut of stretched hides" (p. 83). For

Lars-Goren, too, there is something paternal about his God, something tied to his own father, a connection that leads him "accidentally but firmly to the persuasion that if hell existed it could only exist because God had gone insane. God might be baffling to a human mind . . . but God, if he was sane, was not ultimately dangerous" (p. 84).

God, it is true, might be sane, but the Devil is another case. God might have a plan, but the Devil—the Devil might be "simply crazy, revelling in confusion, urging everyone around him to frenzied activity, having, himself, no idea under heaven what the outcome would be, merely hoping for the best, like an idiot chess-player who occasionally wins by throwing away bishops and queens and confounding his foe" (p. 92). If the Devil is insane—if, in other words, history is out of control and chaotic—what action does a man in the midst of that chaos take? This is the essential intellectual choice. It is the choice that all of Gardner's heroes have to make, and Lars-Goren is no exception. His dilemma is a special one, for he is a man torn between love of family and love of country. On his manor, he is a minor god; he must make decisions, life and death decisions, and assume responsibility for those decisions. "There are evils in the world that a man can't take the blame for, evils that nobody can do anything about" (p. 127), declares Lars-Goren, evils that are a part of one's times. Justice, for an instant, becomes dark and blurred. A woman is burned as a witch, and Lars-Goren is troubled with nightmares, a persistent vision of the dead woman's face: "She stared straight ahead of her, with an expression he could not fathom, as if she were looking at something no one else could see, perhaps a steel-bright light like the light he'd seen in the clouds as he rode home, but a light that came not from the clouds but from everywhere at once, as if the whole physical world had vanished, consumed by that terrible brightness" (p. 140). Light blinds a staring Devil. The witch, like the victims on Sodermalm hill, is transfixed by the light. Lars-Goren returns to Halsingland, realm of clear light. Eyes stare-squint at the light. The image refuses to die, is resurrected in Bernt Notke's statue of St. George and the Dragon, which Lars-Goren and his family go to Hudiksvall to see. Lars-Goren's eyes fix upon

> the blank, staring face of the knight, gazing straight forward, motionless, as if indifferent to the monster, gazing as if mad or entranced or blind, infinitely gentle, infinitely sorrowful, beyond all human pain. I am Sweden, he seemed to say—or something more than Sweden. *I am humanity, living and dead.* For it did not seem to Lars-Goren that the monster below the belly of the violently trembling horse could be described as, simply, "foreigners," as the common interpretation maintained. It was evil itself; death,

> oblivion, every conceivable form of human loss. The knight, killing
> the dragon, showed no faintest trace of pleasure, much less pride—
> not even interest. (pp. 147–48)

The face, the staring eyes are the face and eyes of all those who "looke
asquint on the face of truth." The truth is blinding, brilliant, numbing.
Lars-Goren feels it, the crowd about him feels it, even his insightful
young son Erik feels it: "His son met his eyes, but his face now showed
nothing, as blank as the face of the knight staring straight into the sun"
(p. 148). This truth is the very light that shines through all of Gardner's
fiction—the light in *The Sunlight Dialogues,* the light in "John Napper
Sailing through the Universe," the light in *October Light*—and it is the
light that becomes most clearly the central image in *Freddy's Book.*

If Lars-Goren's Halsingland is a region of light and clarity, Gustav's
Stockholm is a city awash in confused and murderous darkness. The
Devil, as always, has been busy. The economy is near bankruptcy, the
land is barren, and, as if they were a part of nature, political plots abound.
Gustav trusts, perhaps justifiably, no one. Even Bishop Brask is drawn
into a plot against the king, though he is attracted more by the curiosity
of the thing than by its potential for success. For Brask, the plot is just
one more way of coming to know the Devil.

> Bishop Brask understood the Devil. Perhaps he could even outwit
> him, he sometimes thought, if he could summon up enough of his
> heart's former warmth to make it worth it; but that was something
> he was in no mood to expect. It was a curious venom, the poison
> that flowed from the Devil. Say that all human life is idiotic, all
> human feeling an absurdity, effect without due cause; say that to
> weep at the death of one child after the deaths of a million million
> children . . . say that all this is a shameful humiliation, an outrage
> not to be put up with; say that love and sorrow, considered from
> the peak of the mountain of eternity, are as paltry and insignificant
> as the wild, ravished hymning of blue-glinting flies on the four-
> day-old corpse of a mongrel. Say these things, yes, say all this once,
> thought Bishop Brask—say it once with conviction—and how are
> you to rise without revulsion to even the emotion of a heart-felt
> objection to the death you've just swallowed? Dry as a spider, the
> old bishop listened to the dessicate kiss of his rhetoric, the gro-
> tesquely chiming rhymes: *conviction, revulsion, emotion, objection.*
> How was he to feel anything worthy of even the debased coin
> "feeling," he asked himself, limited forever to the predictable
> trapezoids of his mind's drab spiderweb, language? (pp. 168–69)

Brask the spider, the rhetorician, the voyeur. He is a spindly, malaise-ridden, almost hopeless little man in a land of giants.

Yet "almost hopeless" is not equivalent to despair. "The childish impulse to tell the truth was still alive in him . . . indeed he still believed, in some back part of his brain, that there existed some truth to tell" (p. 170). For an instant, Brask feels the urge to open up, to communicate, to tell the truth in a letter to Lars-Goren. The urge passes, a wild "lunatic impulse," but anyone who knows Gardner knows that the lunatic impulse is one to be acted upon; and the development of Hans Brask is the development of his willingness finally to act, to exist on the fringe, to "outride the edge" of his rhetoric.

His king eventually gives him that opportunity. Gustav squelches the abortive revolt by his advisers (a revolt from which Brask safely removes himself before the final hour), and decides that "the time has come to seek out the Devil" (p. 194). For this chore, Gustav selects Brask and Lars-Goren, his closest enemy and his closest friend, and two distinct intellectual opposites. They head northward toward the home of the Devil, the land of the Lapps, the source of beaming light. Their journey is both a mission and a revelation, as personal and worldly mysteries are illuminated in the brightness of the land and sky and the temper of the people.

Between Stockholm and Lars-Goren's home in Halsingland, the two men argue (in typical Gardner dialogue fashion) political and biological theory, Brask spinning a Spencerian world of survival and selection and the sifting out of men and governments and ideas. "Truth will be whatever survives, generation on generation" (p. 204), Brask declares, and he is partly right, believing with Gardner that truth in whatever form—religion, philosophy, art—is what endures in the intuitive minds of the people. Truth and morality will out.

But Brask has no patience with faith: "That's one of the Devil's main tricks, of course. Fill a man with faith. What evils, what absolute horrors the noble sword of faith sends pouring into the world" (p. 207). Faith breeds action, yes—"You act on it! That's the beauty of faith"—but the act often times is senseless, ambitious, savage, ignorant. Brask argues out of despair and disillusion. He is a man who locks up the secrets of his own history, whose heart is "weighted down with fieldstones." One of the truths behind Brask's scorn is the love he once felt as a young man for a friend, a young prior. Brask recalls how the man's words opened up his heart, how the "whisper of his skirts at the door was slaughtering, his scent unearthly" (p. 209). These memories rise, are resurrected through the course of Brask's journey; they are given up grudgingly, like coins, to Lars-Goren's honest interest and patience. Once again the truth, just for an instant, comes leaping up in him "like a shock of excitement, a remembered nightmare" (p. 209), before it is crushed by the weight of Brask's despair. The unlocking of Brask's heart comes slow.

By the time the two men reach Halsingland, Brask significantly has come to think of Lars-Goren as a friend, a thought Brask probably has not known since the days of a younger man's memory. Brask sees the effect of Halsingland, of the knight's manor, on Lars-Goren himself; he also sees the possible flaw behind such an existence. He draws a major historical point for Lars-Goren, marking for him the distinction between city and country, between the reality of Stockholm and the pleasant myth of Hal-singland. The city is complexity, confusion, power, and wealth; the country is clarity, order, contentment, and temperance. Precivilized Europe, the Europe before the city—before the "Fall"—was the Europe of signifi-cant religion and significant art. Postcivilized Europe, postcity and post-Fall Europe is a Europe strangely familiar to the twentieth century: "Great cities rise, artists grow wealthy, their vision grows confused and complex. What a pity! Irony comes in. Paradox. Soon the only powerful emotion artists feel is nihilism" (pp. 216–17). There are "failures of vision." People refuse to act, to communicate, to love. It is the Old Testament ethic conceived by a nation of shepherds and farmers and rural philosophers, and it is outdated. That is why, Brask tells Lars-Goren, "it's unreal, this Eden you live in, this Platonic Form of right behavior. It's refreshing, I don't deny it! It fills a man with hope and good sense, rejuvenates his spirit. But what if it's all snare and illusion? . . . We like to say gloomy, grim cities are the haunt of the Devil, but tradition is against us: it places his home in the unpopulated North—perhaps some such pastoral scene as that valley there below us, shining like a garden" (p. 219). The serpent in the garden. Brask is correct—the Devil inhabits the northland, and power corrupts the city and its citizens. All of Brask's rhetoric and logic, however, is not enough to convince Lars-Goren to forsake his home and family. It takes the King's troops and the King's threats to drive the knight and his bishop (recall the chess-playing Devil) on to Lappland, to the Devil's mountain.

On Lappland's outer rim, Brask and Lars-Goren confront the spirit of the woman burned for witchery on Lars-Goren's estate. She appears be-fore them to condemn the knight, and to damn him for his "devilish complacence":

> Though it may not bring me to rest, I have been given the chance
> to say what I have to say to you: that if I am damned, then you are
> ten thousand times damned, Lars-Goren. You are called a great
> fighter and a wise counsellor, and you are praised as a man who is
> afraid of nothing in the world except the Devil. But I have come to

tell you you are a coward and a fool, for you shiver at a Nothing—mere stench and black air, for that is what he is, your wide-winged Devil—and in the presence of the greatest evil ever dreamt of, the fact that we exist in the world at all, helpless as babes against both evil and seeming good, you do not have the wit to blanch at all. (p. 226)

She turns the curse about, heaping judgment upon judgment. Her eyes are dead, but only in the sheerest physical sense, for they stare at Lars-Goren with "the indifference of a judge, or perhaps the indifference of a divine messenger" (p. 224). The specter sees and issues the truth, bearing on her face the same sort of blankness and amazed neutrality as do all those who stare at the sun. Brask berates her for her selfishness, her ignorance, her single-mindedness and lack of purpose. But Lars-Goren sees dimly through to the truth, telling Brask, "She's right, and you're right. We all are. . . . It's right to cry out for justice beyond anything else. If *we* can dream of justice, surely God can too, if he's still conscious. No harm that she blames me for her misfortunes. We taught her the system, we aristocrats. 'Look to us,' we said. 'We'll take care of you.' If we too were victims of a stupid idea, that's not her fault" (p. 230). The Devil is just a part of the general chaos. The human imagination and the human will, these too are ordering and disordering forces. Gazing ahead into the white Lappland landscape, staring "blankly into the light," Lars-Goren nails his fear: "It was rage that made me tremble; fear that the chaos is in myself, as in everything around me" (p. 231). The fear, the rage, the chaos, the guilt, the Devil—they all exist because we feel they exist. They are not, as Brask lamely argues, mere words, linguistic constructs; Brask himself knows that pain exists. People struggle against the darkness, stare squint-eyed into the sun searching for the truth, and what they get is sometimes the truth, sometimes the half-truth, and sometimes mere sunlight. But even mere sunlight illuminates.

In the end, history becomes the sum of human action. Forces collide, combine, synthesize, and we are pushed this way and that into action. Brask and Lars-Goren stumble into Lappland through the might of the King, the perversity of the Devil, and the insistent tapping of a Lapp shaman on a drum of reindeer skin.

Lappland is a mystical land, a land radiant with light and snow where Lapp and reindeer are strangely akin, dark-eyed and deep. Lappland logic is magic; second sight is as natural as wisdom teeth, and events are foretold in the dance of small stones from a reindeer's belly. Existence is incredibly simple there, too simple, as Lars-Goren's son realizes: "The trouble is, it's not possible to be like the Lapps" (p. 150). They live isolated in their icy, white otherland, content with the different worlds of matter and spirit, unworried by the Devil who sleeps atop their mountains. With their reindeer eyes they peer into the light of snow and sun and stare down truth—and live that truth, that simplicity unbeset by scheming, pride, or fear. The Lapps call the reindeer "six-eyes," and Lars-Goren (part Lapp himself) senses the applicability of the image to the Lapps, as well. The Lapp, too, "was a creature of six eyes: in tune with the wind and snow, the heartbeat of the reindeer, the mind of God. It was true, of course, as his son had said, it was not possible to be like the Lapps. Yet also it was true that it was good to know that Lapps existed, not dreams or illusions, real people, living at the extreme" (p. 238). Cities, kings, wealth, bishoprics: none of these exist for the Lapps. There is only the sphere of sun and light and truth.

It is a marvelous place to kill the Devil, who perches on his mountain peak, blinded by the gleam of snow and ice all about him. The Devil knows something is afoot, senses the fear that has trailed him ever since all this business in Sweden began, knows even that the knight and the bishop have come to kill him. He goes so far as to appeal to them each in their separate dreams, talking to Lars-Goren of evil as "bad luck" and trying to badger him into killing Gustav for the sake of justice and country; and whispering to Brask of "the Devil's lies"—books, love, God— trying to maneuver one last intellectual trick. The Devil, at last, is a fool, caught by his own indifference and inability to take things seriously.

Even Bishop Brask, feeling the nearness of extinction, pauses to revel in his pride, "a bursting star of intellectual energy." Yet for all of his intellectual energy, Brask cannot totally understand the transformation he senses himself undergoing, this intense shift from ennui to exhilaration, from cynicism to hope:

> Even to Hans Brask it was a strange business, a kind of miracle. He had meant to cry out from despair, as usual, and he had reason enough: he was beyond pain, numb to the heart; yet what he felt was the wild excitement of a child or an animal. He would not be fooled by it. He was a sick man, and he knew there was no chance of getting back from here alive. Bishop, man-of-God, whatever, he had no faith in God. As surely as he knew he was alive he knew God was dead or had never existed. What was this euphoria but an animal pleasure in existence at the margin—the joy of the antelope when the tiger leaps? Yet the joy was real enough. Absurdly, for all his philosophy, he was glad to be alive and dying. (p. 242)

Brask's is a typical Gardner "miracle": a man dying in a dead philosophy is resurrected through action and involvement in life. The reality of existence—the movement of blood, the fever of exuberance, the vehement affirmation of the quality of things—turns bad logic into a ghost. Climbing the Devil's throat, all the while exclaiming the futility of the act, Brask becomes for one last instant a human being; his actions belie what he takes for belief. And at the last, as the Devil breaks his bones and takes his life, Brask's face goes "as blank as the face of Bernt Notke's carved statue" (p. 245), blank with the realization that the heroic action is possible, blank with the knowledge that death is not a loss but a transmogrification of body into spirit.[9]

All that is left is the slitting of the Devil's throat. As the knife of reindeer bone rives the dragon's skin, the sky turns blood red, the earth groans—and history does not change. Kings and tsars continue to scheme, families continue to love, and "the yellow light of cities" continues to shine bleakly. With the Devil dead now, though, human beings become terrifyingly responsible for the course of events. The Enlightenment turns people "reasonable," and trashes the remnants of medieval superstition, mysticism, and intuitive belief. Humanity is suddenly rational.

That is part of the beauty and part of the significance of *Freddy's Book*. Gardner hurls his characters—some fictional, some real—into a vortex of swift, irrational historical change, and he charts their actions, writes his psychohistory. The Middle Ages had one distinct advantage going for them: an implicit belief in God and Devil, in forces actively at work for good and evil. How do you eradicate chaos? You slay the Devil, you send your worthiest knight to perform the ultimate heroic act. You send a lunatic, a fool on a fool's errand. And the novelist, hopeful dreamer that he is, writes a fool's story of a fool's deed. That, according to Gardner, is the only way to come to the truth. The knight slays the dragon. The artist—Bernt Notke, John Gardner—retrieves and re-creates that act, turns virtue into wood or black print, in order to touch each man and woman with that heroic spirit. The artist transfixes each of us with the brilliance of the act, with the blinding bright lucidity of the sun that is moral belief and truth. We squint, we stare, and ultimately (Gardner hopes) we see.

Chapter X

The Art of Living and Other Stories

Mortal things like you and I
must bear innumerable crosses.
    —"Dream Vision"

With *The Art of Living* (1981), Gardner brought together nearly all of his previously uncollected short stories and satisfied an old desire to consolidate all of the random fiction he had floating about in various journals and magazines (only the title story had been unpublished). Curiously, while none of the stories in this collection is as intensely personal as the patently autobiographical "John Napper Sailing through the Universe" in *The King's Indian,* at least three of the stories—"Redemption," "Stillness," and "Come on Back"—draw unmistakably upon Gardner's own history for their substance. In a way, *The Art of Living* is a working through of problematical parts of Gardner's past, a sort of therapy in prose by which Gardner comes to at least a temporary truce with private emotional bogies.

More important, though, *The Art of Living* demonstrates with amazing consistency one of Gardner's larger philosophical obsessions: the relation of the artist to his art and to his life. All but three of the stories in this volume deal directly with art in one of its forms or another, and two of those remaining stories ("Come on Back" and "The Art of Living"), while not concerned with bona fide artists, do examine the roles of what might be called "unsuspected artists," or people who work artistically in unusual or even quite mundane ways.[1] That, in fact, is the lesson of *The Art of Living:* there is the artistry of creation (the art of the composer, the painter, the writer) and there is the artistry of life (the art of the individual who lives life as it should be lived, artistically). For Gardner, life should and must be transformed into art, or into *an* art. In some way, the artist should be better equipped to live the artistic and (Gardner would say) moral life, but even he must sometimes be made to see the transformative possibilities of his art and to accept the responsibilities that are inherent in the nature of the artist. Contrarily, the "unsuspected artist" often lives the artistic life, masters the "art of living" unconsciously, and only in epiphanous moments of brilliant clarity and emotional crisis is made aware of the blinding power of art in life. Art, Gardner believes, is infectious and undeniably effective; it has the ability to chastise death, to negate loss, and—as all of Gardner's fiction tells us—to illuminate the darker and more painful mysteries of our existence.

In the first story in the collection, "Nimram," Gardner examines one of his favorite "games of opposites": the matter of good and bad luck. Benjamin Nimram is a toweringly successful symphonic conductor, a man blessed with comfortable public and private lives. He is one of those creatures who occasionally seems to loom over the rest of mankind, a man larger than his name or reputation. He rages and loves like a god, yet he is consciously aware, behind his "Beethoven frown," that he is "a fortunate accident, a man supremely lucky."

> Had he been born with an ear just a little less exact, a personality more easily ruffled, dexterity less precise, or some physical weakness—a heart too feeble for the demands he made of it, or arthritis, the plague of so many conductors—he would still, no doubt, have been a symphony man, but his ambition would have been checked a little, his ideas of self-fulfillment scaled down. Whatever fate had dealt him he would have learned, no doubt, to put up with, guarding his chips. But Nimram had been dealt all high cards, and he knew it. He revelled in his fortune, sprawling when he sat, his big-boned fingers splayed wide on his belly like a man who's just had dinner, his spirit as playful as a child's for all the gray at his temples, all his middle-aged bulk and weight—packed muscle, all of it—a man too much enjoying himself to have time for scorn or for fretting over whether or not he was getting his due, which, anyway, he was. He was one of the elect.[2]

Gardner, like Taggert Hodge in *The Sunlight Dialogues,* believes in the separation of the lucky and the unlucky, believes that we are born with certain portions of good and bad fortune, and that those who ascend are those who are randomly, unforeseeably blessed. It is totally illogical, and impossible to rationally explain.

Nimram himself does not understand it, as he discovers on his flight to Chicago. Nimram shares a first-class seating with a teen-aged girl named Anne, a girl whose physical features could, in another life, have made her

Nimram's daughter. Anne is dying; she is one of the negatively elect. Death is an immediate, inescapable fact for her, yet she fears it, as she fears her plane ride, her first, only when she thinks about it, when she puts the fact into words and declares it. Anne is the symbol of life's most unbearable paradox: death is neither just nor reasonable, but accidental. Time, which Nimram had "consumed too fast to notice he was losing it . . . was time the girl would never get" (p. 19). Gardner throws two of the "chosen" together, juxtaposes good and bad fortune to bring home to Nimram the tragedy that sits beside him. Nimram's sense of responsibility and his singular sense of fear for others throw him into a general metaphysical confusion of doubt and wonder, and make him uncertain of his own thought and feeling:

> It wasn't pity he felt, or even anger at the general injustice of things; it was bewilderment, a kind of shock that stilled the wits. If he were religious—he was, of course, but not in the common sense—he might have been furious at God's mishandling of the universe, or at very least puzzled by the disparity between real and ideal. But none of that was what he felt. God had nothing to do with it, and the whole question of real and ideal was academic. Nimram felt only, looking at the girl—her skin off-color, her head unsupported yet untroubled by the awkwardness, tolerant as a corpse—Nimram felt only a profound embarrassment and helplessness: helplessly fortunate and therefore unfit, unworthy, his whole life light and unprofitable as a puff-ball, needless as ascending smoke. He hardly knew her, yet he felt now—knowing it was a lie but knowing also that if the girl were really his daughter it would be true—that if Nature allowed it, Mother of tizzies and silences, he would change lives with the girl beside him in an instant.
> (pp. 19–20)

How do you behave if you are one of the elect, one of the walking gods on earth? How do you deal with the injustice that sprouts in the gap between good luck and bad? Nimram's heart opens up, almost upon human reflex, with love for the doomed girl, but that is intellectually not enough. Nimram, the fortunate, temporary hero-god must act to redeem that injustice through his art.

Which is what Nimram does the following night in a performance by the Chicago Symphony of Mahler's Fifth, a performance which Anne attends. The moment is compactly epic, epiphanous. The god descends; Nimram springs upon the stage "like a panther," light angling off his hair like lightning flashes, and draws the orchestra into him, commands them with his presence, makes player and conductor one. Anne feels the magic of it all:

> He threw back his shoulders and raised both hands till they were level with his shoulders, where he held them still, as if casting a spell on his army of musicians, all motionless as a crowd in suspended animation, the breathless dead of the whole world's history, awaiting the impossible. And then his right hand moved . . . and the trumpet call began, a kind of warning both to the auditorium, tier on tier of shadowy white faces rising in the dark, and to the still orchestra bathed in light. Now his left hand moved and the orchestra stirred, tentative at first, but presaging such an awakening as she'd never before dreamed of. Then something new began, all that wide valley of orchestra playing, calm, serene, a vast sweep of music as smooth and sharp-edged as an enormous scythe—she had never in her life heard a sound so broad, as if all of humanity, living and dead, had come together for one grand onslaught. The sound ran, gathering its strength, along the ground, building in intensity, full of doubt, even terror, but also fury, and then—amazingly, quite easily—lifted. (pp. 26, 29)

Art, in all of its brilliant lucidity, redeems for an instant the tragic darkness of life. Nimram becomes god-pilot-conductor, turning death's scythe into a life-giving arc of sound; man does not descend, but ascends into that realm of spirit and light where time and space fade, where the souls of past and present conjoin, where death is defeated. The act of the artist elevates man, transforms matter into spirit in a sort of aesthetic holiness. It is an act that is repeated throughout Gardner's collection, and one which ultimately closes the book, in a gathering of living and dead, in a direct echo of this first story.

This theme of art as redemptive force comes through most clearly and most intensely in the second story, "Redemption," which is Gardner's personal attempt to redefine a particularly painful part of his memory. The story is based on the tragic death of Gardner's younger brother Gilbert in a farming accident in the home-fields of Batavia, New York. Gardner talked of this memory in an interview in *The Paris Review,* and explained how the story served as a deliberate exorcism: "Before I wrote the story about the kid who runs over his younger brother . . . always, regularly, every day I used to have four or five flashes of that accident. I'd be driving down the highway and I couldn't see what was coming because I'd have a memory flash. I haven't had it once since I wrote the story. You really do ground your nightmares, you *name* them."[3] Guilt, it should be clear by now, is an integral part of Gardner's universe, and in "Redemption" Gardner attempted a reconciliation with his own private nightmares and misplaced responsibilities.

Death is typically most brutal in its effect on the living, and the tragedy of David Hawthorne's death is felt most clearly by his family. Dale Hawthorne, the father, is profoundly affected, is in fact "nearly destroyed by it":

> Sometimes Jack would find him lying on the cow-barn floor, crying, unable to stand up. Dale Hawthorne . . . was a sensitive, intelligent man, by nature a dreamer. . . . He loved all his children and would not consciously have been able to hate his son even if Jack had indeed been, as he thought himself, his brother's murderer. But he could not help sometimes seeming to blame his son, though consciously he blamed only his own unwisdom and—so far as his belief held firm—God. Dale Hawthorne's mind swung violently at this time, reversing itself almost hour by hour, from desperate faith to the most savage, black-hearted atheism. Every sickly calf, every sow that ate her litter, was a new, sure proof that the religion he'd followed all his life was a lie. Yet skeletons were orderly, as were, he thought, the stars. He was unable to decide, one moment full of rage at God's injustice, the next moment wracked by doubt of His existence. (pp. 30–31)

This disparity, as Nimram calls it, between the real and the ideal hits at Hawthorne as it hits at every person blasted by tragedy and the world's illogic. His mind turns, at times, to suicide and a sort of metaphysical escape, but he ultimately settles on literal physical escape, becoming a fugitive from his family and home. He abandons responsibility, leaves his son, daughter, and wife to mourn their loss among themselves, to survive as *he* hopes to survive.

His wife, Betty, survives in her changedness. She weeps alone at night, and embraces her children "whenever new waves of guilt swept in." She is the emotional center who through her strength of character and sense of love keeps "her family from wreck." Phoebe, the daughter, survives through an abiding child's belief in a God whose wisdom outruns his logic and justice; she sticks unthinkingly, as a girl her age would do, to her faith, tested for the first time by the world's unpredictability.

Jack Hawthorne, too, survives, through a long ordeal of doubt and guilt and sorrow. He doubts his own ability to love and to feel for anyone or anything: "He'd never loved his brother, he raged out loud, never loved anyone as well as he should have. He was incapable of love, he told himself. . . . He was inherently bad, a spiritual defective. He was evil" (pp. 33–34). Jack plummets to the depths of philosophical despair, damning himself for the accident of his brother's death. Like his father, Jack eventually comes to doubt the necessity of his existence, bemired as he is in the certainty of his own damnation: "The foulness of his nature became clearer and clearer in his mind until, like his father, he began to toy—dully but in morbid earnest now—with the idea of suicide" (p. 37). The facticity of death, as Gardner has illustrated before, is the ultimate moral test. It drives us down, sinks us, and challenges us to submit or to respond. If we submit, we become nihilists; if we respond heroically, we rise to love and to believe once again.

Dale Hawthorne responds by returning to his family, who surround him in a tableau of forgiveness: the prodigal father come home. He is a man much changed by his experience; the luster has left his eyes and his body seems empty of its old energy. There is a new sobriety about him that tells you he has faced down tragedy and survived—not necessarily prevailed, but survived. Jack does not immediately perceive the agony his father has suffered, and so rages at him with a censorious sort of hatred. He isolates himself from the family, refuses the consoling, healing influence of those who love him, and turns to his music and to his French horn for solace and some sort of intuitive philosophical comfort.

At the end of the story, Jack visits his horn teacher in Rochester, Arcady Yegudkin, "the General." Yegudkin is an old man, an artist and a sufferer and, with his misshapen wife, a survivor. He is pathetically human—"In his pockets, in scorn of the opinions of fools, he carried condoms, dirty pictures, and grimy, wadded-up dollar bills"—but when he plays the horn, he becomes a god, a transformer of matter into spirit:

> In that large, cork-lined room, it was as if, suddenly, a creature
> from some other universe had appeared, some realm where feelings
> become birds and dark sky, and spirit is more solid than stone. The
> sound was not so much loud as large, too large for a hundred
> French horns, it seemed. . . . As if charged with life independent of
> the man, the horn sound fluttered and flew crazily like an enormous
> trapped hawk hunting frantically for escape. It flew to the bottom
> of the lower register, the foundation concert F, and crashed below
> it, and on down and down, as if the horn in Yegudkin's hand had
> no bottom, then suddenly changed its mind and flew upward in a
> split-second run to the horn's top E, dropped back to the middle
> and then ran once more, more fiercely at the E, and this time burst
> through it and fluttered, manic, in the trumpet range, then lightly
> dropped back into its own home range and, abruptly, in the middle
> of a note, stopped. The room still rang, shimmered like a vision. . . .

> Jack Hawthorne stared at the instrument suspended in space and at his teacher's hairy hands. (p. 47)

On the outer limits of art exists a transmogrified world, a world "suspended in space" and time, a world that Jack Hawthorne longs to know and to explore. For now, however, he can only cry, like Stephen Dedalus, at the beauty and the elusiveness of his vision, and fall once more into the arms of the world around him: his family, his art, his ability to love. There is much to suffer and to enjoy before he can transform the world as Yegudkin can, to take someone soaring and dipping as this artist has taken him. There is always the promise, though, that one's art can and will redeem, will erase the guilt and assuage the pain, will return one's faith and peace-in-sleep. That is the magic of art.

Gardner goes after the quality of this magic in "Stillness," another autobiographical story. It is one of two Carbondale stories in the book, and seems clearly modeled on Gardner's past: Joan and Martin ("Buddy") Orrick are surely John ("Bud" as his parents call him) Gardner and his first wife Joan, and Orrick with his crewcut, leather jacket, and "unpublishable novels" is the Gardner in the jacket photo of the rare hardback edition of *The Resurrection*.

In this story, however, the remembrances belong to Joan Orrick, who while on a lecture trip with her husband, recalls her days as an accompanist in a dance school in St. Louis. Like Jack Hawthorne in the previous story, Joan Orrick has artistic dreams of grandeur: she wants to go to Paris, to play piano, to find the magic. She plays for Pete and Jacqui Duggers—Duggers School of Dance—and she remembers the artistry, the "magic" of Pete Duggers when he moved:

> The speed and lightness with which Pete Duggers danced were amazing to behold, but what was truly miraculous, so that it made you catch your breath, was the way he could stop, completely relaxed, leaning his elbow on empty air and grinning as if he'd been standing there for hours, all that movement and sound you'd been hearing pure phantom and illusion. That was unfailingly the climax when he danced: a slow build, with elegant shuffles and turns, then more speed, and more, and more and still more until it seemed that the room spun drunkenly, crazily, all leading—direct as the path of an arrow—to nothing or everything, a sudden stillness like an escape from reality, a sudden floating, whether terrible or wonderful she could never tell: an abrupt hush as when a large crowd looks up, all at the same moment, and sees an eagle in the sky, almost motionless, or then again, perhaps, the frightening silence one read about in novels when a buzz-bomb shut off over

London. He stood perfectly still, the piano was still, his young
students gaped, and then abruptly reality came back as the piano
tinkled lightly and he listlessly danced and, as he did so, leaned
toward his students and winked. "You see? Stillness! That's the
magic!" (pp. 54–55)

That stillness is the stillness that occurs as the artistic aftermath; it is the
stillness in the crowd at Hudiksvall as they stare at the statue of St.
George and the Dragon, in *Freddy's Book,* the stillness in the cork-lined
room in Rochester as Yegudkin puts down his horn. For an instant, time
and space are truly suspended; art performs miracles, magic. This is
Gardner's vision.

For Joan Orrick, Paris never comes—at least not in her first forty years.
Married half her life, bogged down in the mundaneness of life with a man
who sleeps "exactly as he'd always slept, winter and summer," plagued by
headaches and sleeplessness—she is a long way from the stillness of that
studio in the heart of St. Louis. The future looms tiresomely certain and
transparent, full of as much disappointment as the past. Hope seems to lie
in the recapturing of that stillness and in the re-creation of that magic—
not necessarily in the same fashion (it could just as easily have been in the
lunatic antics of her great-uncle blasting at tornados with his shotgun),
but with the same intent. To have the world transformed, just briefly, to
see art working at its best, to play in Paris and to turn Paris into an
otherworld: that is the miracle the artist seeks.

The working—and counter-working—of this miracle is the subject of
the story "The Music Lover," which is a rewriting of Thomas Mann's
"Disillusionment" (as Gardner says, "The most gallish thing I've ever
done").[4] The "music lover" in this instance is Professor Alfred Klingman,
a dusty, eccentric old man whose obsequiousness insinuates pain and
pathetic sorrow. However, as Gardner writes, "Every man who survives
in this world has at least one area in which he escapes his perhaps otherwise miserable condition, and for Professor Klingman, this area was music" (p. 66). Music, as it was for the girl in "Nimram" and for Jack
Hawthorne in "Redemption," is an escape and a salvation for Klingman.
At concerts, Klingman scurries in, his eyes like lunatic eyes, his white hair
flying, "looking terrified and slightly insane." Though amazingly ignorant of the technicalities of the music he hears—the number, the key—
Klingman enjoys a profound intuitive knowledge of the work that surpasses the sheer intellectual efficiency of the schooled listener. Indeed, his
sensitivity borders on the embarrassing, for

no one could be more responsive to the anguished wellings and
sweet palpitations of the music itself. When Mahler was played, or

even the coolest, most objective of Bruckner, tears would run streaming down Professor Klingman's nose, and sometimes he would sob audibly, so that everyone around him was made uncomfortable. At musical jokes he would sometimes guffaw, though how a man so ignorant could know that the musical jokes were jokes was hard to see. . . . From the first note to the last, even if the concert was abysmal, Professor Klingman was in heaven. (pp. 67–68)

Klingman allows himself to be transported by the music, to ascend and to swoop as the music directs or takes him. Klingman *feels* the music and the artistry.

One night, however, Klingman attends a concert featuring "three contemporary pieces" of music. The evening is a disaster. The music is dissonant and harsh and obscene: Klingman "wrung his fingers, groaned, covered his eyes, and on one occasion cried out loudly, 'Oh my God! My God!' " Klingman's actions are intuitive, emotional reactions to the inherent perniciousness of the music, a perniciousness intended by the composer, Klingman later learns, when the music's composer draws Klingman into a cafe to drink and to talk with him about the piece.

The composer is a young man, full of anger and disillusionment. Like many of Gardner's anarchists, he is dressed in black, with eyes "unnaturally bright and alert" and with "strikingly long white fingers." The composer tells Klingman of his youth, of his life as a clergyman's son in a home dominated by "a punctilious cleanliness and a pathetic, bookish optimism" (p. 74) that is reminiscent of Bishop Brask in *Freddy's Book*. He breathed, the composer tells Klingman,

> an atmosphere of dusty pulpit rhetoric—large words for good and evil which I have learned to hate, since perhaps they are to blame for all our human sufferings. . . . For me . . . life consisted entirely of those grandiose words, since I knew nothing more of it than the infinite, insubstantial emotions they called up in me. From people I expected divine virtue or hair-raising wickedness; from experience either ravishing loveliness or consummate horror. I was full of avidity for all that existed, and full of a passionate, tormented yearning for True Reality, whatever form it might take, intoxicating bliss, undreamt-of-anguish. (p. 74)

Life, for the composer, was little more than words, language, constructs of an alphabet and a rhetoric. When actually confronted with the stuff of life, then, the composer found existence paltry, dull, and unpromising: again, the disparity between the real and the ideal. Life *is* often unequal to the words that describe it; that is the danger of ignoring life for the descriptions of life. Disillusioned, the composer turned to creating works of antiart, music that joked at life and the art that tried to capture or glorify it. The composer is one of Gardner's artist-cynics, writing, composing, or painting bad, exhausted art. That is why Klingman reacts so violently to the discordance of the music, for he senses the inherent malevolence and destructiveness of the thing. The music curses life instead of showing its manifold nature of good and evil. The composer has "transformed" music into bad rhetoric, has stripped the music of its magic, has replaced the "stillness" with the painful cries of a man betrayed by art.

For Alfred Klingman, art has gone dead. For the narrator of "The Library Horror," however, art comes terrifying close to life, as literary characters fill his library and craze his imagination. Winfred, the protagonist, is a bookish man from "a family of lunatics" (p. 88). He sits one night worrying over Susanne Langer's *Problems of Art,* with its idea of virtual space, or "space that seems as real as any other until the moment we try to enter it, at which time it proves an apparition" (p. 90). Langer argues that artistic creations have a life or "living form" of their own; a literary character, "though it is a created apparition, a pure appearance, is objective; it seems to be charged with feeling because its form expresses the very nature of feeling. Therefore, it is an *objectification* of subjective life, and so is every other work of art."[5] Art has a virtual existence, an "autonomous life."

This, in fact, is what Winfred discovers when he explores the noises that have been coming for the last few days from behind his library door. Penknife in hand, he opens the door and enters the tomblike room:

> Well, no point making high drama of it. Suddenly, there in front of me—leaping out so quickly from behind the third bookshelf that I hardly knew at first where he'd come from—stood a man with an axe. He was a small man, no more than four feet tall. Why this should be I have no idea, but small he was, a perfectly formed midget with terrified, rolling, somewhat slanted eyes, more terrified of me than I had time to be of him, a ferocious little Russian—a student, I imagined—crazily muttering to himself. Dim as the room was I saw everything with dreadful clarity, like a man about to die. His eyes were sunken, his lips wildly trembled, his coat came almost to his ankles. On the blunt side of the axe there was blood and what might have been gray hair. I tried to speak, but it was as if all the air had gone out of me. My knees banged crazily together. He drew back the axe, blunt side forward, to strike me, but that

very instant a young woman in English Victorian dress appeared behind him and cried out, "Lord in Heaven! Have you gone loopy?" (p. 92)

In Winfred's library stand Raskolnikov and a woman who might be Becky Sharp, both moral outcasts, but she an outcast "from a morality so different from his own world's as to cast the idea of 'universal human nature' into the trash-heap of ancient *pseudoxia*" (p. 93). They disappear "into the dimness beyond the fourth shelf," worlds and times apart yet similar enough in temperament to go off together as, perhaps, lovers.

The reality of Winfred's vision is the obvious question. Winfred's wife stands outside the door, telling him it is time to go to bed, concerned for his welfare within the library walls. And well might she be concerned, for as her words melt into air a new vision, a new apparition comes rushing from the bookshelf toward Winfred, "brighter than the light from a bursting star, coming straight at me with a clatter and a roar like a lightning-ball" (p. 94). It is Achilles, "the hero of absolute justice, God-sent doom, terrible purgation" (p. 95). Achilles waves his huge sword over Winfred's head, hesitates for a moment at the sound of a woman's voice from beyond the door, then slices downward into Winfred's shoulder: "Not to make too much of it, I knew then and there that I was dying" (p. 95).

An interesting question: is Winfred *actually* or *virtually* dying? Are the characters so real, is Achilles's sword so sharp and so cold that it truly cuts Winfred's flesh? Winfred thinks so, the blood and life running out of him. But perhaps he is just crazy, another lunatic in a long line of lunatics? Even Winfred considers this possibility: "Here sits character *x*, a madman, struck a mortal blow by character *y*, a fiction. What can *x* do, mad as he is, but struggle to maintain justice, normality?" (p. 96). Winfred begins to think of himself as a character in a fiction—which he is. And he also begins to construct a fiction of his own, in an attempt to right a possible injustice and to give immortality to his wife and to his father: "If a fictional character, namely Achilles, can make blood run down my chest (if it is indeed running down my chest), then a living character, or two such characters—my father and my wife—can be made to live forever, simply by being put in a fiction" (p. 96). The loverlike combination of father and daughter-in-law is akin to the coupling of Raskolnikov with the Becky Sharp figure: "He's eighty-two. She's thirty. No one would think him insane except that he once backed his truck through the plate-glass window of my bank" (p. 99). Fiction becomes a convenient means to immortality.

Even Winfred looks for convenience at the end, as the desk fills with blood and his head fills with "planets and stars": " 'Dear Heavenly Father,' I whisper with all my might, for any good fiction will serve in hard times—I clench my eyes against the tumbling of the planets—'Dear Heavenly Father,' I whisper with all my might" (p. 100). Winfred's prayer trails off into silence, the story ending without punctuation, without proper finish. It is left incomplete by Gardner, who creates Winfred as a character in his own fiction and who believes, with Langer, that art has a virtual existence of its own. That is part of Gardner's aesthetic, that art is the objectification of subjective feeling. Such things *could* happen.

Toward the end of his story, Winfred begs of Achilles, "No justice . . . enough of justice!" Winfred has had enough of the cold-handed, clear-eyed justice of the gods and the godlike. Justice among the divine and the fictional is much easier than among the human here on earth. The story "The Joy of the Just" makes this point clear as it details one woman's half-comical search for her due. This story is the second of the Carbondale stories in this collection, and it has all the flavor of a piece of rural, southern humor, something from Faulkner or Welty. It is also a story of grotesques, those bizarre, outsized people who emerge from the backwoods with the looks of lunatics on their wrinkled faces and the wit and knavery of thieves.

Aunt Ella Reikert is an old, lame, near-blind woman who is a victim of more than just her body. She is turned into an avenging angel when she is run off the road by the Preacher's wife, and when no one believes, but Aunt Ella, that it is by the Preacher's wife. Ella becomes involved in a classic feud with the Preacher, anxious to "git justice," to see the Bible's words turned to truth and action. Of course, Ella has a way of turning the Bible's words to her advantage, answering her niece's husband's warning with convenient biblical injunctions of her own:

> Leon said, "It is better to dwell in the wilderness than with a contentious and an angry woman."
>
> "It is a joy to the just to do judgment," she said, "and destruction shall be to the workers of iniquity." She stood up. She felt more cheerful now. There was nothing she liked better than quoting Scriptures. Also, she had a plan. (p. 110)

Ella is convinced of her justness. She knows she is right, knows that she must seek justice for her wrong. But where, Gardner asks, does justice end and vengeance begin?

The problem with Ella is that she so *enjoys* her vengeance. The "joy" she describes is mingled with perversity and malicious delight. After she dupes the Preacher into selling her his much-prized horse, Ella feels the blood running through her old husk of a body once more: "Inside, she was jumping up and down with glee. She felt ten years old again. She felt the way she'd felt the time she broke out all the schoolhouse windows, seventy years ago now" (p. 117). And after her plan to trick the Preacher and his wife into drunkenness ends in the burning of the church, the scolding she receives reminds her of the scolding her father had given her after "she'd murdered the cat" (p. 128). Ella is part angel, part senile old woman, and part vicious young child. She comes to confuse justice with vengeance, feeling "a radiant joy like revelation" when her final plan comes to her.

In the end, Ella is proven right. The Preacher's wife did run her into the ditch, Ella's eyes did see clearly. "There's all kinds of justice," the narrator tells us at the beginning of the story, and Ella achieves her own personal brand. However, there's a certain cruelty to it all that leaves you uncomfortable and squirming. It is a mean sort of justice, the sort of justice that comes from man pretending he is God.

If "Joy of the Just" is a tale in the vein of rural, countrified humor, "Vlemk the Box-Painter" is a fable or parable for artists. Strictly speaking, "Vlemk" is a novella, one that Gardner published separately in 1979, but in spirit it is a fairytale lesson. In some ways, it is a fabulistic parallel to Gardner's earlier story, "John Napper Sailing through the Universe," for the fictional career of Vlemk follows a line similar to the true-to-life career of the artist John Napper. Vlemk descends and ascends, goes from darkness to light much in the manner of Napper, who had to pass through his own "dark" period before achieving the clarity and light of his present style.

Vlemk, as the title states, is a box-painter, an artist, and a very good one at that. In fact, he is the best:

> Though he was not old and stooped, though old enough by several years to grow a moustache and a beard that reached halfway down his chest, he was a master artist, as box-painters go. He could paint a tiny picture of a grandfather's clock that was so accurate in its details that people sometimes thought, listening very closely, that they could make out the noise of its ticking. He painted flowers so precisely like real ones that one would swear that they were moving just perceptibly in the breeze, and swear that, pressing one's nose to the picture, one could detect a faint suggestion of rose smell, or lilac, or foxglove. (p. 136)

Yet Vlemk, like so many of Gardner's characters, has another side, a monstrous side that sends him reeling into staggering drunkenness and makes friends of villains and thieves and knaves. He is trapped by his monstrousness, just as he is trapped by the metaphors of his art: " 'What a box I'm in!' he would cry, looking up from the gutter the next morning. It had long been his habit to think in terms of boxes, since boxes were his joy and occupation" (p. 137).

One morning, while Vlemk lies passed out in the street-filth, he is noticed by the Princess. Ashamed of his condition and smitten by the woman's astounding beauty, Vlemk resolves to call upon the Princess at her castle home. The Princess is taken by Vlemk's openness and grants him his wish to visit her again, but on one condition: that he paint a picture of the Princess's face so realistic and accurate that it actually speaks.

So begins Vlemk's decline. As he works on the painting, he is besieged by "morbid, unsettling ideas":

> Sometimes it crossed his mind that what the Princess had said to him might be nothing but a grim, unfeeling joke, that she had no intention whatsoever of marrying him, indeed, that her purpose in giving him the seemingly impossible task was simply to make sure that he never again spoke to her. As an artist, he had difficulty believing such things, for if one gives in to the notion that visions of extraordinary beauty are mere illusion, one might as well cut off one's hands and sit on street-corners and beg. With all the strength of his carefully nourished and trained imagination he cast back in his mind to that morning when he'd seen her in the carriage, peeking out through the curtains, and with all his dexterity and technical trickery he labored to set down that vision in paint. He could not doubt the intensity of the emotion that had surged in him or the accuracy of the vision he set down line by line. Every flicker of light in her pale blue eyes was precisely correct; the turn of the cheek, the tilt of the nose, the seven stray hairs on her forehead— all, insofar as they were finished, were indisputable. (p. 144)

Vlemk begins to doubt the condition of beauty in life. He even begins to doubt the purpose of his art and his ability as an artist to reproduce that beauty. He becomes wary of his craft, fearful "that the paint was controlling him, creating not an image of the Princess but something new, a creature never before seen under the sun" (p. 144). Vlemk wants desperately to cling to his belief in the reality of beauty, but he feels a need tugging him to redefine that reality. His painting turns into something of itself, attains a life—altogether different from what he had planned—of its own. The face reveals things better left unshown, "faint but unmistakable hints of cruelty, vanity, and stinginess." And as these traits emerge, so does Vlemk's repressed doubt: "He began to perceive clearly the fact that he'd known all along but had never quite confronted: that Beauty is an artist's vain dream; it has, except in works of art, no vitality, no body" (p. 146).

Paradoxically, though, his painting does spring to life, asserts its vitality, its "virtual existence," as Langer would call it. The face on the box becomes Vlemk's personal "library horror." All the while Vlemk is at work finishing the portrait, he is conscious of one thing: "Having come to understand the Princess, both the best and the worst in her, poor Vlemk had fallen hopelessly, shamelessly in love" (p. 150). Yet that is not the worst of Vlemk's dilemma, for the picture is indeed so lifelike that it begins to speak, and its first words are a fitful, doomful curse upon the unlucky box-painter: "You shall never speak a word until I say so!" Vlemk, then, is doubly cursed. He is held by the Princess's demand to create a painting so true to nature that it shall speak, a curse of horrible intensity for the artist; then he is cursed to dumbness when he is close to lifting the initial curse with his painting.

Part of Vlemk's problem is that he receives such bad advice. He talks with a world-weary old monk (shades of Bishop Brask) who tells him that beauty is evanescent, "momentary in the mind," and that "by the highest standards I am able to imagine, I have never known a beautiful woman . . . or even a good woman, or even a relatively good mother" (p. 147). Vlemk's trio of mismatched friends do him no better. One is a poet who no longer writes poetry because no one is capable of learning anything from it: "My audience . . . has, collectively, the brains of one pig. . . . Perhaps I underestimate pigs" (p. 162). He now filches people's jewelry and kidnaps people's children. One is a violinist who no longer makes music because his audience is his enemy and his music noise. He now steals and pilfers the pockets of the wealthy: "There's no real money in it, but the response of the crowd is tremendous" (p. 164). The third is an axe-murderer—though he has yet to claim his first victim. He is the least agreeable of all: "He had a mouth made unpleasant by small, open sores, and eyes that seemed never to fix on anything but to stare with fuming discontent in whatever direction his small, shiny head was turned" (p. 164). The axe-murderer is a nihilist, a believer in "the power of evil," Sartre's brute existent in the flesh:

> I give you my assurance—experience is the test—chop off the heads of a family of seven, let the walls and the floors be splashed with their blood, let the dogs howl, the cats flee, the parakeets fly crazily in their filthy wicker cages, then ask yourself: *is* this or *is this not* Reality?—this carnage, this disruption of splendid promise? Take the blinders from your eyes! Death and Evil are the principles that define our achievements and in due time swallow them. Ugliness is

our condition and the basis of our interest. Is it our business to set down lies, or are we here to tell the Truth, though the Truth may be unspeakably dreadful? (p. 166)

Of course, the axe-murderer speaks only in theory; his experience is merely in language and in dream. All three men, in fact, are dreamers, ineffectual, cynical, dried-up artists who have rejected their art for weak lies and poor opinions. Nihilism, Gardner seems to say, is little more than intellectual sour grapes.

Vlemk, unfortunately, is ripe for such unwisdom. His art first turns sterile, dry, and Vlemk gives up his skill. Then it turns vicious and vile as he explores the darkest sides of the Princess, probes the ugliness and evil that he has been told is the sum of our existence. He paints "Reality boxes" that portray the varieties of man's potential monstrousness, and he achieves a new sort of mastery: "He was painting, after all, as no other box-painter in the world could paint, making discoveries as rare as any scientist's. He was coming to such a grasp of life's darkest principles—and at the same time discovering, as he chased his intuitions, such a wealth of technical tricks and devices—that not a dozen fat books could contain what he had learned in one day" (p. 172). Vlemk spends his days turning out boxes each "more sinister than the last, more shamelessly debauched, more outrageously unfair in the opinion of the picture that could talk, which she now did rarely, too angry and too deeply hurt to give Vlemk the time of day" (p. 173). Art turns into a mean obsession that pleases no one, not even the axe-murderer, not even Vlemk. There is no joy (it is only delusion), no miracle, no magic in Vlemk's art. The light has given way to the darkness. Vlemk's vision is all bleakness and scorn.

The Princess, meanwhile, has begun a personal moral lapse of her own. She sees in the picture of herself (which Vlemk has left her as a gift) the same disturbing traits that had bothered Vlemk, and she is so molested by these "hints of cruelty, vanity, and stinginess" (p. 187) that she considers tossing the painting into the fire. The painting's conscious perversity drives the Princess to distraction and to a sort of enlightenment, pointing up that persistent disparity between what is and what seems to be, between what the Princess "felt to be her best self and knew to be her worst" (p. 188). Still she rejects the several portraits in Vlemk's studio as falsities, coming to see them as veritable curses upon her, or as symbols of the curse that Vlemk himself has placed upon her. What that curse is, the Princess hardly knows, but even her father the king feels it and implores her to "go to the box-painter. Beg him to remove the curse. Otherwise we're doomed" (p. 200).

The curse, as it turns out, is the fact of the love that both Vlemk and the

Queen (as she becomes upon her father's death) feel, but fail to openly acknowledge. The Queen visits Vlemk, and sees in him a changed man and a changed artist. And she falls beneath the spell of that change:

> Yes, she must learn to be like Vlemk the box-painter. Learn to dismiss with absolute indifference the antics of mere mortals! She must live for the imperishable! She'd been wrong about him, she saw now. He had not mellowed, gone soft. In the end he had dismissed even rage and scorn, even the young artist's hunger for Truth. He had moved beyond silence to a terrible kind of comedy, painting nonsense with unholy skill—landscapes, animals, all that dying humanity foolishly clings to. (p. 208)

The Queen apes Vlemk's descent (or mock-descent) into cynicism, joining in disguise the cutthroat world of the tavern. She misreads the curse, defining it as a fear instead of a joy. Rule turns into misrule; the kingdom reverts to chaos and lunacy, but not a beneficent, blessed lunacy. Not until the Queen learns to deal with the portrait—"She's your own very self, a picture so real it can speak. Surely you can find a way to live with your own very self!"—can she return the country and herself to order and sanity.

Vlemk considers helping her by repainting the picture on the talking box, but each time he resolves to try, he fails because "the terrible truth was that he loved with all his heart that saucy, incorrigible little picture on the box—and no doubt also the Queen, since the two were identical" (p. 229). Fraught with his impotence, Vlemk returns one evening to the tavern and to his three old friends, who have suddenly turned commercial. The ex-poet writes verses for a cardboard-box company ("Got troubles? Out-fox 'em! Box 'em!"). The ex-violinist writes music for advertising jingles for the cardboard-box company, pickpocketing symphony themes instead of overcoats. And the axe-murderer: "I chop up wooden boxes to make the phosphor sticks people buy in those little cardboard boxes. They're getting to be all the rage, these phosphor sticks. They're easier than a flint. Also, sometimes children burn down hotels with them. Ha ha!" (p. 231). The three failures have turned into successful, if compromised, frauds. Reality has shifted once again. And it drives Vlemk home to repaint the Queen's face—but without its flaws and insinuations of malice. In the magic of the moment and the repainting, Vlemk reverses the curse, turns the painting mute, leaving both artist and art dumbstruck when they go to see the Queen.

The Queen is near death, a symptom of the painting's effect upon her soul and of her misinterpretation of Vlemk's character. She is intent upon dying and seeks atonement for her sins; she wants to be retrieved, if only for a last moment, from the despair that has tugged her down. Reality, however, is not always as it seems to be. When the box is thrown into the fire, it cries out to Vlemk for salvation; the curse—well, there was no curse upon the box, for it could talk all the time. It merely wished to spite Vlemk, just as the Queen had wished to spite him, for the portrait is indeed the Queen's "own very self." The Prince, the Queen's suitor, reveals himself a married man and leaves, but not before revealing a part of Vlemk's puzzle to him: "Surely . . . my dear Vlemk, you painted what you *thought* was a picture of perfection, but it came out exactly as it had been before you started!" (p. 239). The Queen, like the rest of us, is a hapless mixture of good and evil, perfection and fault. That is what Vlemk had painted, what the portrait had harped upon, and what the Queen had denied. Eventually, the box itself proposes the odd but obvious solution: a marriage of box-painter and Queen ("It's *odd* of course. . . . No doubt we'll have our critics."). Love finally emerges through all of the hatred and doubt, and people "muddle through." The kingdom—like other of Gardner's kingdoms—turns to a rule by art. Strange things happen in such a kingdom—opposites attract, artists marry queens, seasons change unpredictably and instantly. The castle doors open upon a winterscape where there previously was autumn. Art has worked its magic: "In every direction except straight above, the world was white and lovely, as if the light came from inside the snow. Straight above—or so it seemed to Vlemk, standing with one hand on his beard, the other in his pocket—the sky was painfully bright, blinding, as if someone had lifted the cover off the world, so that soon, as usual, everything in it would be transformed" (p. 244). Reality and matter and the world are transmogrified by the lunacies of love and art. Darkness gives way to light, blinding light, the sort of light that blinds the Devil in *Freddy's Book* and illuminates the hero's eyes, the sort of light that turns the Vermont landscape mystical in *October Light,* the sort of light that pierces the blackness of John Napper's painting and bursts upon Queen Louisa's kingdom. It is the same redemptive and transformative light that shines through all of Gardner's fiction.

With "Vlemk the Box-Painter" Gardner caps his study of the "acknowledged artist," of the artist-by-profession, and in his final two stories he takes a realistic look at the "unsuspected artist" whose art is in his living. "Come on Back" details, in a closely autobiographical way, the workings of art to redeem (as it did in "Redemption") mankind from sorrow and loss. The story is set in Remsen, New York, a town very near Gardner's own Batavia. Remsen is infected with the magic of its Welsh settlers; it is almost a fairyland where myth is nearly as real as fact and where the young narrator's imagination is filled with legends of a people who really seem to believe in angels. It is a world of light, where music is a form of communion and exhilaration and art, so that the singing festival—the Cymanfa Ganu—becomes a sort of holy expression and catharsis.

One of the paradoxes of light is that it cannot exist without the parallel existence of darkness. In Remsen, the darkness runs beneath the surface, is hinted at, in the character of the narrator's Uncle Charley. Charley's world is the world of the song, of the Cymanfa Ganu. The boy's grandmother tells him: "Singing's got its place. But a body can get to thinking, when he's singing with a choir, that that's how the whole blessed world should be, and then when he comes down out of the clouds it's a terrible disappointment" (p. 250). When the darkness strikes, as it so often does, in the form of an accident to Charley, the man's world begins to crumble. His body weakens and fails, his flesh goes thin, and his will fades to a whimper. Accidents bring guilt, even to those who are not responsible, even to the young boy who stands aside and tries to make sense of all the confusion going on about him. The boy sees his uncle drifting into use-lessness and impotence, a man wasted by sudden despair, cynical even of his own Welsh myths.

Eventually, the boy attends his first Cymanfa Ganu ("Means 'Come on Back' . . . 'Come on Back to Wales' "), and despite—or perhaps because of—his youth he feels the magic of the celebration:

> They sang, as Welsh choruses always do, in numerous parts, each as clearly defined as cold, individual currents in a wide, bright river. There were no weak voices, though some, like Uncle Charley's, were reedy and harsh—not that it mattered; the river of sound could use it all. They sang as if the music were singing itself through them—sang out boldly, no uncertainties or hesitations; and I, as if by magic, sang with them, as sure of myself every note of the way as the wisest and heartiest in the room. Though I was astonished by my powers, I know, thinking back, that it was not as miraculous as I imagined. Borne along by those powerful voices, the music's ancient structure, only a very good musician could have sung off key. And yet it did seem miraculous. It seemed our bones and blood that sang, all heaven and earth singing harmony lines, and when the music broke off on the final chord, the echo that rang on the walls around us was like a roaring Amen. (p. 266)

It is all a part of that mysterious, magical, miraculous uplift and ascension that is art. For a moment the soul is suspended, removed from the material world, and transported; several souls become one, a unity.

Sometimes, though, even the magic is not enough. Charley drifts off, disappears, finally reappears to the family a suicide, a victim of his despair. Sorrow splinters and deadens the family; the union is temporarily broken; the voices lapse: "Slowly the whole conversation died out like embers in a fireplace, and as the stillness deepened, settling in like winter or an old magic spell, it began to seem that the silence was unbreakable, our final say" (p. 269). This is the stillness that *precedes* art, part of the same magic at work in "Stillness" and "Vlemk." The silence lasts until the first timid voice breaks through, inviting others to join it in a personal, familial Cymanfa Ganu, a welcoming back to Wales of Uncle Charley, a resolution of the combined guilt and sorrow of those left behind in Remsen. Art has redeemed the souls of both the dead and the mourning, defeating time and space in the instant of a song.

In the final and title story, "The Art of Living," Gardner repeats this celebratory motif, demonstrating how there is indeed an art to living, how we are all sorts of unsuspecting artists, how we all participate in the miracle that is art. Arnold Deller is a cook, a man of seemingly ordinary talents who takes an extraordinary approach to his work. Food, to Deller, is an "art," and Deller himself a self-described "artist." He is also a sufferer. He has lost his son in Vietnam, a loss that has transformed him into a human-monster reminiscent of Henry Soames in *Nickel Mountain*. Finnegan, the recollecting narrator, describes Deller: "Cooks are notoriously cranky people, but Arnold was an exception. Why he should have been so even-tempered seems a mystery, now that I think about it—especially given his fondness for rant and given the fact that, as we all found out, he was as full of pent-up violence as anybody else at that time. Nevertheless, even-tempered he was. Sometimes when certain kinds of subjects came up, his eyes would fill with tears; but he never swore, or hardly ever, never hit anybody, never quit his job in a huff" (p. 271). Deller possesses that "lidded wrath" that consistently threatens to turn man into a beast, that outruns the modes of expression and converts itself into violence and overwhelming emotion. It is that bit of Grendel in all of us.

Deller is also a philosopher and a humanist. He has (to quote another Gardner fiction) "first-class opinions." The world is in chaos, Deller tells Finnegan's gang, and the temptation is just to back off, to turn irresponsible: "But it's no good, leads straight into craziness. The thing a person's gotta have—a human being—is some kind of center to his life, some one thing he's good at that other people need from him, like, for instance, shoemaking. I mean something ordinary but at the same time holy, if you know what I mean. Very special. Something *ritual*—like, better yet, cooking!" (p. 282). Man must have an art and a purpose. Man's potential for artisthood, in fact, is one of the things that distinguishes him from other forms of life: "People can get the idea life's just instinct, no trick to it. But we're not animals, that's our great virtue and our terrible dilemma. . . .

We've got to think things out, understand our human nature, figure out
how to become what we are" (p. 282). And part of that understanding is
learning how to love, which is in truth learning how to live: "Love by
policy, not just instinct. That's the Art of Living. Not just instinct; something you do on purpose. Art!" (p. 286).

Deller begins talking the lunacy that is art. The narrator feels the craziness of things in the rushing of his blood, like a drunkenness, to his head.
He feels the dead son rising in Deller's memory as it always does when the
cook unleashes his emotion: "My boy Rinehart had a certain dish over
there in Asia, a certain dish you might think no American would touch,
given our prejudices. But it was made so perfectly, it was so downright
outstanding, sooner or later you just had to give in to it. . . . It wasn't just
food, it was an *occasion*. It was one of the oldest dishes known in Asia. Sit
down to that dinner . . . you could imagine you were eating with the
earliest wisemen in the world" (p. 287). The dish is cooked dog. The
occasion is art, a ritual, a celebration. It is the artist's responsibility to create
that occasion, that ritual, that celebration:

> If he's an artist, what a man does, or a woman, is make things—
> objects which nobody asked him to make or even wanted him to
> make, in fact maybe they wanted him *not* to. But he makes them,
> and once people have them in their hands or standing there in front
> of them, people for some reason feel they would like to take them
> home with them or eat them, or if the object's too big to take home
> or eat, have it hauled to some museum. That's what it's all about.
> Making life startling and interesting again, bringing families
> together, or lovers, or what-not. (pp. 288–89)

The artist's function is to redeem, through his art, the lost and sorrowed
and guilty. We have seen it in "Nimram," in "Redemption," in "Vlemk,"
in "Come on Back"—and we see it here.

Despite their doubts ("It was all pure bullshit"), the gang finds a dog
for Deller, assists in the celebration of the ritual. For Finnegan, the narrator, the action springs from love and from an intuitive sense of the necessity of the thing. He knows that Deller is "crazy-serious," but he also
knows that Deller believes in the morality of the covenant of the artist and
in his sanctioned lunacy:

> What's an artist? How's he different from an *ordinary* nut? An artist
> is a man who makes a covenant with tradition. Not just dreams,
> grand hopes and abstractions—no, *hell* no—a covenant with
> something that's *there*, pots and paintings, recipes: the specific that
> makes things indefinite come alive. . . . The artist's contract is, come

hell or high water he won't go cheap, he'll never quit trying for the best. Maybe he fails, maybe he sells out and hates himself. You know it can happen just like you know you can stop loving your wife, but all the same you make the promise. Otherwise you have to go with ordinary craziness, which is disgusting. (305–6)

The artist possesses an inherent conviction of the rightness of his art and is obliged to an aesthetic and holy fidelity to it. The failed artist "sells out," turns cynical and spiteful. The faithful artist maintains his madness.

So the celebration finally comes off. The repugnance, the horror, the violence—all are overcome in the transcendence of the moment. What begins in doubt ends in affirmation as the magic of art once again works its transforming wonder:

> There was no sign of the thousands and thousands of dead Asians, or of Rinehart either, but it felt like they were there—maybe even more there if there's no such thing in the world as ghosts, no life after death, no one there at the candlelit table but the few of us able to throw shadows on the wall. Say that being alive was the dinner candles, and say they burned forever over this everlasting meal of Imperial Dog. Then we were the diners there now, this instant, sent as distinguished representatives of all who couldn't make it this evening, the dead and the unborn. Everybody was feeling it, the importance of what we were doing—though it wasn't *what* we were doing that was important. . . . We were all, even Arnold, a little shocked, but in the darkness beyond where the candles reached, Rinehart nodded, and a thousand thousand Asians bowed from the waist. (pp. 309–10)

The essence of the celebration, of the art, is what matters. The overpowering emotion of the ritual is what manifests itself as art. The method might vary—a Mahler symphony, a Welsh hymn, a dinner of Imperial Dog—but the end is the same. The souls come together from the corners and the depths of the world. Art brings life to death and light to darkness. For one lost moment in time, there are no roots, no ties, no connections to the material world. For that one moment all is strangely holy. For that one moment one captures the art of living.

Chapter XI

Mickelsson's Ghosts

and I must turn my smarting eyes
to those loves I'm committed to,
must love where nothing satisfies
but death, if worms, like higher forms, are true.
　　　　　—"Desire on Sunday Morning"

Fate was doubly harsh upon John Gardner when it stole the wheels out from under him in September 1982. It took his life, and at the same time robbed him of the chance to redeem himself, to hoist himself up and out from the despondency that had plagued him for many months before his death. His last complete work of fiction, *Mickelsson's Ghosts,* had been published just three months before, and except for some scattered praise, the novel was scorned by most readers and reviewers. Benjamin De Mott's remarks in the *New York Times Book Review* were typical: "[*Mickelsson's Ghosts*] transforms the stuff of its own potential vision, not into a thesis, but into canned goods—a standard-brand thriller with a queer Gothic hum in the background."[1] While *Mickelsson's Ghosts* is, as I hope this analysis will show, a better book than most people think it, it did deserve much of the criticism it received. And that, in part, is the unfairness of it all, for Gardner's career finished weakly, his final novel far from his best. The voice in *Mickelsson's Ghosts* is a voice that is windy, parenthetical, Jamesian, a voice that lacks the direction and purpose of Gardner's finest fiction. It is as if Gardner found himself, for once, uncertain and unconfident.

Mickelsson's Ghosts failed, in part, because Gardner consciously tried to be something he wasn't: a popular, bestselling author of a popular, bestselling book. "What I basically was trying to do . . . was a thriller which is thrilling on every level—intellectually, spiritually and physically,"

Gardner said in his last published interview.[2] What he achieved was a disappointing confusion of thought and style and action.

Gardner also intended the novel as a half-facetious response to all those who had jumped on his aesthetic sermonizing in *On Moral Fiction*. When Peter Mickelsson, Gardner's philosopher-protagonist, looks over the reviews of his last book, he bristles at the accusation (à la John Barth) that his was a "shrill pitch to the philosophical right"; Gardner apparently was still sensitive to certain public wounds and embarrassments. A look at the novel's acknowledgments confirms his lingering, half-humored uneasiness: every possible personal, artistic, and scholarly debt and borrowing is noted. There would be no room for the sort of controversy that shadowed *The Life and Times of Chaucer* and *Freddy's Book*. It's as though Gardner was trying to exorcise those particular ghosts with a charm, a totem, an apology.

Yet there are other, more important ghosts Gardner tries to purge in this novel, and that is probably what made the book's failure most painful. *Mickelsson's Ghosts* is acutely autobiographical. Peter Mickelsson's old house outside of Susquehanna, Pennsylvania, is Gardner's old house outside of Susquehanna, Pennsylvania. The dining room rebuilt by Mickelsson is the dining room rebuilt by Gardner. The town and people of Mickelsson's Susquehanna are those of Gardner's Susquehanna. Mickelsson and Gardner share faculty positions at SUNY-Binghamton, penchants for gin and for tobacco, childhoods on dairy farms.

They share, too, more touching and more afflicting concerns. Both are beleaguered souls, hounded by the IRS, troubled by rancorous divorces and scattered families, bled by alimony payments. Gardner invests his Mickelsson, in other words, with the intensely private and powerful woes of his own life. Certainly, Peter Mickelsson is not John Gardner, in a very limited and limiting sense. Rather, Gardner is a small part of Mickelsson in that both are contemporary men haunted by very real and contemporary problems. Life, it seems, has become a matter of survival, of outrunning the perdurable evils, of outhaunting the ghosts of our age.

Peter Mickelsson exists in a world that, for him, has turned disastrously disordered. A professor of philosophy, a teacher of ethics, Mickelsson senses both a personal and a universal decline. His apartment weighs upon him, crowds him in with its dinginess and shadow; his poverty aggravates his desire; the city of Binghamton depresses him with its stark ugliness. And "the feeling that his life was hopeless—and his misery to a large extent undeserved (like everyone else's, he began to fear)—would drive him down to the maple- or oak-lined streets at night, to prowl like a murderer, looking in through strangers' windows with mixed scorn and envy."[3] Mickelsson is slowly sliding into monstrousness. He turns voyeur, peeking into other people's lives (like Will Hodge and Fred Clumly in *The Sunlight Dialogues*), existing vicariously. His own life is barren; he is professionally and emotionally impotent ("Lately, of course, he'd been publishing nothing"), vaguely asocial, drifting into a "shadowy world of withdrawal" (p. 74). He even grows capable of killing, cudgeling a dog into senselessness on a dark Binghamton street ("In Providence he wouldn't have killed the dog"). It is life on the edge of the abyss.

Mickelsson the moralist is turning amoral. Existence is uneasy. Gnawing at his consciousness is "the peripheral sense of dread that comes when a dream begins to decay toward nightmare" (pp. 9–10). Survival is difficult enough for an ordinary man. For a philosopher, though, for an ethicist, it is nearly impossible to survive without betraying oneself. Mickelsson feels that truth, senses the "slippage" in his life. He recognizes the "increasing tendency to lie to himself," to play his ethical system false.

Salvation, Mickelsson speculates, lies in an exchange of worlds. The chance of escape from Binghamton's drear bleakness to the otherworld of the "Endless Mountains" teases him with the hope of clarity. What he does not realize is that he is inheriting another collection of metaphysical worries, ghosts, implacable forces that will haunt him even more fiercely than the black sterility of Binghamton. Susquehanna possesses a singularity, a certain quality of light, a "special, seemingly magical tint" that recalls his days as a youth on a Wisconsin farm. It is also a light that transports Mickelsson outside of time—beyond the "perishability of time," as he puts it. It is the very transmogrifying light that bathes so much of Gardner's fiction. The earthly turns spiritual. Past and present are fused, and the living mingle with the dead. Mickelsson remembers his father, and his second-sighted grandfather (note how often second-sightedness turns up in Gardner's work). Ghosts share Mickelsson's house, fill it with the aroma of baking bread and the creak of echoed voices in the hallways. We are in a different, haunted landscape here. Anything seems possible.

It is also a threatening landscape. There are rumors of rattlesnakes, a thought that, in a strange and philosophical way, satisfies Mickelsson:

> Except in zoos, Mickelsson had never seen a rattlesnake. The idea that they were here, all around him in the woods, was interesting, faintly disquieting, nothing more. But no, that was not quite right, he corrected himself. He was pleased that there were snakes. He'd looked at a house, about a month ago, in a town called Jackson, a few miles south of Susquehanna, where a day or two earlier two large trees beside the road had been torn out by the roots by a twister. It was that, he'd realized when he thought about it, that had led him to consider buying the place. He knew the theory—

Nietzsche, Sorel, Karl Jaspers when he spoke of "the abysses which lie on each side of the footpath"—that the human spirit comes alive in the proximity of danger, or perhaps one might better say, with Sartre, the presence of temptation—the temptation to sink back into Nature: bestiality and death. (pp. 52–53)

Here, in a geography that Gardner surely saw as closely akin to the world of southern Illinois, Mickelsson tests his spirit, challenges the resurrective powers of harm and the existential temptation to monstrousness. What does it take, asks Gardner, to haul a man into or out of that abyss, closer to or farther away from "bestiality and death"? And as conditions of his test, Gardner hurls at Mickelsson the "ghosts" of this enchanted world: "Rattlesnakes, housebreakers, animals in the cellar, big-chested big-cocked devils on dirt bikes" (p. 180).

Not all of Mickelsson's problems, however, are so spectral and queer. He is tangled in a web of personal and sexual relationships that grows increasingly complicated with his decline. He is in the midst of extricating himself from a messy divorce, one fraught with animosity, regret, and financial chaos. The marriage had been a battle of wills and egos, a contest of deceits, a history of unfaithfulness that eventually left both parties hopelessly distant: "They'd both been idealists. They'd been brought up, both of them, in families where fidelity was assumed, the marriage bond inviolable; and when they'd left that pattern, following the fashion of their friends and time (Ellen smiling, Mickelsson looking dangerously intense), enjoying the usual excitement of the chase and the cheap thrill of liberation, they'd become like lost children. Decency striking back. They'd become anxious. Soiled" (p. 90). It is the new age of throwaway relationships, Gardner says, of abdicated responsibilities, and for someone as inherently ethical as Mickelsson, such breakups leave scars. Children are left behind, worried about; love seems to have no object. Suddenly Mickelsson realizes his inability to protect his children—Mark and Leslie—and memories turn bittersweet and tighten his stomach with fear. He craves reunion and reassurance.

There is something special about familial ties—for Mickelsson, for Gardner—that is more affecting when disrupted than any other sort of relationship. We carry with us a sort of genetic inheritance that influences us emotionally, psychologically, and intellectually. Mickelsson feels this influence most strongly through the contrasting figures of his father—a farmer, an eminently pragmatic and hopeful man—and his grandfather. Mickelsson's grandfather was a Lutheran minister, and like Luther himself he believed in devils, in visible and nagging temptors and testers of man's faith and will. He was too, almost by necessity, a mystical man:

"He'd been the dullest man on earth, except for one oddity. In his seventieth year he'd developed second sight" (p. 20). The grandfather, despite his supposed dullness, becomes for Mickelsson the embodiment of Lutheran spirituality with its disdain of worldly and excremental existence. He is the opposite of everything Mickelsson believes himself to be, and is one of the two philosophical standards against which he tests his ideas and action.

Thesis-antithesis. That is how Mickelsson (and much of Gardner's fiction) works. And nowhere is this plainer than in his emotional-sexual relationships. As in so many of Gardner's books, the women in *Mickelson's Ghosts* are antithetically opposed creatures. On the one hand, there is Jessica Stark: professor of sociology, widow, athletic, beautiful, unapproachable. On the other, there is Donnie Matthews: prostitute, perhaps twenty, plain, all too readily available. When Mickelsson first meets Donnie in a Susquehanna bar, the contrast—physical, emotional, psychological—is evident: "Her dress was a light flowerprint, almost transparent, wide open at the throat and plunging; no bra. Her white cleft instantly aroused him. He thought guiltily of Jessica Stark. The girl's face, in spite of the slight look of drunkenness, was as innocent and open as a child's. Compared to Jessica, she was as common as a kitchen sink" (p. 142). Jessica is Mickelsson's symbol of queenly virtue, a latter-day Wealtheow, the essence of spirituality and rightness. Donnie is the symbol of concupiscence, all physicality and sensualness. The trouble, of course, is that Mickelsson is profoundly attracted to Donnie, desires her with all the unregenerate lust (so he thinks) of a demon. He is pulled between these two poles, these two forms of desire—holy, lustful—never able to totally banish either from his mind. And so he wrestles with the consequences, the guilt and the shame. And, too, with the subtle transformational powers of Donnie's outright sexuality. After his first tryst with the prostitute, Mickelsson returns home to find things—his world, his wants—changed:

> His visitors were long gone when Mickelsson got home that night, or rather that morning; the sky was already beginning to lighten, and birds were singing in every bush and tree, like poor Mickelsson's heart. It was not that he'd ceased to feel guilty. Intellectually he had no doubt that what he'd done was very wrong, inexcusable in fact, and no doubt that if there were in fact a God, He ought to be shot for creating a world where young women so sweet and essentially innocent could be turned into playthings of masculine pleasure. But when he climbed out of the Jeep . . . it was not solid ground but dewy air he stepped on. It had of course not

escaped his attention that she'd outrageously tricked him. . . . But the truth was, he liked the trick, liked its bold, teasing wantonness—liked it almost as much as he liked her sweaty, plump young body, or the way she'd somehow banished from his mind all fear of going limp, or her oral expertise, or her shyness when he'd come out of the bedroom and caught her with her glasses on. (p. 148)

Mickelsson's world is, indeed, transformed, but it is a problematical transformation. For at heart, Mickelsson is sick, and is sickened by the rawness of his behavior. In a book where sexual intercourse figures largely as metaphor, as a shape-shifting symbol of human love or human lust, Mickelsson's relations with Donnie emerge as animal rage and need, a base expenditure of desire upon a girl no older than his daughter. Mickelsson's actions fail, as they will continue to fail, to jibe with his moral theory. This disparity between action and belief hastens his decline; to mend the chaos of his existence, Mickelsson must reconcile these moral and emotional differences.

Even in Mickelsson's social life, there are contrasts and complications which only seem to disorder his world the more. He moves within two social realms: the world of Susquehanna, and the world of Binghamton and the university. In Susquehanna, Mickelsson's first and closest friend is Tim Booker, the thirtyish real estate agent who (like Gardner) dresses in jeans, boots, and motorcycle jacket, and who, he intuits, possesses a hint to the mystery of Susquehanna:

> From the moment he'd met him Mickelsson had been hard put not to like him. He seemed obviously honest, blessed with the heartiness and dependable gentleness Mickelsson had associated since childhood with dairy farmers. . . . Tim had been his first real introduction to the character of the people who'd be his neighbors if he managed to get the Bauer place. From the outset the signs had been promising. Even Tim's accent was a pleasure, or anyway interesting, a sort of key to the place—a set of clues, if Mickelsson could figure them out, to the ungraspable phantom meaning he'd felt up at the house. The secret of wholeness, perhaps, if he was lucky. His cracked-up life's second chance. (p. 33)

It is Booker who sells Mickelsson the Bauer place, his new Susquehanna home and shelter of ghosts and unexplained histories. It is Booker, too, who does eventually provide the key, who does finally help patch up Mickelsson's "cracked-up life."

There are others—businessmen, storeowners, farmers, policemen—

who make up the substance of Mickelsson's Susquehanna life, people who are intimately connected to one another by a sort of geographical kinship. Susquehanna is a community of attuned hearts and minds; people know about one another, know the shadowy content of each other's lives. Relations are struck almost mystically. When Mickelsson visits the young farmer, Lepatofsky, about his Jeep, Mickelsson catches something in the thoughtful look of Lepatofsky's daughter, Lily, "a silent, shyly smiling red-head, something wrong about her eyes—maybe just a dreamer" (p. 69). These mystical relations are what save Mickelsson in the end: a red-haired troll doll, a biker friend, a puzzlingly patient policeman.

Mickelsson's professional world, naturally, is much different. The university community seems to thrive on bitterness and jealousy and intrigue. There really is *no* community at all. Mickelsson's chairman, a hunchbacked and devious man, exists to torment Mickelsson (who, admittedly, gives back his share of headache); the torment, which begins as a purely professional matter, eventually turns painfully personal, as Mickelsson's antagonist turns into his rival. It is Tillson, the chairman, who introduces into Mickelsson's world Michael Nugent, a crisis-ridden student who comes like another ghost: "The young man . . . had such glassy eyes and pallor of skin, color like a dead man's, that Mickelsson was for an instant thrown. . . . The leaden skin, the reddened eyelids, the nervous, weak mouth like a child's all gave ominous warning" (p. 11). Nugent carries within him an entire filamented mystery, which he wraps around Mickelsson, and which unravels as slowly and as horridly as the several lives it touches.

By the end of part one (the novel is divided into three parts), Gardner has laid the structure for his multifaceted "thriller." At the center is Susquehanna and Mickelsson's house (the Bauer place), with its ghosts and legends, which ultimately brings Mickelsson face to face with the murderousness at the novel's heart. Part of the history of the house—and the most important element of Gardner's mystery—is the legacy of the Mormons: of Joseph Smith and his vision. As one of Mickelsson's friends informs him: "I b'lieve one might call it *spiritual* country—though to my mind it's downright peculiar, what with the Mormons starting up there and all. Why, Peter, you're dwelling on *holy land!* That's where Joseph Smith had those *divine* visitations, where those *fabulous* tablets were given into his *very hands*" (p. 111). Add to this the Pennsylvania Dutch, hex signs, witches, klansmen—and Gardner has a wonderland of fancy and fright and suspicion. Mickelsson's house is broken into, there are rumors of illegal chemical dumpings, and a chemistry professor dies under suspicious circumstances. Gardner's mystery is every bit as chaotic as the life that swirls around Mickelsson; indeed, his life *is,* in essence, that very mystery, and Gardner forces him to try to make some sense of it. In doing so, Mickelsson (and Gardner) drive the mystery even deeper, turn it more opaque, watch it become a maze of events and personalities and philosophies.

In part two, Gardner poses the question: Under what conditions will a seemingly moral man commit murder? Or put perhaps more accurately, given a specific set of conditions and forces, can a seemingly moral man commit murder? In Mickelsson's case, it is not, strictly speaking, an act of murder; it is, however, an act that is certainly criminal and arguably immoral. Gardner studies, in this middle section of the novel, the sorts of pressures and confusions that pursue a man into violence and depravity. Mickelsson is faced with a very practical and very tortuous ethical dilemma: the contravention of the ethical by a professor (in both the academic and personal sense) of ethics.

In this section, the several mysteries in Mickelsson's life grow more complex as they supposedly grow more revealed. The dead chemistry professor, Warren, it turns out, was murdered by someone he knew: ". . . let in the murderer, apparently had a chat with him" (p. 255). Warren was a friend of Mickelsson's student, Nugent, who saw Warren as

> a clown in a way. The sort of person who liked to go on—you
> know—intellectual benders. . . . When I say he was a "clown" all I
> mean is— . . . You know how it is in the circus. The acrobat does
> something, and the clown tries to imitate it, but the clown's not
> human, like the acrobat, he's just this creature with straw in his
> head. That's why clowns are at the same time funny and sad: they
> imitate exactly what human beings do, and if the *Nichomachean
> Ethics* were right, they really would become human. But no matter
> what they do they remain just clowns. (p. 223)

Nugent is echoing Gardner here.[4] Mickelsson runs the risk himself of turning into a clown—as did Agathon and Clumly and Henry Soames before him. He must learn to *act* like a human being, not merely mimic as a clown—as a man in descent—must do.

Actually, Mickelsson's relationship with Nugent thickens the mystery, for it is Mickelsson who recommends to Nugent the class of his colleague, the solitary Edward Lawler. Lawler is huge and balding, "curiously baby-faced, as if nothing had ever happened to him, no griefs, no joys, no wind to dishevel him but the harmless wind of words" (p. 354). Lawler's appearance is deceiving. Mickelsson and Lawler discuss the problems of young Nugent in a fashion that belies Lawler's knowledge of and interest in the student. All the conversation does for Mickelsson is reinforce his growing guilt: "One thing was certain. He ought to take Michael Nugent aside, have a heart-to-heart talk with him. *Ought,* he brooded. A stupid word, no force. A word for weaklings, Nietzsche would say. A word for survivors, something he apparently was not. No paradox, for Nietzsche. *The species does not grow in perfection: the weak are forever prevailing over the strong"* (p. 356). *Ought.* A word for survivors, for weaklings, for clowns. Mickelsson's existence is plagued by things he *should* do. Nor is it merely a question of acting: it is also a question of which action to take once one does decide to act. Mickelsson wants desperately to survive. Right now there is no real question of prevailing.

Unfortunately, Mickelsson's hesitancy costs him. He receives (apparently) a phone call from Nugent, a person in powerful and evident distress, and Mickelsson sinks beneath the same sort of moral ineffectiveness that paralyzed him before: "He felt a kind of sickness sweep over him, a strange and baffling feeling like absolute despair, the very soul's prostration. He knew what he should say. . . . The boy's anguish, whatever its cause, was so strong that Mickelsson could feel it himself, a sensation of teetering on the rim of the abyss" (p. 390). For Nugent it is too late: an apparent suicide three days (again apparently) *before* his phone conversation with Mickelsson. Mickelsson's world is suddenly both more tragic and more confused. He, like Nugent, stands peering into the abyss, almost waiting for the final, killing nudge.

That abyss, maddeningly enough, is a shape-shifter. In one form it mirrors back the growing psychological disorder that is crazing Mickelsson's consciousness. Rumors of UFOs and "falls"—"frogs falling out of the sky, or blood, or fish . . . stones" (p. 215)—confound Mickelsson as surely as the spell of the land around Susquehanna and his farmhouse. Witches and superstitions pass in and out of his mind as freely as the memory of his grandfather, whose "gift" of second sight reminds Mickelsson of his own history of breakdowns and psychic failures. As a sort of therapy Mickelsson sets to restoring his house, restructuring in the process his own frail mind and personality ("It was magic, not madness"). Like Jay Corby in "The Old Men," Mickelsson works at building something real and positive through human physical effort. The attempt is simultaneously a cure and a harm, for while it offers him a chance to purge both mind and body of guilts and woes and metaphysical debts, it also masks (a masking intensified by his constant drinking) the true nature of his predicament. The physical effort is not enough: Mickelsson must come to final and authentic terms with his "ghosts."

Here is where the house truly becomes a symbol of Mickelsson's psychology, for as his moral confusion grows, so do the manifestations of the ghosts which genuinely haunt his home. What are first mere scents and sounds soon become visions, embodiments of the past's dead. The spell of the land, the spell of the house work their magic: Mickelsson is "taken over" by ghosts (much in the fashion of James Chandler in *The Resurrection*). And in the process he connects with not only his second-sighted grandfather but also with his grandfather's psychic ancestor, Martin Luther, who battled with his own private demon. Unlike Luther, however, Mickelsson feels threatened by his haunters; they highlight his emotional and physical vulnerability, mock his intellectual conceit, and remind him of the interminable mystery that has literally swallowed him.

Ironically, while Mickelsson feels the increasing presence of his ghostly friends, he also feels the increasing separation from his more corporeal friends. The loneliness scares him, makes him anxious, hastens his physical and psychic breakdown. Nugent gives him a book, *The Broken Heart*,[5] which details the debilitating effects of loneliness and lovelessness on the human heart, and which seems to speak directly to Mickelsson: "Reading through Nugent's book, case after dreary case of cardiac fatality in the single, the unhappily married, and the divorced, Mickelsson had begun to feel like a man encountering his own obituary" (p. 213). Mickelsson's heart, like his mind, has grown frail and fragile from the worrisomeness of his emotional, sexual (and nonsexual) relationships. His attraction to Jessica Stark nurtures his fantasy and erotic need, but as "always when he'd made imaginary love to her, what he felt now was not relief but shame and revulsion. If any man had ever been truly in love, he thought, he, Peter Mickelsson, was in love with Jessica Stark. . . . But he was thinking: he understood now the agonies of the silly courtly-love poets, moaning and groaning over the holy unattainable" (p. 270). In one of Gardner's favorite images—the knight and the maid—Mickelsson comes to see Jessica as an ideal, unpossessable. Yet he does eventually possess her, and is transformed in the possessing: "Soon a motion he could not control came over him—over her as well—a terrible mechanical power he'd never in all his years been taken by, a mighty and yet effortless rocking that made him feel shaman-like, as if the curtain of illusion had parted and they'd fallen to the beginning of things. Her face shone, her smile wide. When at last the explosion came, he felt light, as if turned from heavy flesh into thin, shining air" (p. 301). The sexual act becomes (in Gardner's scheme) an artistic act. Flesh, in one of those singular moments, is transmogrified into spirit, transcends the "illusion" of time and space; the world fills with luminousness and peace. Mickelsson ascends into love in a true human transformation.

For every rise, however, there is a fall, and with Mickelsson that fall comes in his relationship with Donnie Matthews, whose "base, uncomplicated love" he finds physically and simplistically fulfilling. It is nearly a death wish. Love—or at least sex—can kill a person: "The sexual coupling of an older man and a younger woman, especially one not his marriage partner, was apparently only a little less deadly than cyanide. In the end, of course, the heart's real, physical demand for love was not just a matter of sex: the heart—whatever the mind's objections—demanded company, security, trust" (pp. 213–14). Not only might Donnie turn Mickelsson into a clown, but into a corpse as well. In his depths Mickelsson knows what his heart requires—what his *soul* requires—but he lacks the will to act upon the knowledge. Instead, he philosophizes, constructs an elaborate symbology, transmutes himself into a penitent monk battling with concupiscence and obscene desire:

> In his mind Jessie had become for him (though part of him knew that it had nothing to do with reality) a sort of Platonic beacon of immaculacy, secular equivalent to Luther's "Lord's Supper," the point at which the finite and infinite touch. And Donnie, poor kid, had become for him the soul and vital symbol of all things lubricious and lewd, meretricious, debauched, profligate and goatish— the dark side of Luther's symbolism of the privy in the monastery tower. The more he brooded, self-flagellating, turning his bullish will against itself—striking out in his mind first at Jessie, then at Donnie—the more angry, confused, and anxious he became.
> (p. 338)

Mickelsson's Luther-like anguish (and its link with his grandfather) is nettlesome enough while it remains an emotional issue, but when Donnie informs him that she is pregnant she forces the *ethical* issue upon Mickelsson. It turns from an examination of what Mickelsson feels to an examination of what Mickelsson believes—believes strongly enough to act upon.

The immediate issue is abortion, about which he has genuine doubts. The more distant issue, as one of Mickelsson's students puts it, is the battle between the Angels of Life and the Angels of Death, between the traditional Gardner ideas of affirmation and denial. The Angels of Life, for Mickelsson, are represented by his family, his friends, and the pull of affection and need. Mickelsson recalls (recollection is his principal mode of thought, it seems) his daughter costumed for Halloween as a fairy princess, "large transparent wings that seemed lighter than air," looking like a "Sumerian goddess": "He stood motionless, baffled as by a psychic vision, and he was not himself until his daughter came to him, obscurely smiling, and, raising her star-tipped silver wand, lightly—impishly— touched him with it on his nose. He stood grinning, dazed" (p. 204). Her beauty transmutes reality, a human work of art. Mickelsson's son is forced underground, an exile from his father's love, an object of his father's miserable worry and doubt. Mickelsson's friends—what few sincere ones he has—bear him through his oddness with a guarded patience that, unfortunately, eventually wears out. And there is the anticipated "miracle" of his house, which he works maniacally at "transforming." These are the preserving, saving forces in Mickelsson's life.

Standing opposed to these powers are the philosophical figures of Luther and Nietzsche, Mickelsson's metaphysical and ethical bogies. Like his grandfather, Mickelsson slowly falls under the influence of Luther's word and image, in a not altogether reassuring way:

> His simultaneous hatred and admiration grew day by day. He began to know the doctor's stylistic tics as he knew his own— indeed, he began to see, to his horror, more and more similarities between his own personality and Luther's. Sometimes, brooding as he worked on the house or as he walked the streets of Susquehanna, doing errands, he felt as if the old fiend were right at his shoulder, listening in; and once, in a drizzling winter rain, just as he was coming out of the hardware store, he actually thought he saw old Dr. Martinus in the flesh. . . . He was dressed in black, as he'd been in life, his back turned to Mickelsson, the coarse hands folded behind his prodigious ass, and instead of coat and hat he wore a hooded sweater, exactly what one might expect of a former monk. Mickelsson froze in his tracks, knowing already that it wasn't really Luther, yet staring on, stupefied, some dim, ancient part of his mind unconvinced. Then the enormous creature turned, as if aware of someone behind him, and Mickelsson saw that it was the fat man from Donnie's apartment building. (p. 337)

An interesting connection here between Luther and the man Mickelsson finally shocks into death, and an interesting identification of Mickelsson with the ghost of Dr. Martinus; Mickelsson even goes so far as to adopt Luther as his private confessor. He also adopts Luther's ghosts, his devil, just as his grandfather had done. It is Luther, in fact, in league with his "disciple" Nietzsche, who pushes Mickelsson over the edge.

Mickelsson turns smartly aware of the gap between his own appearance and his own reality; there is the image of Mickelsson as lover and friend, and there is the image (his own image) of Mickelsson as villain and beast, and this realization makes clearer, he realizes,

> old Luther's doctrine, and Mickelsson's grandfather's, of all flesh as filth. "The world not only is the devil's, it *is* the devil." And he understood more clearly than ever before, it came to him— understood in his bowels—Luther's observation that never is God's

wrath more terrible than in His silence. Nietzsche's starting point.
That once mankind discovers that it has lost God, the only possible
result is universal madness. If God is dead, Nietzsche had claimed,
human dignity is gone, all values are gone. Cold and darkness begin
to close in. . . . No alternative now but the old, mad Luther's
imperious longing for death, the sad old fiend limping on gouty
legs from room to room, shaking his fists, demanding release from
this wicked virgin-shit world, and the sooner the better. . . . It was
too late now even to cry out, fervently indignant, for death. Peter
Mickelsson was living in the cynical, long-suffering age Nietzsche
had foretold. Rhetoric was exposed; and suicide—all human
feeling, in fact—was rhetoric. (p. 339)

We have heard, of course, all of this before. We have heard it from the
Dragon in *Grendel,* from the Sunlight Man in *The Sunlight Dialogues,* and
from Bishop Brask in *Freddy's Book.* Here, in *Mickelsson's Ghosts,* Gardner
traces the twentieth-century malaise of existential doubt and dread and
negation to Martin Luther, and to an earlier expression of a similar idea:
Die Welt als Scheiss. In such a world, Nietzsche saw, moral right and
responsibility rested within the individual, the particularly superior individual. The need for guilt, regret, repentance vanished—and so Mickelsson rejects his confessor's offer of absolution: "I feel sorry for all the
people I'm hurting. . . . That's my best offer" (p. 342).

As Mickelsson recognizes, Luther had his devils, Nietzsche had his
Übermensch, but contemporary man has no real ethical scapegoat for his
unethical actions: "What was one to do if he knew that every movement
of the spirit was poisoned at the source, as if by uremia?" (p. 402). His
conclusion is surprisingly and disappointingly simple: "Better to act with
fully conscious stupidity: for instance, steal the fat man's stolen money"
(p. 403). "Conscious stupidity" seems the best modern man can do. A
futile denial of conscience. In one instant, Mickelsson convinces himself
of the guilt he would feel should he steal the man's money, and in the
next, "he saw himself smashing through the fat man's door, then shook
his head, banishing the thought as he would a nightmare. One impression
remained: he would not feel especially guilty" (p. 403). Mickelsson comes
round to the ways of thought of Luther and Nietzsche, uses their peculiar
disdain to his moral advantage, and acts, finally, from the darkest of his
furious instincts.

Mickelsson goes to Donnie, argues with her about the abortion, and,
pushed by the disordering forces of the moral confusion, the dismay of
Nugent's death, the wrongheaded appeal of Nietzsche's *Übermensch,*
breaks down the door to the fat man's apartment to steal the stolen

money, and confronts another of his ghosts. They are two clowns, two sorrowful, pitiable mock-ups of human beings in error:

> They stood facing one another in the room's yellowed dimness, clutter all around them, two huge animals squared off, each more frightened than the other. . . . Mickelsson stood motionless, trapped in a nightmare, but now the fat man's mouth opened, round as a fish-mouth, showing blackness within, and he bent a little, as if cringing in shame, and slammed the fist that held the gun toward his own chest, clutching himself, his mouth still open, eyes narrowing to slits, squeezing out tears. Though Mickelsson's mind wheeled, one thought came through clearly, as if someone else were thinking it: *he's having a heart attack.* "The broken heart," he remembered, and felt, along with his own heart's pain, a vast surge of pity. . . . Again and again Mickelsson told himself that he must shout for help, and never mind the consequences to himself—no one knew the arguments better than he—but each time, he did nothing, mentally begging the man to die quickly, lose that expression of pain and, worse, bottomless, childlike disappointment. At last the fat man's knees buckled, a strained, babyish cry came from his throat—a cry to Mickelsson for help—and, turning toward the bed, trying to reach it but too far away, he tumbled like a load of stones onto the carpet. Mickelsson bent down for a look at the eyes. They squeezed shut, dripping tears, then weakly fell open and were still. . . . He looked in horror at the silver, lioness-headed cane and imagined it flashing down, sinking into the fat man's temple. "Holy God in Heaven," he whispered, fully understanding at last that, though not with the cane, he had murdered the man. (pp. 409–10)

With this pathetic act, with this self-conceived tragedy—the broken heart, the silent death, the pained denial—Mickelsson traps himself in a nightmare of his own making. Thought turns to deed, a clown dies a man, and Mickelsson heaves himself deeper into an ethical vortex.

In part three of the novel, Gardner explores the emotional and metaphysical consequences of Mickelsson's act, tracing a familiar pattern of descent, discovery, and redemption. The mysteries multiply, clear, and more or less resolve themselves. Mickelsson begins in abandonment: "Partly he felt . . . that whatever happened to him from this point on was fated, as all things material are. He seemed not his own man, only an agent—the submissive means by which evil powers he could not understand did their work" (p. 413). He acts instinctively, "without thought," out of that same "conscious stupidity" which drove him to act immorally in the first place. He finds himself increasingly indifferent and unafraid, experiencing "existence on the edge," life at the rim of the abyss: life as lived by the *Übermensch*.

Yet it is a life with which he is supremely uncomfortable. He lies in bed on Christmas Day, wallowing in his isolation and withdrawal, awash with memories, "each one more painful than the last." All the myths and legends and stories, in the black honesty of his mind, turn to falsehoods:

> Oh, cruel holiday! Infinitely more terrible lie than Santa Claus! Day of agonizing human love, awful promise that God would be equally loving and—against all odds, against all reason—would ultimately make everything all right. . . . Redemption, resurrection . . . what ghastly, unspeakable lies, if they were lies! He, Peter Mickelsson, was the frozen, buried world, and the deep snow that buried him and would never be melted was his murder of the fat man, that and much, much more: his swinish misuse of Donnie Matthews, his failure to love his wife as she'd deserved, his betrayal of Jessie— sins, failures, death-stink blossoming on every hand! (p. 436)

Some of this, surely, is histrionics and self-pity, but much of Mickelsson's feeling is genuine, private despair. He has betrayed, through his silence and his removal from human intercourse (symbolized by his snowbound-ness), certain trusts, has reneged on certain responsibilities; in turn, he assumes exaggerated guilts and moral debts. These are all symptoms of his developing metaphysical madness, a darksome lunacy that plagues him as surely as his more "material" ghosts.

And even these have proliferated, making more frequent appearances: "He was haunted all the time now, which in theory should have con-vinced him that he was mad, but he could not be sure, turn it over as he might" (p. 449). The ghosts are evidence of his further slippage into an emotional paralysis: "Unable to feel, unable to function; living, as if there were nothing more mundane, in a house inhabited by ghosts more vital than himself" (p. 521). Mickelsson is becoming one of his own ghosts, more specter than human. The guilt, the ghosts, the house, the woods: all are getting to him, shoving him toward some sort of breakdown, some sort of ultimate disbelief in the worth of the human self.

There is, in truth, very little to encourage Mickelsson toward recovery. He sees around him dislocation and rootlessness. Love is excluded by the condition of modern existence: "Alas, the fidelity the heart required was no longer among the world's possibilities" (p. 432). Betrayal is a fact of life. Mickelsson sits through an agonizing session in court, watching the breakup of his family, the disbursement of a relationship gone hideously wrong. Despite the legitimacy of his claims—his poverty, his resourcelessness—he still flinches at his wife's anger and charge of treachery, sensing the truth of his betrayal of her. His daughter's trusting love simply exacerbates Mickelsson's misery: "He'd wanted tears, sobs, rage at the world's betrayal" (p. 469). And when what seems the ultimate betrayal comes—the discovery of Jessica and Tillson, the realization of Jessica's role as mistress—Mickelsson becomes convinced of the world's "shittiness," and of his own role in its scheme of betrayal.

Mickelsson temporarily sees this long chain of fear and disappointment and deceit as a cleansing and purification, a preparation toward a new clarity: "It was as if all he had been through, these past months, had stripped him of the last vestiges of herd opinion, so that from his dark pit of guilt he saw with eyes like an innocent's. . . . He'd achieved, perhaps, Nietzsche's higher consciousness" (p. 473). He casts off his grandfather's "righteous, stern opinions," his ungiving Lutheranism, and adopts the icy cynical eye of the amoralist, the man beyond human connection, the neutralist. At the same time, he still cannot rid himself and his soul of what he calls the "primal faith in magic": the puissance of psychological symbols, the power of transformation, the connection between human action and higher human value. It was this sort of "faith" that had carried his father through the workings of change: "That was how his father had lived his whole life: rebuilding, letting the light in. He, not Nietzsche's Prussian officer—much less the artist, philosopher, or saint—was the Übermensch" (p. 475). The true *Übermensch* is the illuminator, the bringer of light, the authentic Sunlight Man.

A similar, well-hidden but inherent belief temporarily lifts Mickelsson from his despondency, gives him a semblance of health, a recuperative obsession: "Even now, in his hopelessness and guilt, he could not deny that his knowledge of the house around him, restored by his hands to something like its former beauty, miraculously cleaned up like the world of Noah, gave a kind of security, however tentative; a place to stand" (p. 475). Mickelsson is in desperate need of such a miracle. The transmogrification of his soul begins with the resurrection of the house, which had "become his expression, a projection of the self he meant to be, visible evidence that what he hoped for in his life and character might perhaps be attainable" (p. 477). He turns away from an existence that is anomistic and destructive, turns toward an existence that stresses effort, labor, and the building of "things": gifts, walls, relationships.

In the midst of all this reconstruction, however, comes the second great crisis of Mickelsson's life (or at least of his novelistic life). Appearances again prove deceiving. Edward Lawler visits him, masked as a philosopher-humanist, at heart one of the world's killers. Lawler tantalizingly reveals the coils of mystery and deceit and murder that he has manufactured in the name of religious fanaticism. He tells Mickelsson: "Your kind of dream is finished, you see, your admirable but deadly liberalism. Life must defend itself against the mad raging horde. . . . Believe it or not, most people *want* to give up all traces of their humanness to some authority that frees them to be comfortable, healthy beasts. . . . We don't make people weaker than they are. We make them *profoundly* what they are!" (p. 543). Mormonism is just another guise of the institution perverted, a religious Reich that plays to people's weaknesses and faults and fears. Lawler, a perfect emblem of that perversion, is cold-hearted—or perhaps heartless—and amoral. Lawler, and the machine he represents, is implacable. All, he tells Mickelsson, is arranged:

> "Once a man's *in* with us—given our various 'support systems,' as the mealy-mouths say—there's not very much he can do, you see. Oh, a few slip through the net, turn against us. We put pressure on, of course. You can see where we'd be if such defections became common. But if the odd fish proves recalcitrant enough, we let him swim away. On the whole, however . . . on the whole the Saints are pretty much in *your* situation." He seemed to smile behind the mask. "Not a prayer except, possibly, prayer." (p. 549)

Lawler attempts to bring down the already weakened framework of Mickelsson's reconstructed soul, just as he forces him to wreck the house that symbolizes that soul. A man points a gun at you. Death is immediate and real. How do you act?

Mickelsson, taking a clue from Lawler's own cynicism, retreats to that same "primal faith in magic" that saved his father and others like him. He issues a "psychic cry for help," an expression of his belief in the connectedness of things, a connectedness that he at first feels is inane, but which in his extremity comes to be as real to him as the house that is crumbling at his hands. *"Help me! Please!"* cries Mickelsson to the otherworld, Nietzsche standing by "cackling in admirable and scornful glee." Mickelsson stands helpless, his soul "bellowing," echoing Grendel's cry to his mother. And then slowly, perceptibly, the transformation begins: "Mickelsson was swinging the pick as if he'd just begun, all his tiredness gone, more aching, thudding power in his legs and arms than he could remember ever having felt before." His exhausted body revives itself, regains its strength, the spiritual investing the physical. The phone rings. Mickelsson persists in his cry:

> Suddenly he was conscious of a headache so fierce he was amazed that he didn't pass out. Almost the same instant he noticed the headache, it was gone—*all* bodily sensation was gone. He could

have been floating a thousand feet above the earth. *Help me, please,*
he thought, far more clearly than before. . . . The sheen of the
wallpaper startled him, and—his thought elsewhere—he bent
closer. The wallpaper brightened more. He felt alarm—terror—
though for a moment he couldn't tell why. He drew his head back.
The light on the wallpaper dimmed. Before he knew what he was
testing, he moved his head forward again, and the wallpaper
brightened as if a candle had come near. He was thinking all this
while, *Please, please, please!*—pouring the thought out as if it were
his life. He turned around to look at Lawler. The man's eyes were
wide, astonished, but there was something else on his face, too:
terrible despair. Then, as when one's ears pop on an airplane,
Mickelsson heard the real world's sounds again. Someone was
knocking loudly at the door. (p. 553)

Mickelsson becomes the essence of illumination, a sort of human light
that transmogrifies and spiritualizes all it comes near. The "terrible despair" on Lawler's face is ambiguous: it reflects both the effect of Mickelsson's change, and the portentous knocking at the door. Mickelsson's cries
have been heard; the troll doll and the odd and silent little girl and
Mickelsson's soul connect to save his life. Mickelsson, "nothing in his
mind," falls upon Lawler, acting from pure instinct and pure instinctual
justice, in a reversal of his earlier attack on the other "fat man." The proof
of the affirmation has been made. All that remains is the restoration and
reunification of the rest of Mickelsson's world. The disparate parts must
coalesce.

The tying-up of loose ends begins with a phone call from Donnie
Matthews, now relocated in California; the pregnancy has been aborted,
the money, ridden with guilt, thrown into the ocean. Mickelsson thinks:
"*Sublimieren. God be with her*" (p. 530). The strong take care of themselves. Mickelsson, not being quite so strong, relies on the strength of
others. The town of Susquehanna enfolds him, helps him heal. Lily, the
young girl, and Tim Booker, the suspected witch, come to Mickelsson
and save him. The sheriff, Tinklepaugh, dismisses Mickelsson's prime
ethical dilemma by blinking the knowledge of his involvement in the
death of the fat man, but not without an explanation. Susquehanna becomes, in the sheriff's words, a microcosm, an emblem of the world's
"fragility":

You'd be surprised how delicate the balance is, place like this. Man
runs up a pile of debts, then skips out, or something happens to
him—somebody's business could go under. That's how fragile it
can get. Everybody knows that, these dying small towns. Different

places you live got different ways of being, of course. But that's how it is here. People take care of each other, when they're all living right on the edge—they better, anyway. The worse it gets, the more careful they all got to be. Somebody stops pulling his weight—somebody breaks the agreement, you might say—that's trouble. Anything can happen. . . . We just all gotta be careful, I guess, keep things in perspective, watch out for each other . . . and watch each other. (p. 569)

Gardner's lawmen are startlingly wise. Existence is a kind of tenuous agreement among those who live it; there are obligations to uphold, faiths to buttress, errors to overlook. This, says Gardner, is one of the truest "ways of being."

So Mickelsson makes his agreement, his "truce" with the universe. He learns "that one could live with guilt, that the existentialists were to this extent right: one was free to move on" (p. 570). One, in fact, *had* to move on, refuse to submit to despair and hopelessness. Once Mickelsson begins reconnecting the pieces of his life, reality returns, "bleak as a stone. For all his nightmares, he hadn't seen the ghosts in days" (p. 571). The magic temporarily deserts Mickelsson, just as he temporarily deserts the world: "He would not die, that was his decision; in a small way, he would let the world die. Resignation" (p. 577). Mickelsson must redefine reality, shed the ghosts of error—of Nietzsche and his satanic anger—and await the miracles.

The first miracle comes with the return of his son, Mark, who appears seemingly out of nowhere. Indeed, Mickelsson at first thinks him another of his ghosts:

> Yet he felt a strange uneasiness creeping up on him, as if there were something important that he was supposed to do and had not done. Suddenly it came to him that the feeling was not free-floating guilt but fear, increasing by leaps and bounds. He held his breath and confirmed what a part of him had known for minutes now: he was not the only one breathing in the room. . . . In the doorway between the kitchen and livingroom he stopped, staring in astonishment. His son had arrived. He lay asleep in his rumpled clothes on the couch in the destroyed, now cleaned-up livingroom. Carefully Mickelsson approached and touched him, to see if he was real, then sniffed his hair, as if the sense of smell might be more worthy of trust than touch. (pp. 578–79)

Mark is part of that magical realm of light and order who brings with him the ghosts that had departed from Mickelsson. The "new, more narrowly circumscribed life" that Mickelsson has vowed to lead is turning mystical; he has paid his penance, the past has been somewhat absolved, and he can now begin to understand the present as he should. He grows "dismayed by the direction he must go to escape the fly-bottle"—Nietzsche's fly-bottle—but he does go. He realizes what he must do, how he must abandon his isolation and rejoin the human community. It is the last of his miracles.

Dressed like another sort of clown—Liberty tie, scarlet huntsman's coat, face powdered with plaster dust—Mickelsson stands outside Jessica's house a parody of the courtly lover, attired in "the knightly garb with which he'd meant to stun his Cosima, kingly suitor arriving in tarnished splendor to ask his lady's hand" (p. 581). Inside the house he sees the shapes of the people he has spurned, hurt, betrayed, and he affirms his Luther-like love for them, speaking to the darkness: "Sentimental, you may say . . . but perhaps you judge too quickly. These are all we can honestly call our own, these shitty human beings" (p. 582). Mickelsson reclaims the world around him, gathers in, embraces all that a human being can embrace.

To genuinely do so involves the ultimate reclamation—the reclamation of his love for Jessica. Fortunately, he is not alone; the ghost of Jessica's dead husband welcomes Mickelsson, almost encourages him in his suit, blesses his desire. Mickelsson declares his love: "I'm not crazy. . . . I'm just faking because I'm scared. I'm not drunk either. Smell my breath. . . . To make a long story short . . . I love you. . . . I want to marry you." He admits his fear and his flaws and his past: "Jessie . . . it's true that the get-up is a fraud. But the craziness is real. You have to help me. If I had my way, I'd come to you as the perfect lover, flawless golden lion." Mickelsson reaches beyond Renaissance rhetoric to frankness, to an open statement of his love as well as his guilt, and it draws Jessica in.

And then the final miracle happens. Mickelsson and Jessica stand in her bedroom, Mickelsson grappling with her clothes: "The room was full of ghosts, none of them very solid yet, some with their hands to their jaws, looking thoughtful, some grinning obscenely, some timidly looking away. The sky outside the windows glowed, then darkened" (p. 589). All reality is falling apart: "Beyond the farther window, blood was falling, swooshing and boiling as it hit. From high in the night overhead came silvery human laughter." Mickelsson and Jessica make love—literally, in true Gardner fashion, make, create love—and the mystical transmogrification completes itself, spirits rising from the dead and the immaterial and the irresurrectable:

> Now the bedroom was packed tight with ghosts, not just people but also animals—minks, lynxes, foxes—more than Mickelsson or

Jessie could name, and there were still more at the windows,
oblivious to the tumbling, roaring bones and blood, the rumbling
at the door, though some had their arms or paws over their heads—
both people and animals, an occasional bird, still more beyond,
some of them laughing, some looking away (Mormons, Presby-
terians), some blowing their noses and brushing away tears, some
of them clasping their hands or paws and softly mewing, shadowy
cats, golden-eyed tigers (Marxist atheists, mournful Catholics) . . .
pitiful, empty-headed nothings complaining to be born. (p. 590)

The act of love (particularly in this most sexual of Gardner's fictions) is an
act of spiritual rebirth. All at once, what is truly significant in life is
illuminated. All else is obliterated or ignored or turned silly. Love and art
act as one and the same: they summon ghosts (they are there in *Nickel
Mountain, October Light,* "The Art of Living"), they celebrate the laugh-
ably human quality of our existence, they affirm the lunacy of faith and
the compelling magic of human need. Love—like UFOs and "falls" and
ghosts—is a madness, a fool's belief. But, says Gardner, love is the single
most sustaining madness, the healthiest sort of madness we possess.

If *Mickelsson's Ghosts* is a study in survival, then what Gardner contends
is that love is what survives. Love is what pulls Mickelsson through. Love
is what clarifies the mysteries. Love is what convokes the ghosts. In a
tragic way, there is something appropriate in the fact that *Mickelsson's
Ghosts* is Gardner's last fiction, for love is what survives death, is what
ultimately will have us survive. John Gardner's art—and the love contained within it—survive him. The tragedy is that that truth had to be
proved so early.

Epilogue

At the time of his death, John Gardner was working—as he had been, off and on, for eight years—on a novel that he believed would explain and affirm his moral vision, that would be "a summary of everything I've done, a recapitulation." The book was called *Shadows,* a "metaphysical detective story" set in southern Illinois, its hero a drunken detective. Gardner once predicted it would "be either the most pompous stupid thing in the world, or it [would] be a mindbreaker."[1] We quite possibly will never know the true nature of this book. Gardner, however, clearly thought it a novel that would finally establish his metaphysical system—and, perhaps, his artistic reputation.

Gardner, himself, was fairly certain of his place among his contemporaries. He thought himself one of the best of the serious writers working, and one of the few practicing their craft in the tradition of Homer and Dante and Tolstoy—practicing what he called the "new seriousness."[2] Nor was his reputation solely a matter of aesthetics. *Where* a reader or critic was reading Gardner's work was almost as important as how he was reading it. It was a question of geography: "I'm absolutely loved in the Midwest and West. . . . In Kansas City, Los Angeles, Chicago, I'm God"[3] A slightly drunken and fully fatuous declaration, but Gardner sincerely believed his work a victim of the East Coast literary establishment, of the *New Yorker* mind and temperament.

Gardner, of course, was partly to blame for the animosity—personal and critical—that ran between himself and the eastern critics. *On Moral Fiction* made Gardner fewer friends than enemies. And there is no arguing the fact that in that book Gardner often fell to ranting and (as John Barth put it) shrillness. Yet angry men do rant, turn shrill: "I wrote that book in 1964. I had not yet been published. I was furious—just enraged at those guys with big reputations—and I wrote a vituperative, angry book."[4] Gardner later apologized for the nastiness and error of some of his attacks, but he clung to his belief that contemporary American fiction was misdirected, shoddy, impermanent. The times, it seemed, demanded a Jeremiah (or, as Gardner put it in *On Moral Fiction,* a Thor), and Gardner assumed the role.

However accurate or inaccurate Gardner's assessment of his contemporaries might have been, it is important and imperative to make some sort of judgments upon his own work. Gardner was a major American artist. He changed the face of twentieth-century fiction, partly by returning it to its beginnings, partly by defying popular custom and championing old, neglected values. He reconnected, as it were, contemporary art with a tradition that had been disrupted by a postmodernist heresy (as Gardner might have called it), describing magical landscapes in a manner both realistic and philosophic, reviving exhausted forms and ideas.

Gardner was a fairly prolific writer. Ten works of serious fiction in thirty years' time (if we take for fact his claim that *Nickel Mountain* was begun when he was seventeen) is a respectable achievement, and when considered beside his other published works—his children's books, his medieval scholarship, his poetry—it is perhaps a remarkable achievement. Naturally, like any artist, Gardner wrote with varying degrees of success (though never with total failure). Not all of his work will endure the pressures and scrutiny of time. There are among his writings books that will survive as significant samples of twentieth-century fiction. There are others that will stand as near-misses, books that rise and fall on flaws inherent in their content and structure. And there are still others that will likely pass unnoticed, often unread, and (at best) always undervalued.

Within this lower range would go such books as *The Resurrection, The Wreckage of Agathon,* and *Freddy's Book,* his two earliest and one of his latest published works. *The Resurrection* fails because Gardner's imagination fails. Gardner does more "telling" than "showing," and his characters turn flat and sometimes just unlikeable. *The Resurrection* was also one of Gardner's first attempts at being the "philosophical novelist" that critics later so conveniently labeled him; unfortunately, the philosopher, not the storyteller, bears a heavy hand in the novel. *The Wreckage of Agathon* is a failure of a different sort, for here Gardner does succeed in making his ideas palatable, but at the cost of undermining the spirit of the book. Gardner's Agathon is both endearing and despicable; we enjoy his wit and cynicism, but we despise his viciousness and irresponsible cowardice. The dual narration of the novel alleviates some of the book's nastiness, but it also weakens its unity. The same is true of *Freddy's Book,* where the radical shifts in time and place that occur between the two novellas are tied together by the slightest of thematic and psychological connections. One of the book's other problems is that it comes too late in Gardner's career: it is interesting as pseudohistory, but Gardner had already done the same things technically in *The Wreckage of Agathon* and the same things philosophically in a number of his books. There is the inescapable sense of philosophical rehash about *Freddy's Book* that is ultimately too unsatisfying.

Within the "middle range" would go those books that show flashes of

Gardner's brilliance, which are moderately successful, and which support Gardner's reputation as an important novelist. These are the works that might be minor triumphs, but that fall short of Gardner's truly great writing. *Nickel Mountain* is included here because while Gardner (as he usually does) succeeds in creating authentic and interesting characters, he fails in giving the book a coherent structure. The episodic nature of the book is its downfall. Still, *Nickel Mountain* is curious as a pastoral love story, and as a study of Gardner's animistic universe. *The Art of Living,* by its very nature as a collection of short stories, lends itself to inconsistency and imbalance; ironically enough, however, its real handicap is its over-pressed consistency and insistency of theme. Stories become predictable; we have heard it before. There is, though, some superb literature in *The Art of Living.* Stories such as "Nimram," "Redemption," and "Come on Back" are miniature masterpieces, sparkling proofs of Gardner's ability to deal successfully with the shorter form.

Mickelsson's Ghosts, I suspect, has all the makings of a "sleeper." Most critics panned it, gave it literally no chance of surviving. Yet there is something in the marvelous ambition of this novel that makes it admir-able and promising. It is true that the novel dies in spots, that there are severe losses of creative energy, that Gardner is left bruised by several of the Indian clubs he has whirling in the air. However, there is just enough magic and mystery and intelligence to turn *Mickelsson's Ghosts* into one of Gardner's best works.

If *Mickelsson's Ghosts* suffered at the critics' hands, *Grendel* became very nearly a cult novel, a book that *had* to be read. And of course such success always threatens the serious achievement of a book. Yet despite the risks taken in *Grendel*—the reworking of old material, the animating and hu-manizing of the monster, the contemporizing of character and thought—there is a genuine truth that transcends popular, modern fancy. Gardner elevates the cartoon, in *Grendel,* to high art. We believe in the monster because he is less an anachronism than his killer, Beowulf, and because he reminds us both of our links to life in the abyss and of our secret belief and faith in the hero.

Perhaps the most troublesome of Gardner's books, in terms of its fu-ture, is *October Light,* for its success turns upon the controversy of its structure. What one thinks of *October Light* often depends upon what one thinks of the inner novel. If one accepts the structural relevance and necessity and effectiveness of the inner novel, then one accepts *October Light* as a major twentieth-century novel. If, however, one denies the purpose of the inner novel and perceives it as gimmickry, expedience, and failure, then one judges the book as an interesting but minor work of contemporary art. (There are also those, of course, who prefer the inner novel to the outer novel—cranks and nihilists, Gardner would say.) Ultimately, I think, *October Light* will emerge as one of Gardner's preeminent works by virtue of its rich, imaginative weave of imagery and symbol and story.

Such will also prove the case of *The King's Indian*, which is a marvel of construction and production: it is simply a physically beautiful book. It is a literary triptych of sorts; while each section is vastly different in style and approach, each section does coalesce into a larger thematic landscape in which Gardner traverses vast areas of time and space and form. He is at times realistic, at times lyrical, at times fantastic. But never in *The King's Indian* is he a failure.

The finest of Gardner's efforts, however, must be *The Sunlight Dialogues*, for it is the novel that will eventually stand as one of the great books of the twentieth century, and perhaps as the most important American book in the last three decades. Its ambitiousness is matched by its coherence, its wit by its philosophical seriousness. *The Sunlight Dialogues* is the will and testament of this century's middle age, and yet it affirms its ties with that long tradition—that "great tradition"—of literature that goes beyond the boundaries of time and that survives because it strikes resonantly at common chords in the human soul. *The Sunlight Dialogues* is a novel that will prevail.

There is, of course, something unnerving about making these sorts of literary judgments. It's akin to making aesthetic book: placing odds, figuring distance, picking ultimate winners. Still, what is a "sure thing," it seems, is Gardner's ability to last. He produced a significant body of work, the quality of which has been matched in our time and country by only a handful of writers, and which will certainly rank, in its consistency of worth, with any work by any author of this age. John Gardner took chances—despite his supposed conservatism—and he worked originally and honestly from a moral aesthetic that he thought viable, proven, and trustworthy. After all, it had centuries of practice to recommend it. The universe is no less humane now than it was two thousand years ago; we simply have the power and capacity to turn it back to darkness more quickly, to resurrect the ancient chaos. John Gardner believed in man's ability to sustain the light, maintain the order. It is there in his literature. It is there in his life. He simply wanted us to rediscover it in ourselves.

Notes

Prologue

1. John Gardner, *On Moral Fiction* (New York: Basic Books, 1978), p. 6.
2. Ibid., p. 5.
3. Ibid., p. 14.
4. The sense of morality and of humanity that Beal shares with Gardner is apparent not only in his work but in his remarks, which, except for his references to painting, could easily be attributed to Gardner. For example, in an article by Jane Cottingham in *American Artist* 44 (November 1980), Beal commented: "Painters have the ability, the responsibility to make beauty. . . . That beauty is more than just a good-looking painting; it also has to do with having a good life, a social responsibility" (p. 61).
5. Helprin is a good example of the hybrid nature of the neohumanistic movement, for while his work expresses a clear and sincere human concern, he has personally declared an affection for language that would mark him as a neoclassicist: "I consider myself a sort of a neo-classicist. . . . Most of my reading is in the classics. I read and reread Shakespeare, for example, because he reminds me of what language can do, of what it ought to be. I am quite comfortable being a neo-classicist; because I don't believe that art inevitably evolves. It need not advance but must only be good, for any true work is both an end and a beginning" (*New York Times Book Review,* 1 March 1981, p. 35).
6. I am indebted for this idea to Robert Bergstrom.

I. "The Old Men"

1. "John Gardner," *The Originals: The Writer in America* (PBS, 3 April 1978).
2. Personal interview with John Gardner, Lanesboro, Pennsylvania, 22 February 1979.
3. One might also include in this group a story Gardner wrote as part of his M.A. thesis at Iowa. It is entitled "Nickel Mountain," and it is an early version of the first section of the novel by that name.
4. John Gardner, "The Old Men" (Ph.D. diss., University of Iowa, 1958), p. 3. Subsequent references will be in the text.
5. John Gardner, *The Complete Works of the Gawain-Poet* (Chicago: University of Chicago Press, 1965), p. 71.

II. *The Resurrection*

1. "Conversation with John Gardner on Writers and Writing," originally published in the *Detroit Free Press,* 23 March 1975. Reprinted in *Authors in the News,* ed. Barbara Nykouk (Detroit: Gale Research Company, 1976), p. 169.
2. Marshall Harvey, "Where Philosophy and Fiction Meet: An Interview with John Gardner," *Chicago Review* 29 (Spring 1978): 82.

3. Gardner, *On Moral Fiction,* p. 144.

4. Leo Tolstoy, *Resurrection,* trans. Rosemary Edmonds (London: Penguin Books, 1966), p. 564.

5. Personal interview with John Gardner, Cleveland, Ohio, 13 March 1974.

6. Alan Donagan, *The Encyclopedia of Philosophy,* ed. Paul Edwards, 2d ed. (New York: Free Press, 1973), 1:140.

7. Gardner, *On Moral Fiction,* p. 10.

8. John Gardner, *The Resurrection* (New York: Ballantine Books, 1974), p. 7. Subsequent references will be to this edition. Neither the 1974 Ballantine edition nor the 1966 New American Library edition is currently in print. However, the later version of *The Resurrection* contained many stylistic and syntactical changes made by Gardner prior to the book's publication. It is this edition, therefore, that will be used here for discussion.

9. Don Edwards and Carol Polsgrove, "A Conversation with John Gardner," *The Atlantic Monthly* 239 (May 1977): 47.

10. There are a good many autobiographical connections in *The Resurrection.* As mentioned earlier, Batavia is Gardner's own birthplace and his parents still work a farm outside of town. Like Chandler, Gardner made the trip from Oberlin to San Francisco during his professional career. Also like Chandler, Gardner, as a child, took piano lessons from one of the "old ladies" of Batavia, Laura Stanley. Furthermore, the geographical realism of the novel is acute; while the town has changed, the streets, houses, and part of the ambience remain the same. We will see a similar phenomenon in *The Sunlight Dialogues* (which is also set in Batavia) and in *Mickelsson's Ghosts.*

11. Polsgrove and Edwards, "Conversation," pp. 44–45.

12. Gardner, *On Moral Fiction,* pp. 160–61.

III. *The Wreckage of Agathon*

1. Joe David Bellamy, *The New Fiction: Interviews with Innovative American Writers* (Urbana: University of Illinois Press, 1974), p. 75.

2. Gardner has privately acknowledged (in response to my questioning him upon it) one definite source in his novel: Plutarch's *Lives of the Noble Grecians and Romans.* Indeed, there are many passages in *The Wreckage of Agathon* that are merely touched-up renderings of Plutarch. At times Gardner modernizes or humorizes Plutarch, but there is never any doubt of where he is finding his material. There are at least twenty-three such borrowings in the novel, some of which match the original nearly word for word.

Gardner, it should be said, is in no way reluctant to confess his foraging in Plutarch; he makes his borrowings, instead, an integral part of his work. For the sake of bibliographical thoroughness, I include a listing of the passages in *The Wreckage of Agathon* that I have found to be derived from Plutarch's *Lives.* The page references in *Agathon* are from John Gardner's *The Wreckage of Agathon* (New York: Harper & Row, 1970). Both this edition and the 1972 Ballantine paperback edition are currently out of print, so I am using the original 1970 edition here and in subsequent references. The page references in Plutarch are taken from *Plutarch's Lives of the Noble Grecians and Romans,* trans. John Dryden, revised by Arthur Hugh Clough (New York: The Modern Library, n.d.).

Agathon	*Subject*	*Plutarch*
pp. 14–15	King Sous & the Clitorians	p. 50
p. 15	Lykourgos & his sister-in-law	pp. 50–52
p. 21	Lykourgos's absence from Sparta	p. 52

Agathon	Subject	Plutarch
p. 22	Consultation of oracle & establishment of senate	pp. 52–53
pp. 22–23	Lykourgos's outlawing of wealth	pp. 55–56
p. 24	Lykourgos's outlawing of "superfluous arts" and luxury	pp. 56–57
pp. 24–25	Lykourgos & Alkander	p. 57
p. 28	Lykourgos & public burial	p. 70
p. 30	Unwritten law	p. 58
p. 31	Humiliation of Helots	p. 71
p. 71	Solon's father	p. 97
pp. 72–73	Solon & his Megarian plan	p. 101
p. 81	Training of Spartan troops	pp. 64, 67
p. 82	Draco's laws	p. 107
pp. 97–98	The Krypteia	p. 71
pp. 112–13	Solon and Kroesos	pp. 113–14
p. 114	The taking of the Spartan bride	pp. 60–61
p. 114	Sexual privilege	p. 61
pp. 114–15	Draco's laws	p. 107
p. 115	Solon's reforms of courts	pp. 104, 107–8
p. 134	The earthquake	p. 71
p. 136	Lykourgos's farewell to city	pp. 71–72
pp. 220–21	Lykourgos's death	p. 72
p. 232	Striking of Lykourgos's crypt by lightning	p. 74

A brief sample of Gardner's adaptations might serve to illustrate the way in which he makes use of Plutarch. This is a characteristic passage:

Gardner

Aesop, the man who writes the fables, was in Sardis at the time of Kroesos's invitation—an old friend of Solon's— and he was troubled that Solon was so ill received as a result of his own mulishness. "Solon," said he, "when a man gives advice to kings he should make it pert and seasonable."

Solon nodded as if abashed and said softly, feebly, for he was well up in years: "Or short and reasonable. Or curt and treasonable. Or tart and please-him-able."

Aesop sighed. Though a person of the greatest sobriety, he was always unmanned by a jest. (p. 113)

Plutarch

Aesop, who wrote the fables, being then at Sardis upon Croesus's invitation, and very much esteemed, was concerned that Solon was ill received, and gave him this advice: "Solon let your converse with kings be either short or seasonable." "Nay, rather," replied Solon, "either short or reasonable."
(p. 114)

Gardner flavors Plutarch, at times making his writing less anachronistic and more attractive than Dryden's rendering. Nowhere, though, does he perform injustices upon the original; he always borrows with the greatest respect. It is a reflection of Gardner's long-held esteem for history that this novel takes no advantage of the terrific time-gap between present and past. One might contrast it to John Barth's awesomely humorous book *The Sot-Weed Factor,* which re-creates the seventeenth-century American scene, peoples the landscape with characters fictional and real, but makes no point beyond its wit and parody. Gardner, I think, is after something more significant; while *The Wreckage of Agathon* is, in places, a funny book, it is substantially a serious novel. Laughing pokes of hindsight are easy and sometimes cheap. Gardner would rather have us learn from the past than chuckle at its ironies and anachronisms.

3. In a personal interview with Gardner at his home in Lanesboro, Pennsylvania (22 February 1979), he spoke to me of this idea: "In *The Wreckage of Agathon* I set up different kinds of contrasts. The contrast between Sparta and Athens parallels the West (with its Goldwater attitude) and the New York, megalopolis, whatever—the East Coast. They're both wrong, obviously wrong." The novel is also wide open to other political interpretations. The date of its composition avails it of a possible connection with the Nixon-Vietnam era, and even of a comparison of communistic and democratic traditions of government. That the book's political overtones did nothing to hurt its modest popularity is certain.

4. Thaletes's cellblock disquisition on the "brute existent" (p. 186) is from Sartre's *Being and Nothingness,* and the takeoff has its purpose. Gardner commented on this section several times. In an interview with Harvey ("Where Philosophy and Fiction Meet,") Gardner explains:

> Sartre writes like an angel. That's the kind of thing that fascinates me. Sartre is my great love-hate, kind of because he's a horror intellectually, figuratively, and morally, but he's a wonderful writer and anything he says you believe, at least for the moment, because of the way he says it. In *The Wreckage of Agathon,* I take one of his most glorious passages, the passage on the brute existent. He talks about a mountain, and the image that he uses is so powerful that you believe everything he says. So in that passage I just made the substitution and everything else I translated directly from the French. (p. 75)

In a more recent interview with James Harkness in the State University of New York *Forum/The News* 8 (April 1979), Gardner adds: "When [Sartre] presents a position as he does on the brute existent, which is so moving because of the gorgeous image of the Alp, you have to show what that position becomes when you substitute a vulgar or disgusting image. Then the argument doesn't hold anymore" (p. F-2). Gardner's replacement of the mountain with an elephant serves well to strip Sartre's original passage of its rhetorical eloquence, and at least partly batters his argument. It was not the last time that Gardner was to take Sartre to task.

IV. *Grendel*

1. Harkness, "Interview: John Gardner," p. F-7. Gardner has also remarked that "one of the virtues of Grendel is that it is not very clear," which could also account for the book's diverse appeal and its susceptibility to misinterpretation.

2. In a letter to me, dated 6 December 1977, Betty Anderson at Knopf elaborated on this relationship between author, artist, and publisher:

> We have always illustrated John Gardner at his own insistence. He feels very strongly that works of fiction should be illustrated now just as they were in the nineteenth century. As for the selection of the artist, this has been a shared activity. *The Sunlight*

Dialogues, The King's Indian, and the *Life and Times of Chaucer* were all illustrated by acquaintances of John Gardner. In each instance, he recommended their use and we were quite happy to go along with his selection. In the case of *Grendel, Nickel Mountain, October Light,* and *In the Suicide Mountains,* we found an artist and got Gardner's approval before proceeding with the work. In every instance, we have been responsible for commissioning the artist. However, we have always felt that we arrive at happier results if people work together. We have therefore always made arrangements for Gardner to meet with the artist when the artist has been unknown to him and we have always shown Gardner the rough sketches as well as the finished art. The art has always been corrected to agree with his wishes when ever that was necessary.

3. While Gardner's work was afforded respect at Knopf, it was still treated roughly by less careful editors. In the October 1971 issue of *Esquire* there appeared "Song of Grendel," a long section from the novel that had been operated on (without Gardner's knowledge) by the magazine's fiction editor, Gordon Lish. The changes ranged from the cleansing of obscenities to vast alterations in intention and character. In fact, much of the "new" material in the story was written by Lish himself.

4. Personal conversation with Gardner, 28 October 1978. In his interview with Bellamy in *The New Fiction,* Gardner elaborated on this idea: "In *Grendel* the subject matter is Anglo-Saxon, but the treatment is what Walt Disney would have done if he hadn't been caught up in the sentimentality of smiling Mickey Mouse" (p. 175).

5. Perhaps Gardner's briefest comment on Sartre came in the interview with Harvey, "Where Philosophy and Fiction Meet": "I use Sartre a lot. What happened in *Grendel* was that I got the idea of presenting the *Beowulf* monster as Jean-Paul Sartre, and everything that Grendel says Sartre in one mood or another has said, so that my love of Sartre kind of comes through as my love of the monster, though monsters are still monsters—I hope" (p. 75). There is scarcely an interviewer who does not ask Gardner to talk of Sartre. Of the several critical looks at Gardner's use of Sartre, the best are Craig Stromme's "The Twelve Chapters of *Grendel*" in *Critique: Studies in Modern Fiction,* vol. 20, 1978, which hits upon the various intellectual ideas used by Gardner; and K. Clif Mason's unpublished essay, "Of Monsters and Men: *Beowulf* and Gardner's *Grendel,*" which is an exhaustive treatment of Gardner's approach to Sartrean existentialism.

6. Gardner, *The Complete Works of the Gawain-Poet,* pp. 38–39.

7. *The Republic of Plato,* trans. Francis MacDonald Cornford (London: Oxford University Press, 1945), p. 142.

8. *The Nichomachean Ethics of Aristotle,* trans. Sir David Ross (London: Oxford University Press, 1969), p. 138.

9. From an interview with C. E. Frazer Clark, Jr., in *Conversations with Writers,* ed. Matthew Bruccoli (Detroit: Gale Research Company, 1977), 1:83.

10. John Gardner, "Fulgentius's *Expositio Vergiliana Continentia* and the Plan of *Beowulf*: Another Approach to the Poem's Style and Structure," *Papers on Language and Literature* 7 (1971): 227–62.

11. *The Originals: The Writer in America.*

12. In a personal interview with Gardner of 28 October 1978, Gardner mentioned that the twelve chapters correspond to the twelve Aristotelian virtues. Though I don't think this a major organizational or thematic point—particularly in that it is difficult to locate exactly *twelve* virtues in the *Nichomachean Ethics*—I do think the idea helps illuminate parts of the book. Listed below for convenience, then, are twelve Aristotelian virtues, one or two slightly stretched, and their corresponding chapters in *Grendel.*

Chapter 1—Indignation   Chapter 8—Unnamed virtue—
Chapter 2—Courage   between ambition & nonambition
Chapter 3—Temperance   Chapter 9—Ready wit
Chapter 4—Magnificence   Chapter 10—Truthfulness
Chapter 5—Liberality   Chapter 11—Good-temper
Chapter 6—Friendliness   Chapter 12—Grandeur of soul
Chapter 7—Shame

Two articles have dealt in fair depth with Gardner's use of the "12 numerology." One is Susan Strehle's "John Gardner's Novels: Affirmation and the Alien" in *Critique: Studies in Modern Fiction,* vol. 18, 1976, pp. 86–96, which dives halfway into the astrological and intellectual connections of the twelve chapters; the other is Stromme's aforementioned "The Twelve Chapters of *Grendel,*" which is the most complete study of the astrological and philosophical symbolism of each chapter.

13. John Gardner, *Grendel* (New York: Alfred A. Knopf, 1971), p. 8. Subsequent references will be to this edition.

14. Mason, "Of Monsters and Men," p. 10. Mason is a member of the English Department at Bellevue College in Bellevue, Nebraska.

15. Bellamy, *The New Fiction,* p. 179.

16. Gardner is very clear on his feeling toward the dragon. He told Bellamy:

> The Dragon looks like an oracle, but he doesn't lay down the truth. He's just a nasty dragon. He tells the truth as it appears to a dragon—that nothing in the world is connected with anything. It's all meaningless and stupid, and since nothing is connected with anything the highest value in life is to seek out gold and sit on it. Since nothing is emotionally or physically connected you make piles of things. That is the materialistic point of view. Many people spend their lives, rightly or wrongly, doing nothing but filling out their bank accounts. My view is that this is a dragonish way to behave, and it ain't the truth. (*Ibid.,* p. 175)

17. The dialogue between Grendel and the dragon is echoed and expanded in the four dialogues between Clumly and the Sunlight Man in *The Sunlight Dialogues.* The characters and their actions and reactions are significantly similar, and Gardner seems to have exploited this early device to later good advantage, making it the framework for his larger novel.

18. The dragon also makes good use of Alfred North Whitehead, quoting him in his lecture to Grendel on time and space. Stromme, in his "Twelve Chapters of *Grendel,*" was the first to note Gardner's indebtedness to Whitehead, though Gardner has also commented on the subject:

> When I was a kid in college, the most interesting course I ever had, in a way, was a course in philosophy. And the way I really came across it was in Plato. I had read Plato but before the course I didn't understand him. And when I came to Whitehead my head went off because—not so much that he's a great philosopher, although he is, but—I felt he said what I would say. That is to say his world-view, incredibly, was like the world-view I had developed—born with it or whatever—so that a lot of times when I'm working with a philosophical question or problem of some kind, I think, "What would Whitehead say?" and then I try that out, dramatizing it; or "What would Whitehead do with this?"

See Harvey, "Where Philosophy and Fiction Meet," p. 74.

19. This idea of Grendel's inability to understand Wealtheow's sexuality was introduced by Helen B. Ellis and Warren U. Ober in their article, "*Grendel* and Blake: The Contraries of Existence," *English Studies in Canada* 3 (Spring 1977): 87–102, where they write that

Grendel "is trapped by an evolutionary dead end: it is perhaps possible for men to accept both the queen's sexuality and the ideal of the queen, but Grendel, of the monster's race of Cain, has known only one female, his mother: shuffling, wordless, ugly, foul-smelling" (pp. 98–99).

20. Gardner's system of naming and the clue to the identity of Red Horse are mentioned in an interview in *The Paris Review:* "I've used real characters in every single novel, except in *Grendel* where it's impossible—they didn't have our kinds of names in those days—but even in *Grendel* I used jokes and puns that give you clues to who I'm talking about. For instance there's a guy named Red Horse, which is really a sorrel, which is really George [*sic*] Sorel. And so on." See Paul Ferguson et al., "John Gardner: The Art of Fiction LXXIII," *Paris Review* 21 (Spring 1979): 59.

21. Gardner commented on the use of this symbol in an interview of 28 October 1978: "The spider is the poet—a weaver, a creator, and a killer."

22. The lines are from Thomas Kinsella's poem "Wormwood."

23. Ellis and Ober, in their article on *Grendel* and Blake, say that this section in *Grendel* is strikingly similar to lines from Blake's *Marriage of Heaven and Hell.* Their article is one of the most illuminating and rewarding approaches to this novel.

24. Gardner has interpreted, quite sensibly and thoroughly, this shape-shifting of Beowulf:

> As a medievalist, one knows there are two great dragons in medieval art. There's Christ the dragon, and there's Satan the dragon. There's always a war between those two great dragons. In modern Christian symbolism a sweeter image of Jesus with the sheep in his arms has evolved, but I like the old image of the warring dragon. That's not to say Beowulf really is Christ, but that he's Christ-like. Actually he is many things. When Grendel first sees Beowulf coming, Grendel thinks of him as a sort of machine, and what comes to the reader's mind is a kind of computer, a spaceman, a complete alien, unknown. The inescapable mechanics of the universe. At other times, Beowulf looks like a fish to Grendel. . . . On other occasions, Grendel sees other things, one after another, and for a brief flash, when he is probably hallucinating— he's fighting, losing blood very badly because he has his arm torn off—Grendel thinks he's fighting the dragon instead of Beowulf. At the end of the story, Grendel doesn't know *who* he's fighting. He's just fighting something big and horrible and sure to kill him, something that he could never have predicted in the universe as he understood it, because from the beginning of the novel, Grendel feels himself hopelessly deter- mined, hopelessly struggling against—in the profoundest sense—the way things are.

See Ferguson et al., "John Gardner," pp. 44–45.

25. This same old Welsh song Grendel sings is used as an epigraph to *The Resurrection,* and later appears in its full form as "Setting for an Old Welsh Line," in Gardner's *Poems* (Northridge, Calif.: Lord John Press, 1978).

26. Gardner has explained this transformation from monster to poet:

> Grendel is seduced by the Shaper; he wants to be a part of that vision. Unfortunately, he can't get in because he's a monster. But at the end of the novel Grendel himself becomes the Shaper. Beowulf bangs his head against the wall and says *feel.* Grendel feels—his head hurts—so Beowulf makes him sing about walls. When the first Shaper dies, a kid is chosen to succeed him, but the real successor is Grendel. In the last pages of the book Grendel begins to apprehend the whole universe: life and death, his own death. Poetry is an accident, the novel says, but it's a great one. May it happen to all of us.

See Bellamy, *The New Fiction,* pp. 179–80.

v. *The Sunlight Dialogues*

1. Personal interview with John Gardner, Middlebury, Vermont, 22 August 1978.

2. Diane Cochrane has written an interesting article on Napper and his work for *The Sunlight Dialogues*. It is entitled "John Napper: The Return of the Illustrated Novel," and appeared in *American Artist,* 23 July 1973, p. 26. Napper's illustrations were also featured in a showing at the Lacarda Gallery in New York City, an exhibition favorably reviewed by John Canaday in the *New York Times,* 16 December 1972, p. 27.

3. The poem originally appeared in *The Southern Review* 4 (January 1968): 162–64. Except for some small changes, it is the same poem Gardner included in the novel. See pp. 310–11 of the edition I am using in this chapter: John Gardner, *The Sunlight Dialogues* (New York: Alfred A. Knopf, 1972).

"A Little Night Music" was published in *The Northwest Review* 4 (Spring 1961): 30–40. Among the characters in this story are Chief Clumly, one of the two protagonists of *The Sunlight Dialogues,* and Charley Tree, who is mentioned in *The Resurrection* (p. 63), and whose probable relative, Jim Tree, is named in *The Sunlight Dialogues* (p. 104). Also named is Maude Stanley, one of the trio of elderly sisters in *The Resurrection* (though in that novel she is called Maud Staley).

"A Little Night Music," along with the stories "Redemption" and "Come on Back" (in *The Art of Living*), completes the "Batavia group," which also includes *The Resurrection* and *The Sunlight Dialogues*. All are set in or around Batavia, New York, and all share common themes and characters (sometimes to the point of obscurity: in "Redemption," for example, there appears the famed French horn player Arkady Yegudkin, who is also mentioned by Taggert Hodge in *The Sunlight Dialogues,* p. 534). It all represents just another use by Gardner of elements of his personal history.

4. Daniel Laskin, "Challenging the Literary Naysayers," *Horizon* 21 (July 1978): p. 36.

5. For a complete examination of Gardner's use of Babylonian religious and cultural tradition in *The Sunlight Dialogues,* see the essay by Gregory Morris, "A Babylonian in Batavia: Mesopotamian Literature and Lore in *The Sunlight Dialogues,*" in *Critical Perspectives on John Gardner,* ed. Robert A. Morace and Kathryn VanSpanckeren (Carbondale: Southern Illinois University Press, 1982).

6. A. Leo Oppenheim, *Ancient Mesopotamia: Portrait of a Dead Civilization* (Chicago: University of Chicago Press, 1964), pp. 221, 223.

7. Ferguson et al., "John Gardner," pp. 53–54. Gardner has also talked elsewhere about his intention in using Batavia, giving a somewhat different explanation:

> In *The Sunlight Dialogues* I wanted to tell a story which had the feel of total fabulation, total mystery—magicians—strange things and impossible tricks—so that everybody would have the sudden feeling at some point in the novel that he's caught inside a novel, but with streets that can be recognized, houses which are accurately described, and so on. I wanted to tint the stock and photograph Batavia. I wanted to make people in the novel just as much like Batavians as possible and yet create the feeling that the whole novel is taking place in Oz.

See Bellamy, *The New Fiction,* pp. 191–92. This partially explains Gardner's one obvious indulgence in self-conscious fiction in *The Sunlight Dialogues* when, on p. 621, Taggert Hodge says, "There's always the future, p. 622." The idea of *The Sunlight Dialogues* as a part of the "new fabulation" is a curious and illuminating one, I think.

8. *The Originals: The Writer in America.*

9. This is just one of Gardner's many parodies of Faulknerian prose, an intention he

remarked upon at least twice. In Bellamy's *New Fiction,* p. 173, Gardner says, "In *The Sunlight Dialogues* when the narrator tells about Will Hodge Sr, he throws out long, parody-Faulkner sentences in parentheses: 'Invincible Hodge!' 'Ah, Hodge!' He is carried away by his character." Again, in Ferguson et al., "John Gardner," p. 50, he says, "The whole conception of the book [*The Sunlight Dialogues*] is in a way parodic of Faulkner, among others—the whole idea of family and locale."

10. Personal interview with John Gardner, Lanesboro, Pennsylvania, 22 February 1979. This notion of the Einsteinian universe is important in another way to the novel: *The Sunlight Dialogues* is a printed model of the expanding universe. Its plot, like the planets, moves outward and apart at a rapid pace, unlike the typical architectonic, Dickensian structure in which plot lines tend to converge.

11. Gardner makes a fuller statement on Malory and the narrator of *The Sunlight Dialogues* in his interview with Ferguson et al.

12. There are other evidences of Melville's influence upon Gardner's *The Sunlight Dialogues*. On Congressman Hodge's study wall hangs a "boggy, squitchy painting" (p. 346) that is a replica of the painting that graced the Spouter Inn in *Moby Dick*. There is also some hint of a Pierre–Mrs. Glendinning relationship (perhaps in reverse) between Luke Hodge and his mother, Millie. *Pierre* is even mentioned once as the subject of a family discussion (p. 639).

13. Dante Alighiere, *The Inferno,* from *The Divine Comedy,* trans. Mark Musa, (Bloomington, Indiana: University of Indiana Press, 1971), 3.35–36.

14. In the interview with Bellamy in *The New Fiction,* Gardner commented on this scene:

> At one point Clumly and Mrs. Clumly are lying in bed together. He thinks of her as a chicken—he wouldn't be surprised to see her feet sticking in the air. Later, Mrs. Clumly lies in bed trying to sense what she looks like. It comes to her in a great flash: she looks like a chicken. Mrs. Clumly is the Beatrice of *The Sunlight Dialogues*. She guides everybody because she loves. This is the kind of imagination which holds the world together. (p. 188)

15. Again in the Bellamy interview, Gardner talks of this important scene:

> The two characters who have the most imagination in the novel are Clumly and Mrs. Clumly, because they can see into other people's minds. With his little mole's intelligence, Clumly stares at the Sunlight Man and tries to understand him. He really tries to understand the principle of evil by empathizing with it. During the novel, the Sunlight Man, because of his experiences, sees fire around him. He knows that's crazy, but he keeps on seeing fire. Just before his last speech, Clumly looks through a door and sees it's burning inside: he's gotten inside the Sunlight Man's emotions. He fully understands even though he can't make sense of it. At least he has compassion, which is a kind of imagination. (p. 188)

VI. *Nickel Mountain*

1. Harkness, "Interview: John Gardner," p. F-2.
2. Personal interview with John Gardner, Lanesboro, Pennsylvania, 22 February 1979.
3. Stephen Singular, "The Sound and the Fury over Fiction," *New York Times Magazine,* 8 July 1979, p. 39.
4. For a listing of the previous publication data on the chapters of *Nickel Mountain,* see

John Howell's *John Gardner: A Bibliographical Profile* (Carbondale: Southern Illinois University Press, 1980).

5. Harvey, "Where Philosophy and Fiction Meet," p. 79. For fuller studies of *Nickel Mountain* as pastoral, see David Cowart's *"Et in Arcadia Ego:* Gardner's Early Pastoral Novels," and Samuel Coales's " 'Into the Farther Darkness': The Manichaean Pastoralism of John Gardner," both in *John Gardner: Critical Perspectives,* ed. Morace and VanSpanckeren.

6. Personal interview with John Gardner, Lanesboro, Pennsylvania, 22 February 1979.

7. John Gardner, *Nickel Mountain* (New York: Alfred A. Knopf, 1973), p. 4. Subsequent references will be to this edition.

8. *The Originals: The Writer in America.*

9. George Levine, "The Name of the Game," *Partisan Review* 42 (Spring 1975): 293.

10. In Harvey's "Where Philosophy and Fiction Meet" Gardner commented on the source and role of his Goat Lady: "There was a Goat Lady that came through western New York when I was a kid, and she was a very strange lady. I more or less borrowed her from life and made her a kind of contrast to Henry Soames. That is, the one thing that's noticeable about her is that she's a loving mother. The trouble is that she's an idiot, and Henry Soames is very much like the loving mother, and he is in a certain way an idiot, but in other ways he's not. It was meant finally as a symbolic contrast" (p. 80).

11. One of Gardner's most interesting collection of comments deals with a sure shift taken by *Nickel Mountain* from its original aim: what began as a romantic love story somehow turned into a cosmic love story. When he began, he "was trying desperately to write a book that wasn't tricky. I wanted it to be an enormously simple kind of love story. I thought that was the direction I wanted to go, but I haven't done that." (See Harkness, "Interview: John Gardner," p. F-2). One of the reasons for the change, furthermore, is a basic personal inability to deal with the sexual theme and the complexities of an involved and demanding relationship:

> That's the greatest weakness in my fiction—the lack of real sexual love. The only great artist who ever surmounted an inability to deal with this was Melville. Shakespeare mastered love. Mozart was great. He *knows* about men and women. Chaucer, terrific on it. Dante, fantastic. Homer, just unbelievable. It's one of the motivating forces— and I don't have it. It's partly puritanical shyness. *Nickel Mountain* is a kind of love story, but it really shies away from it. I couldn't handle it. . . . A real love story requires a woman who is the equal of the man. And my women . . . this has been a weakness.

See Singular, "The Sound and the Fury over Fiction," p. 39. In *Nickel Mountain* Gardner transforms an elemental love into something universal and lofty. He makes of Callie more a symbol than a human being; we never really know what she is feeling because of her perplexity. She is also overshadowed (as are almost all of Gardner's female characters, with perhaps the exception of Millie Hodge in *The Sunlight Dialogues*) by her husband, who draws most of the artistic and psychological attention. And not until *Mickelsson's Ghosts* did Gardner really tackle the problem of sexual love—with mixed success.

VII. *The King's Indian: Stories and Tales*

1. For a history of the previous publication of the stories in *The King's Indian,* see Howell's *John Gardner: A Bibliographical Profile.* All of the stories previously published

reappear in *The King's Indian* with little change. The only exception is "The Temptation of St. Ivo," which underwent small additions and revision, only two of which are significant: the added emphasis in the later version of Brother Nicholas's homosexuality, and the new, annexed ending. The increased stress on Nicholas's supposed homosexuality gains interest when examined in light of Gardner's letter to the *Kansas Quarterly* 10 (Winter 1978) explaining his decision as judge of their fiction contest. In this letter, Gardner commented: "I know that stories about homosexuality are inherently trivial (besides, I tend to hate homosexuals)." This remark brought a letter in response, condemning Gardner's attitude and his gall. Gardner explained the situation in a personal interview in Lanesboro, Pennsylvania (22 February 1979):

> That letter was really bad. That's the meanest thing I ever wrote. I wrote that after getting out of the hospital. I was really sick, and I had to get it off. Then I read the stories, and they weren't very good. I was, in effect, asked to judge a contest for $50 that wasn't worth judging. I wrote the letter very, very fast. I never had a chance to read it over. And I got one letter from a guy who was furious at me for something I'd said about homosexuals. He was absolutely right. . . . Anyway, that was a bad moment in my life.

Homosexuals, in fact, come off badly in almost all of Gardner's work. In *The Old Men, The Wreckage of Agathon, The Sunlight Dialogues, Jason and Medeia,* and *Freddy's Book,* as well as in *The King's Indian,* those characters who are homosexual or who exhibit stereotypically homosexual behavior are consistently portrayed unfavorably. Peter Mickelsson, in Gardner's novel *Mickelsson's Ghosts,* probably summed up what was Gardner's own position, describing homosexuality as an "aesthetically unpalatable" way of life.

2. Ferguson et al., "John Gardner," p. 54.

3. John Gardner, "Southern Illinois," *Vogue* 167 (March 1977): 156. Subsequent references are in the text.

4. Harvey, "Where Philosophy and Fiction Meet," pp. 81–82.

5. John Gardner, *The King's Indian: Stories and Tales* (New York: Alfred A. Knopf, 1974), p. 316. Subsequent references will be to this edition.

6. The article was entitled "Nicholas Vergette" and it appeared in *Craft Horizons* 33 (October 1973). The poem "Nicholas Vergette" was also printed in *Craft Horizons* 34 (April 1974). It might also be noted that in Herbert Fink's portrait of the country doctor in "The Ravages of Spring," the face is that of Vergette. In fact, all of the portraits are of people known and close to Gardner and Fink in Carbondale.

7. Gardner has explained the working of *The King's Indian* in the following fashion:

> The way I think the collection works generally is that the opening stories are fairly dark and each one up to the last one in the first section presents a kind of miraculous or "absurd" resurrection. In "Pastoral Care," the minister is caught up in neo-orthodoxy, the kind of thing John Updike is very interested in, which I think is a bad idea, and in the end he loses his self-consciousness, his priggishness, and he's a minister, which is his resurrection. The last story in the group, "The Warden," is about a man who is a destroyer, and the hopeful guy is his father the artist, but the hopeful possibility is muted. "John Napper Sailing Through the Universe" is my fundamental theory of art, which I'm spelling out in a different, more discursive way in a book . . . called *On Moral Fiction,* but what John Napper says is the heart of it: the artist can't just describe the world, "bitter reality"; the artist has to create new and wonderful possibilities. What happens in the Queen Louisa stories is that the princess has died; Queen Louisa has gone crazy; and, having no way to make anything out of

the fact that the princess is dead and everything's awful, she in her insanity creates a new world, which gets better and better. When I get to "The King's Indian," I do the whole thing in a more serious and complex way, using the greatest writers of the American tradition along with the one English poet who had more influence on American fiction, I think, than anybody else. . . . I think the two most important influences on American literature from the beginning to the present have been Keats and Coleridge, and of the two the most important was Coleridge. Anyway, "The King's Indian" uses the Yankee Melville, the Southerner Poe, and the middle-man Twain as a sort of basis, and Coleridge as a sort of background. It's an attempt to create a new world—a vision—which at the same time is a story of the American democracy, a people's self-expression in their ship of state, "The New Jerusalem."

See Harvey, "Where Philosophy and Fiction Meet," p. 81.

8. Gardner may have in mind here the eighteenth-century physician and surgeon, John Hunter (1728–93), who wrote on such wide-ranging topics as the history of teeth, the treatment of gunshot wounds, and venereal disease.

9. As mentioned above in note 1, the original version of this story ended with the confessional scene between Ivo and Nicholas. That Gardner affixed a new ending to his story would indicate: (1) that he wished to emphasize the forest imagery, something he would use more directly and more fully in "Tales of Queen Louisa"; and (2) that he wanted to clarify his point by going beyond the ambiguous and quizzical ending of the first version, showing Ivo (presumably) in the act of his sainthood, and making the connection between Ivo and the rest of mankind.

Brother Ivo's historical existence is something Gardner took into consideration when he created him, but he told me (in the Lanesboro interview) that he had no one certain Ivo in mind at the time. *The Book of Saints,* compiled by Benedictine monks and published in 1921, lists three Ivos, all of whom have been canonized. Only two, however, seem to fit Gardner's own character: (1) Ivo (Yvo). A Breton saint of the fourteenth century and the patron of lawyers. "His gratuitous services to the oppressed and needy earned him the title of 'Advocate of the poor.' . . . He was above all a man of prayer and penance" (p. 144). (2) Ivo of Chartres. A Canon regular of twelfth-century France, Ivo was "distinguished by his learning, as by his piety and zeal in God's service. He reluctantly received consecration at Rome as Bishop of Chartres from the Pope, Blessed Urban II. His long Episcopate was chiefly notable for the untiring war he waged against abuses in Church discipline" (p. 144). Either of the two men it seems could have modeled for Gardner's Ivo, and Gardner admitted to me the appeal (though he was unaware of the fact) of Ivo's being the patron saint of lawyers.

10. This final scene of Ivo, the Knight, and the forest is reminiscent of Italo Calvino's *The Non-Existent Knight.* Gardner has praised Calvino both in book reviews in the *New York Times Book Review* and in *On Moral Fiction,* and the sense of fantasy and surrealism evident in "The Temptation of St. Ivo" surely is due in part to the richly imaginative tales of Calvino.

11. The idea is also an echo of the fantastic genetic theories of John Hunter in "The Ravages of Spring," who manages to perfect the indestructibility of matter by cloning. Thus, matter never melts into spirit, but merely duplicates itself infinitely.

12. This was first brought out in Harkness, "Interview: John Gardner," p. F-2. Harkness's question and Gardner's response are included below:

H: Can we pursue the Sartre connection a bit? In . . . "The Warden," the narrator closes by quoting from an imaginary book he has just refused to purchase from an anonymous "fool." The quoted lines just happen to be the actual first sentence of *Being and Nothingness*. . . . Are most readers likely to make that rather hermetic association? If not, doesn't that affect the story and the likelihood it will be understood?

G: I think the story works either way, or I wouldn't have written it. I never want to exclude any reader from what I write. . . . Anyway, if you've followed "The Warden" dramatically, in terms of simple feelings, what you're afraid of and worried about and so on, you feel, by the time you come to that ending, that the central character in that story is a frightening man, that his position is a dangerous position. Then one reads those lines, and if one doesn't know it comes from *Being and Nothingness*, one thinks, "Oh my god, what a terrifying position." If you do recognize the source, you recognize how cruelly I'm misusing Sartre—but also, in a way, how true and fair it is—then, I think, the reader gets a double pleasure.

13. John Gardner, "Trumpeter," in *The Art of Living and Other Stories*, (New York: Alfred A. Knopf, 1981), p. 80. Subsequent references will be to this edition.

14. The borrowing of Melville's "howling infinite" is not the last time Gardner makes use of Melville's work. Gardner may be the only novelist ever to quote from Melville's long, philosophical poem, *Clarel*. On page 280, the hoary image of Melville arises from the sea foam and shouts a pair of lines (partly misquoted) from his own poetic work:

"Even death may prove unreal at last, and stoics be astounded into Heaven." (From *Clarel*, 4.35, "Epilogue")

"Man, beast, grass, 'tis all one: Bearers of crosses—alike they tend, and follow, slowly follow on!" (From *Clarel*, 4.34, "Via Crucis")

Gardner also takes from *Moby Dick* Melville's question: "Ain't all men slaves, either physical or metaphysical?" (*The King's Indian*, p. 198). Beside the straightforward quoting of Melville, Gardner also uses motifs and techniques and characters that Melville exploited so fruitfully; from Melville, Gardner takes his Captain Dirge-Flint (as awesome and foreboding as Melville's Ahab), his Indian harpooner Kiskawah (just the name is enough to remind one of Queequeg), and the notion of the ship as microcosm.

While all of these borrowings are sure evidence of Gardner's attraction to America's genius of the nineteenth century, he is even more liberal in his use of Edgar Allan Poe. His description of Augusta, for instance, is very close (and in some places identical) to Poe's *Ligeia* (compare p. 252 of *The King's Indian* and this line from "Ligeia": "They were even fuller than the fullest of the gazelle eyes of the tribe of the valley of Nourjahad.") Gardner even mentions "Ligeia" on p. 310.

Gardner draws most heavily, however, from Poe's only novel, *The Narrative of Arthur Gordon Pym*, which provides Gardner with a good deal of his plot and motivation. What follows is a summary of Gardner's forays into Poe's *Pym*. (The edition referred to is that published by Hill and Wang, 1960.)

A. Both Pym and Upchurch own a sailboat, and both boats are "worth about seventy-five dollars" (*AGP*, p. 5). Pym's is called the *Ariel* and Upchurch's the *Jolly Independent*, and both lie wharfed by the lumberyard of Pankey & Co. Both Pym and Upchurch are washed out to sea by the same hellish storm, and both are picked up by whaling ships (compare the nearly identical descriptions—*AGP*, pp. 8–9; *KI*, pp. 212–13).

B. When Pym once more sets out to sea, he sails aboard the *Grampus,* which is the ship which recovers the spurious painting that Flint uses to justify his ghost-voyage (see *KI,* pp. 283, 307).

C. Captain Guy of the *Grampus* sets out to look for the Vanishing Isles or Aurora Islands, and he sets his bearings at 52° 37' 24" S, 47° 43' 15" W. These are the exact headings given by Wilkins (*KI,* p. 266) as he traces Captain Dirge's strange tacking pattern. Although Captain Guy does not succeed in finding the Vanishing Isles, Dirge (and Upchurch) do manage to come upon them—or at least they find the proper heading and smell the unaccountable smell of land where there was no land.

D. When the *Jane Grey* explodes in *Pym* (p. 176), savages and birds yell "Tekeli-li! Tekeli-li!" This is the same cry which bursts from the rigging of the *Jerusalem* as it sets out for home (*KI,* p. 323).

E. Jonathan's near-fall from the mast (*KI,* pp. 237–38), which has one antecedent in *Moby Dick,* is almost directly taken from Poe's description of Pym's vertigo at the edge of the cliff (*AGP,* p. 185). The lines are, in fact, the same in some places. And the fellow who saves Pym, his good friend Dirk Peters, we are later told now lives in Illinois, where of course both Upchurch and John Gardner have lived.

F. Both Poe and Gardner include mutinies in their tales, and Gardner's description (*KI,* pp. 295–96) is a near carbon copy of that written by Poe (*AGP,* pp. 41–42). Moreover, in both accounts the black cook is particularly villainous and bloodthirsty.

G. In "The King's Indian" Jeremiah tells us he sailed with "Captain d'Oyarvido on the good ship *Princess* that found out the Vanishing Isles of the South Pacific" (*KI,* p. 234). Poe confirms the factualness of Jeremiah's voyage, writing: "In 1790, Captain Manuel de Oyarvido, in the ship *Princess,* belonging to the Royal Philippine Company, sailed, as he asserts, directly among the Vanishing Isles" (*AGP,* pp. 130–31).

H. Finally, in "The King's Indian," when Wilkins destroys his dummy and then himself, he lies by the bulkhead upon which sits "the crudely carved but ornate memorial of some mortal presumably dead long since, returned to the universe . . . paroled forever from Discipline, word full of hardness: A. G. P." (*KI,* pp. 309–10). It is as if Gardner is adding the final words to a tombstone, echoing Poe's long distrust of man's penchant for invention; as Gardner said in the Lanesboro interview: "Poe hated the idea of slavery to machines." It is that blasphemous and ignorant grasping for godhood that both men deplore, the belief that man can create a nature that, in its intricate and ingenious mechanics, outdoes the original.

15. The reference to Shakespeare's *Tempest* is only a confirmation of Gardner's intentional use of the play within his tale. By naming his "heroine" Miranda, he makes the connection obvious, and though Flint plays a perverse Prospero, the animalistic Wolff is a fitting counterpart to Shakespeare's Caliban.

16. Personal interview with John Gardner, Lanesboro, Pennsylvania, 22 February 1979.

17. John Gardner, *Jason and Medeia* (New York: Alfred A. Knopf, 1973), p. 269.

VIII. *October Light*

1. Personal interview with John Gardner, Middlebury, Vermont, 8 August 1978.

2. John Gardner, "Amber (Get) Waves (Your) of (Plastic) Grain (Uncle Sam)," *New York Times,* 29 October 1975, sec. M., p. 41.

3. Personal interview with John Gardner, Middlebury, Vermont, 8 August 1978.

4. For Gardner, this experimentation is a genuine artistic technique, one which had a direct effect on the conception and eventual completion of *October Light*. As Gardner explains in *On Moral Fiction:*

> One begins a work of fiction with certain clear opinions—for instance, I myself in a recent novel, *October Light*, began with the opinion that traditional New England values are the values we should live by: good workmanship, independence, unswerving honesty, and so on—and one tests those opinions in lifelike situations, puts them under every kind of pressure one can think of, always being fair to the other side, and what one slowly discovers, resisting all the way, is that one's original opinion was oversimple. (p. 114)

5. The publication history of these articles before they were collected in *On Moral Fiction* can be found in Howell's *John Gardner: A Bibliographical Profile*. Interestingly, the seeds of these articles (and much else in *On Moral Fiction*) can be located in even earlier of Gardner's writings; in particular, in an essay entitled "The Way We Write Now," in *The New York Times Book Review* (9 July 1972, p. 2ff.) and in a brief letter to the editor in *New American Review* 9 (April 1977): 232–35. Of course, other hints of Gardner's critical way of thinking can also be picked up in his numerous book reviews, in which he dealt with many of the writers later taken to task or praised in *On Moral Fiction*.

6. John Gardner, *October Light* (New York: Alfred A. Knopf, 1976), p. 21. Subsequent references will be to this edition.

7. Gardner, *On Moral Fiction*, p. 112. Subsequent citations are in the text.

8. There are still other, smaller ties between the two books. For instance, James's thoughts on "snuff films" (p. 297) are similar to Gardner's own mention of them in *On Moral Fiction* (p. 22). When Peter Wagner, a character in *The Smugglers of Lost Souls' Rock*, claims to fabricate the tragedy of his sister, he is simply prestating Gardner's own comments on William Gass's creation and noncreation of a character. And when Terence Parks ruminates on "pure and subservient art," he is expanding on a theme played by Gardner in *OMF*, where he discusses the imitative function of music (p. 65).

9. Howell states in *John Gardner: A Bibliographical Profile*, that by April 1970 Gardner had "begun, with the assistance of his wife, Joan, *The Smugglers of Lost Souls' Rock*" (p. xvii). This would indicate that the inner novel was completed earlier and inserted much later into the *October Light* manuscript.

10. In one way, *October Light* works as a companion piece to Gardner's adultish children's tale, *In the Suicide Mountains*, which Howell notes was completed several months after the final revision of *October Light* (*John Gardner: A Bibliographical Profile*, p. xix). Both works deal seriously with the subject of suicide, its causes and its effects. Gardner seems to feel that the existential as well as the idealized notions of suicide are wrong, horribly wrong, that they mislead people into a tragedy that is unnecessary and ill-considered. Gardner also implies that one suicide may serve as the model for another; thus, Richard hangs himself partly because of Ira's earlier example, mistaking it for a sign of courageous vengeance. Death, says Gardner, is tragic, not laughable, and to make of suicide something fanciful and ironic borders upon the criminal.

11. Gardner purposely undercuts the seriousness of his inner novel, not only by making it the symbol of everything he detests in bad art, but by playing little self-conscious tricks within the book itself. For example, the book that Peter Wagner was reading, the book that he frequently recalls only snatches of, is actually Gardner's own *The King's Indian*. As he comes to in the hull of the *Indomitable*, Wagner considers: "He lay still, oppressed by a

sense of *déjà vu,* then remembered: all that was happening had happened in some novel he'd read about a hoax" (*OL,* p. 84). And when Alkahest goes to investigate the identity of Wagner, the would-be suicide, he discovers: "The man who had jumped from the bridge had left no trace but the car—no plates, no registration, no engine number, nothing but a paperback in the front seat, something about an Indian" (*OL,* p. 174). In short, *The Smugglers of Lost Souls' Rock* is "The King's Indian" without the hope and the determined faith in art and its ability to redeem. Peter Wagner and Jane are thin, black-comic sendups of Jonathan Upchurch and Miranda, and the *Indomitable* and its Captain Fist a weak reflection of the *Jerusalem* and its demonic Dr. Flint. Gardner even uses Fred Clumly from *The Sunlight Dialogues* as a model for his police chief in the inner novel: "He was enormous: so bloated that the wire things that held on his glasses sank deep into his head. On his desk he had pill bottles, a dozen or more, all prescription" (*OL,* p. 175). The commissioner seems, indeed, a combination of Clumly and the mountainous Henry Soames of *Nickel Mountain.*

Gardner does not stop at using elements of his other fictions in *October Light,* nor at using parts of *October Light* in later works (note that the poems recited by Ruth Thomas appear in Gardner's *A Child's Bestiary*). He goes further by inserting himself as a character in his novel, making an appearance at Merton's Hideaway with his family and some friends (one of whom is Nicholas Delbanco, whose novel *Possession* provides the germ for the tale of Judah Sherbrooke and his "bare-naked wife"). The flare-up between Gardner and his wife, Joan, (p. 295) is quelled by their son Joel, and they rise to leave, drunkenly silent and regretful. James watches as they go: "Furtively, he watched them pay Merton at the bar. At the door the bearded man paused for an instant, and it seemed to James that he was about to turn and look back, straight at him; but if that was what was in the man's mind he thought better of it—or in his drunkenness forgot it—and went out" (p. 296). Gardner is playing a game similar to that played by John Fowles in *The French Lieutenant's Woman,* where Fowles himself appears to one of his characters on a train and in the street. There is, I think, more to this little self-indulgence, however. Recall that Gardner was living and working in Vermont while writing *October Light.* In one interview Gardner remarked that "when I did *October Light,* which came out of a very direct and immediate experience in the East . . ." (Ferguson et al., "John Gardner," p. 55). My guess is that Gardner is describing, in his chapter on James at Merton's Hideaway, at least part of that "direct and immediate experience," that the story of James Page and Sally Page Abbott is derived to some extent from a personal encounter (a figure seen in a bar, a story overheard, a person actually met). Both James and "the bearded man" (Gardner sported a beard for a time) are captivated by one another, worried and moved by each other's looks and behavior. The glances that passed between the two men in the tavern signify the beginning of a fictional connection and an emotional relationship that eventually blossomed into *October Light,* and would indicate, I am sure, the nature of Gardner's feelings toward his main character.

12. Harvey, "Where Philosophy and Fiction Meet," p. 84.

13. Personal interview with John Gardner, Lanesboro, Pennsylvania, 22 February 1979. Gardner explains this dilemma in another fashion elsewhere:

> We all as children feel we are a certain kind of person, and it's a good person. . . . We get a very clear sense in childhood of who that person is. Then, in the process of life, we betray that person, over and over and over, until we begin to believe that we're not that person—although we are. Well, what I think the program of weak fiction is, is to make us comfortable with our betrayals instead of lead us back to the pure self that we were, or that we thought we were. When people become depressed, when people cry out in their dreams, when people are afraid to make commitments,

afraid to lend a beggar money, afraid to do anything, it's because they lost the kid. And I think that fiction and religion and education ought to be in the business of keeping the kid alive, keeping that noble self alive instead of saying, "Look, it's all right, we're all punks." (Laskin, "Challenging the Literary Naysayers," p. 34).

14. Gardner, *The King's Indian*, p. 352.

15. Gardner's symbolic use of the bear in *October Light* evokes the bear in Delmore Schwartz's poem, "The Heavy Bear Who Goes with Me":

> That inescapable animal walks with me,
> Has followed me since the black womb held,
> Moves where I move, distorting my gesture,
> A caricature, a swollen shadow

16. Gardner's most complete statement on the monster in his fiction came in a segment of *The Originals: The Writer in America*, in which Gardner remarked:

> It's true that in my books, monsters are always important. People are monsters, people are called monsters. Really, there are three kinds of things important in my things. One is monsters, another is clowns, another is human beings, and of course they keep shape-shifting. One turns into the other; clowns are always trying to be human beings. What I mean by clowns is this: human beings do things and clowns desperately try to imitate human beings. So the acrobat gets up on the wire and the clown wants to be an acrobat and he tries, but he's a strawman and he can't be. He's always acting, he's always faking, pretending, mimicking. Many of us feel that, about ourselves, all the time. That is to say, we put on masks and never find out who we really are. And one of the things that happens in the novels is that characters who start out as clowns try to earn the grade as human beings, and sometimes they turn into monsters instead. Monsters are those things that I used to go to the Saturday afternoon movies and see. I mean by monsters walking dead, I mean nihilists, people who really have given up on all faith, and act as if the world were evil, and as if all people were either stupid or malicious. They're creatures who have given in to the emotional war that's in everybody.

17. Gardner's comments on Dante and Beatrice illuminate the relationship between James Page and Ariah, and also shed light on a fundamental problem in Gardner's fiction: his admitted inability to deal successfully with women and with personal and sexual loving (see Singular, "The Sound and the Fury over Fiction," p. 39). Gardner, perhaps as a result of his long years as a medievalist, tends to conceive a woman as either a saint or a whore; thus, his female characters are often thin, one-dimensional, and too easily explained. A little later in *On Moral Fiction*, Gardner discusses more extensively his concept of this Beatrice-saint figure:

> Most of us, I hope, have had some child or spouse or friend like Beatrice, someone who by his very nature, his seemingly innate goodness and intelligence, makes us uncomfortably conscious of our lies when we lie. Writers have been noticing and copying down such people for centuries—or making them up, if that can be believed. Literature abounds with these saintly figures—they need not be women or even young—and if the saints in some writers' fictions seem stick figures, like Dickens' Agnes in *David Copperfield* or Julien in Flaubert's *La legende de Saint Julien l'hospitalier*, that does not diminish Chaucer's Knight, Shakespeare's Ophelia, or a dozen heroes and heroines in the fictions of Henry James. (p. 34)

While it is true that some of Gardner's saints are men (Lewis in *October Light,* perhaps Luke in *The Sunlight Dialogues*), it is certain that the majority of such saint figures in Gardner's fiction are portrayed by women. One thinks of Esther in *The Sunlight Dialogues,* Callie in *Nickel Mountain,* Wealtheow in *Grendel,* and Jessica in *Mickelsson's Ghosts.* The same is true of Gardner's demons. Beginning with Ginger Ghoki in *The Old Men* and continuing with Viola in *The Resurrection* and Millie in *The Sunlight Dialogues,* this sort of devil-temptress has always served as a dark counterpoint to the splendid saintliness of Gardner's heroines, like figures from a medieval *exemplum.*

IX. *Freddy's Book*

1. John Gardner, as told to Howell in *John Gardner: A Bibliographical Profile,* p. 70.

2. See William Logan, "Gardner's Book: Myth with Lapses of Imagination" (a review of *Freddy's Book*), *Chicago Tribune Book World,* 16 March 1980, p. 1. Gardner's reply appeared in the *Chicago Tribune Book World,* 13 April 1980, p. 10.

3. Marshall Harvey, "John Gardner: Considerations . . . ," *The Cresset* 42 (September 1979): 21.

4. Sir Thomas Browne, *Religio Medici and Other Writings,* ed. L. C. Martin (Oxford: Oxford University Press, 1964), p. 5. I am quoting John Gardner, *Freddy's Book* (New York: Alfred A. Knopf, 1980), p. 14. Subsequent references will be to this edition.

5. Harvey, "John Gardner," p. 21.

6. Ibid.

7. Gardner's *Freddy's Book* is not the first literary treatment of the reign of Gustav Vasa. Beside the native Swedish epics and ballads, there have been several dramatic works that have dealt with segments of Gustav's role in Sweden's history. The German playwright August Friedrich Ferdinand von Kotzebue (1761–1819) wrote a play entitled *Gustav Wasa,* which soon after its appearance drew from a contemporary, Clemens Maria Brentano (1778–1842), a parodic drama of the same title. In England, the dramatist Henry Brooks (1703?–1783) authored a play entitled *Gustav Vasa, the Deliverer of his Country.* And many years later August Strindberg offered the first serious native effort at explaining this national hero with his "Vasa Trilogy": *Master Olof, Gustav Vasa,* and *Erik XIV.* Even Ibsen, in his *Lady Inger of Ostrat,* dealt indirectly with Gustav in this work that concerns the *daljunker's* machinations in Europe.

8. Brask is very likely, at least in part, a caricature of Gardner's literary nemesis, John Barth. Brask's enslavement to style, to rhetoric, and his later analysis of the decline of the arts into irony, paradox, and nihilism (an analysis that distinctly echoes Gardner's own in *On Moral Fiction* and elsewhere) all characterize Gardner's opinion of Barth and his work.

9. This, anyway, is the manner in which Gardner's Brask dies. The historical Brask, so Michael Roberts tells us, in *The Early Vasas: A History of Sweden, 1523–1611* (Cambridge: Cambridge University Press, 1968), after the Vasteras *riksdag* in 1527,

> had been forced to find sureties for good behaviour, and was now constrained to an onerous "agreement" with the king. He had lost heart; there seemed no more that he could do. He took the opportunity of an episcopal visitation to Gotland to slip away—to Denmark first, and then to Prussia. Inevitably he was drawn into correspondence with other members of the ever-growing band of Gustav's enemies in exile—with von Melen, with Trolle; but his part in Sweden was played out, and he died in a Polish monastery eleven years later. (p. 85)

Gardner's rewriting of history in his life and death of Hans Brask is a particularly good example of his psychohistorical technique in fiction. How much more interesting (and significant) to die scaling the Devil than to waste slowly away in a monastery somewhere in Poland, exiled and desolate and ignored.

x. *The Art of Living and Other Stories*

1. Though "Trumpeter" is a part of *The Art of Living* (and of this count), I discuss it in Chapter Seven (*The King's Indian*), where I treat it as part of the "Tales of Queen Louisa" section.

2. Gardner, *The Art of Living,* p. 8. Subsequent references will be in the text.

3. Ferguson et al., "John Gardner," p. 65.

4. Personal interview with John Gardner, Middlebury, Vermont, 22 August 1978.

5. Susanne K. Langer, *Problems of Art* (New York: Charles Scribner's Sons, 1957), p. 9. Gardner, in response to a question about the generation of ideas for his fiction, once remarked in an interview: "Just recently I was reading a book on aesthetics, which I had heard about for a long time, and I found it very exciting and got three short stories out of it." See Ed Christian, "An Interview with John Gardner," *Prairie Schooner* 54 (Winter 1980–81): 82–83. It's my guess that "The Library Horror" was one of these three stories.

xi. *Mickelsson's Ghosts*

1. Benjamin De Mott, "A Philosophic Novel of Academe" (a review of *Mickelsson's Ghosts*), *New York Times Book Review,* 20 June 1982, p. 26.

2. Curt Suplee, "John Gardner, Flat Out," *The Washington Post,* 25 July 1982, p. H8.

3. John Gardner, *Mickelsson's Ghosts* (New York: Alfred A. Knopf, 1982), p. 5. Subsequent references will be to this edition.

4. Gardner's original statement of this idea, which he copied nearly word for word in *Mickelsson's Ghosts,* came in *The Originals: The Writer in America.*

5. The book, by James J. Lynch, is fully titled *The Broken Heart: The Medical Consequences of Loneliness* (New York: Basic Books, 1977).

Epilogue

1. Suplee, "John Gardner, Flat Out," p. H9.

2. *The Best American Short Stories,* edited by John Gardner, with Shannon Ravenel (Boston: Houghton Mifflin Company, 1982), p. xv. This book was published soon after Gardner's death in September 1982, and the comment comes from his introduction.

3. Suplee, "John Gardner, Flat Out," p. H1.

4. Ibid., p. H8.

Bibliography

The most complete Gardner bibliography is John M. Howell's *John Gardner: A Bibliographical Profile* (Carbondale: Southern Illinois University Press, 1980). What I offer below is a working bibliography of Gardner's major published works (including those that have appeared after the publication of Howell's bibliography), as well as any lesser pieces mentioned in this study.

Novels

Freddy's Book. New York: Alfred A. Knopf, 1980.
Grendel. New York: Alfred A. Knopf, 1971.
Mickelsson's Ghosts. New York: Alfred A. Knopf, 1982.
Nickel Mountain. New York: Alfred A. Knopf, 1973.
October Light. New York: Alfred A. Knopf, 1976.
"The Old Men." Ph.D. dissertation. University of Iowa, 1958.
The Resurrection. New York: New American Library, 1966; rev. ed. Ballantine Books, 1974.
The Sunlight Dialogues. New York: Alfred A. Knopf, 1972.
Vlemk the Box-Painter. (A novella). Northridge, Calif.: Lord John Press, 1979.
The Wreckage of Agathon. New York: Harper & Row, 1970.

Short Story Collections

The Art of Living and Other Stories. New York: Alfred A. Knopf, 1981.
"Four Short Stories." M.A. thesis. University of Iowa, 1957.
The King's Indian: Stories and Tales. New York: Alfred A. Knopf, 1974.
"A Little Night Music." *The Northwest Review* 4 (Spring 1961): 30–40. (An uncollected published story).

Poetry

Jason and Medeia. New York: Alfred A. Knopf, 1973.
Poems. Northridge, Calif.: Lord John Press, 1978.

Letters, Articles, Essays

"Amber (Get) Waves (Your) of (Plastic) Grain (Uncle Sam)." *New York Times*, 29 October 1975, sec. M., p. 41.

"Cartoons." In *In Praise of What Persists,* edited by Stephen Berg. New York: Harper & Row, 1983.

"Fulgentius's *Expositio Vergiliana Continentia* and the Plan of *Beowulf:* Another Approach to the Poem's Style and Structure." *Papers on Language and Literature* 7 (1971): 227–62.

"John Gardner's Letter to the *Chicago Tribune.*" *Chicago Tribune Book World,* 13 April 1980, sec. 7, p. 10.

"John Gardner's Letter to the Editor." *New American Review* 9 (April 1977): 232–35.

"John Gardner's Statement Designating the Fiction Award Recipients." *Kansas Quarterly* 10 (Winter 1978): 6–8.

"Southern Illinois." *Vogue* 167 (March 1977): 156–57.

"The Way We Write Now." *New York Times Book Review,* 9 July 1972, pp. 2, 32–33.

Critical and Scholarly Books

The Alliterative Morte Arthure. Carbondale: Southern Illinois University Press, 1971.

The Complete Works of the Gawain-Poet. Chicago: University of Chicago Press, 1965.

The Construction of Christian Poetry in Old English. Carbondale: Southern Illinois University Press, 1975.

The Construction of the Wakefield Cycle. Carbondale: Southern Illinois University Press, 1974.

The Life and Times of Chaucer. New York: Alfred A. Knopf, 1977.

On Becoming a Novelist. Foreword by Raymond Carver. New York: Harper and Row, 1983.

On Moral Fiction. New York: Basic Books, 1978.

The Poetry of Chaucer. Carbondale: Southern Illinois University Press, 1977.

Edited Works

The Best American Short Stories 1982. Edited with Shannon Ravenel. Boston: Houghton Mifflin Company, 1982.

The Forms of Fiction. Edited with Lennis Dunlap. New York: Random House, 1962.

MSS: A Retrospective. Edited with L. M. Rosenberg. Dallas: New London Press, 1980.

Tengu Child: Stories by Kikuo Itaya. Edited and translated with Noboko Tsukui. Carbondale: Southern Illinois University Press, 1983.

Plays

Death and the Maiden. Dallas: New London Press, 1981.

The Temptation Game. Dallas: New London Press, 1980.

Opera Libretti

Frankenstein. Dallas: New London Press, 1979.

Rumplestiltskin. Dallas: New London Press, 1978.

William Wilson. Dallas: New London Press, 1979.

Children's Books

A Child's Bestiary. New York: Alfred A. Knopf, 1977.
Dragon, Dragon and Other Tales. New York: Alfred A. Knopf, 1975.
Gudgekin the Thistle Girl and Other Tales. New York: Alfred A. Knopf, 1976.
In the Suicide Mountains. New York: Alfred A. Knopf, 1977.
The King of the Hummingbirds and Other Tales. New York: Alfred A. Knopf, 1977.

Cited Interviews with John Gardner

John Howell has estimated recently the number of interviews given by Gardner at nearly two hundred. Therefore, what I give here is a collection of those interviews referred to in this study. For a more complete listing, consult Howell's *Bibliographical Profile*.

Bellamy, Joe David. *The New Fiction: Interviews with Innovative American Writers*. Urbana: University of Illinois Press, 1974, pp. 169–93.
Christian, Ed. "An Interview with John Gardner." *Prairie Schooner* 54 (Winter 1980–81): 70–93.
"Conversation with John Gardner on Writers and Writing." Originally published in the *Detroit Free Press,* 23 March 1975. Reprinted in *Authors in the News,* edited by Barbara Nykouk. Detroit: Gale Research Company, 1976, pp. 168–69.
Edwards, Don, and Carol Polsgrove. "A Conversation with John Gardner." *The Atlantic Monthly* 239 (May 1977): 43–47.
Ferguson, Paul F., John R. Maier, Frank McConnell, and Sara Matthiessen. "John Gardner: The Art of Fiction LXXIII." *Paris Review* 21 (Spring 1979): 36–74.
Harkness, James. "Interview: John Gardner." *Forum/The News* [State University of New York] 8 (April 1979): F-1–F-2, F-7–F-9.
Harvey, Marshall L. "Where Philosophy and Fiction Meet: An Interview with John Gardner." *Chicago Review* 29 (Spring 1978): 73–87.
———. "John Gardner: Considerations . . ." *The Cresset* 42 (September 1979): 21.
"John Gardner." In *Conversations with Writers*. Vol. 1. Detroit: Gale Research Company, 1978, pp. 82–103. Interviewed by C. E. Frazer Clark, Jr.
"John Gardner." *The Originals: The Writer in America*. Produced and directed by Richard O. Moore. PBS, 3 April 1978.
Laskin, Daniel. "Challenging the Literary Naysayers." *Horizon* 21 (July 1978), pp. 32–36.
Morris, Gregory L. Unpublished interviews with John Gardner, 13 March 1974, 22 August 1978, 28 October 1978, 22 February 1979.
Singular, Stephen. "The Sound and the Fury over Fiction." *New York Times Magazine,* 8 July 1979, pp. 13–15, 34, 36–39.
Suplee, Curt. "John Gardner, Flat Out." *The Washington Post,* 25 July 1982, pp. H1, H8–H10.

Cited Studies, Articles, Reviews

Coales, Samuel. " 'Into the Farther Darkness': The Manichean Pastoralism of John Gardner." In *Critical Perspectives on John Gardner,* edited by Robert A. Morace and Kathryn VanSpanckeren. Carbondale: Southern Illinois University Press, 1982.
Cowart, David. "*Et in Arcadia Ego:* Gardner's Early Pastoral Novels." In *Critical Perspectives on John Gardner,* edited by Morace and VanSpanckeren.

De Mott, Benjamin. "A Philosophic Novel of Academe." (A review of *Mickelsson's Ghosts*.) *New York Times Book Review,* 20 June 1982, pp. 1, 26.

Ellis, Helen B., and Warren U. Ober. "*Grendel* and Blake: The Contraries of Existence." *English Studies in Canada* 3 (Spring 1977): 87–102. Reprinted in *Critical Perspectives on John Gardner,* edited by Morace and VanSpanckeren.

Hutman, Norma. "Even Monsters Have Mothers: A Study of *Beowulf* and John Gardner's *Grendel.*" *Mosaic* 9 (Fall 1975): 19–31.

Levine, George. "The Name of the Game." *Partisan Review* 42 (Spring 1975): 291–97.

Logan, William. "Gardner's Book: Myth with Lapses of Imagination." (A review of *Freddy's Book*.) *Chicago Tribune Book World,* 16 March 1980, sec. 7, p. 1.

Mason, K. Clif. "Of Monsters and Men: *Beowulf* and Gardner's *Grendel.*" An unpublished essay.

Milosh, Joseph. "John Gardner's *Grendel:* Sources and Analogues." *Contemporary Literature* 19 (Winter 1978): 48–57.

Morace, Robert A., and Kathryn VanSpanckeren, editors. *Critical Perspectives on John Gardner.* Carbondale: Southern Illinois University Press, 1982.

Morris, Gregory L. "A Babylonian in Batavia: Mesopotamian Literature and Lore in *The Sunlight Dialogues.*" In *Critical Perspectives on John Gardner,* edited by Morace and VanSpanckeren.

Ruud, Jay. "Gardner's *Grendel* and *Beowulf:* Humanizing the Monster." *Thoth* 14 (Spring/Fall 1974): 3–17.

Stromme, Craig. "The Twelve Chapters of *Grendel.*" *Critique: Studies in Modern Fiction* 20, no. 1 (1978): 83–92.

Secondary Works

Alfred North Whitehead: An Anthology. Selected by F. S. C. Northrop and Mason W. Gross. New York: The Macmillan Company, 1961.

Brodie, Fawn M. *No Man Knows My History: The Life of Joseph Smith.* Alfred A. Knopf, 1966.

Browne, Sir Thomas. *Religio Medici and Other Writings.* Edited by L. C. Martin. Oxford: Oxford University Press, 1964.

Cochrane, Diane. "John Napper: The Return of the Illustrated Novel." *American Artist* 37 (July 1973): 26–31, 65, 70.

Cottingham, Jane. "For Real: Paintings by Jack Beal." *American Artist* 44 (November 1980): 58–63.

Dante Alighiere. *The Divine Comedy.* Translated by Mark Musa. Bloomington, Indiana: University of Indiana Press, 1971.

Delbanco, Nicholas. *Possession.* New York: William Morrow and Co., 1977.

The Encyclopedia of Philosophy. Edited by Paul Edwards. 2d edition. New York: Free Press, 1973.

Great Dialogues of Plato. Translated by W. H. D. Rouse. Edited by Eric H. Warmington and Philip G. Rouse. New York: New American Library, 1956.

Haile, H. G. *Luther: An Experiment in Biography.* New York: Doubleday & Co., 1980.

Hare, R. M. *Essays on the Moral Concepts.* Berkeley and Los Angeles: University of California Press, 1972.

Langer, Susanne K. *Problems of Art.* New York: Charles Scribner's Sons, 1957.

Lynch, James J. *The Broken Heart: The Medical Consequences of Loneliness.* New York: Basic Books, 1977.

MacIntyre, Alasdair. *After Virtue: A Study in Moral Theory*. London: Duckworth, 1981.

Maguire, Daniel C. *The Moral Choice*. Garden City, New York: Doubleday & Co., 1978.

Melville, Herman. *Clarel*. Edited by Walter E. Bezanson. New York: Hendricks House, 1960.

The Nichomachean Ethics of Aristotle. Translated by Sir David Ross. London: Oxford University Press, 1969.

Oppenheim, A. Leo. *Ancient Mesopotamia: Portrait of a Dead Civilization*. Chicago: University of Chicago Press, 1964.

Plutarch's Lives of the Noble Grecians and Romans. Translated by John Dryden. Revised by Arthur Hugh Clough. New York: The Modern Library, n.d.

Poe, Edgar Allan. *The Narrative of Arthur Gordon Pym*. New York: Hill and Wang, 1960.

The Republic of Plato. Translated by Francis MacDonald Cornford. London: Oxford University Press, 1945.

Roberts, Michael. *The Early Vasas: A History of Sweden, 1523–1611*. Cambridge: Cambridge University Press, 1968.

Sartre, Jean-Paul. *Being and Nothingness*. Translated by Hazel E. Barnes. New York: The Citadel Press, 1969.

Schwartz, Delmore. *Selected Poems (1938–1958): Summer Knowledge*. New York: New Directions Books, 1967.

Steiner, George. *The Death of Tragedy*. New York: Alfred A. Knopf, 1968.

Tolstoi, Leo. *My Confession*. Vol. 17 in *The Novels and Other Works of Lyof Tolstoi*. Edited by Nathan Haskell Dale. New York: Charles Scribner's Sons, 1911.

———. *What is Art?* Vol. 20 in *The Novels and Other Works of Lyof Tolstoi*. Edited by Nathan Haskell Dale. New York: Charles Scribner's Sons, 1911.

———. *Resurrection*. Translated by Rosemary Edmonds. London: Penguin Books, 1966.

Wise, William. *Massacre at Mountain Meadows*. New York: Thomas Y. Crowell, 1976.

Index